I0812761

IMAGES
of America

RAPPAHANNOCK COUNTY

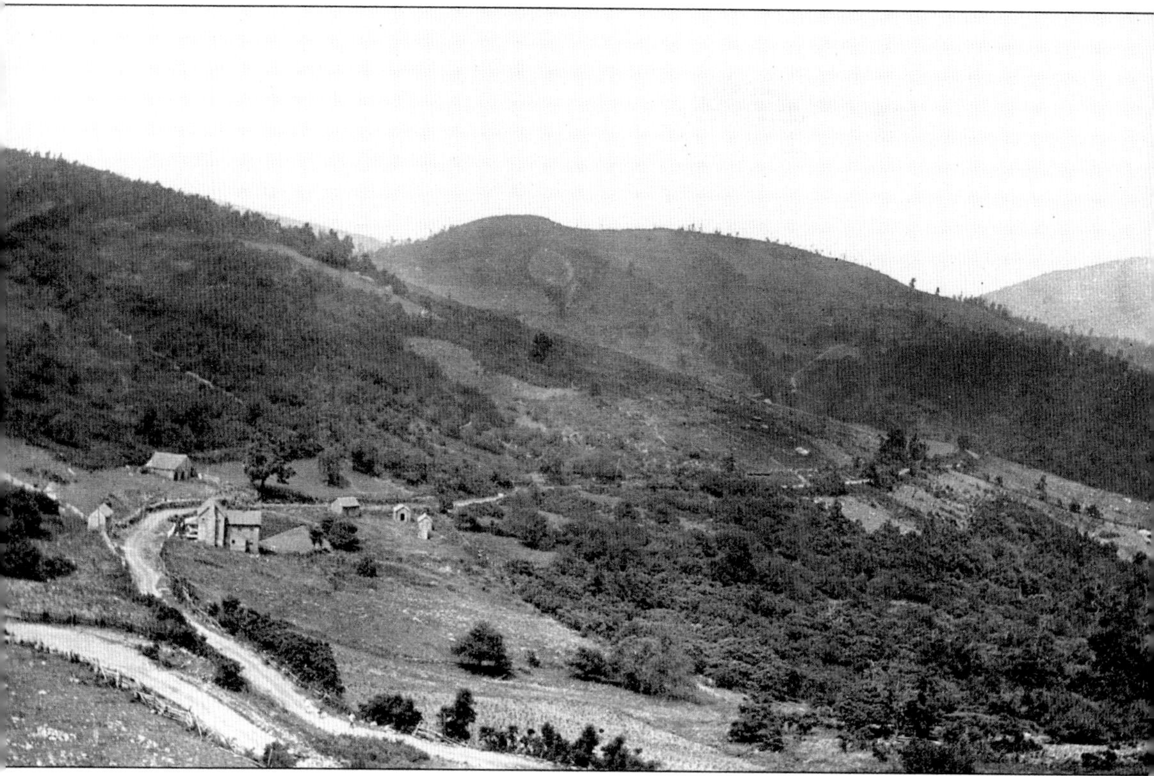

The Lee Highway passing through Thornton Gap in the 1920s was narrow and only recently paved. Just prior to establishment of the Shenandoah National Park, homes dotted the sides of the highway and, unlike the dense forest cover of today, much of the land in the surrounding mountains was under cultivation or used for grazing livestock. (Courtesy of the Shenandoah National Park Archives, Reed Engle.)

ON THE COVER: The Rappahannock National Bank has been an integral part of the community since its establishment in 1902. (Courtesy of the Rappahannock Historical Society.)

IMAGES
of America

RAPPAHANNOCK COUNTY

Kathryn Lynch
and the Rappahannock Historical Society

ARCADIA
PUBLISHING

ISBN 978-0-7385-4384-0

Published by Arcadia Publishing
Charleston, South Carolina

Printed in the United States of America

Library of Congress Catalog Card Number: 2006933974

For all general information contact Arcadia Publishing at:
Telephone 843-853-2070
Fax 843-853-0044
E-mail sales@arcadiapublishing.com
For customer service and orders:
Toll-Free 1-888-313-2665

Visit us on the Internet at www.arcadiapublishing.com

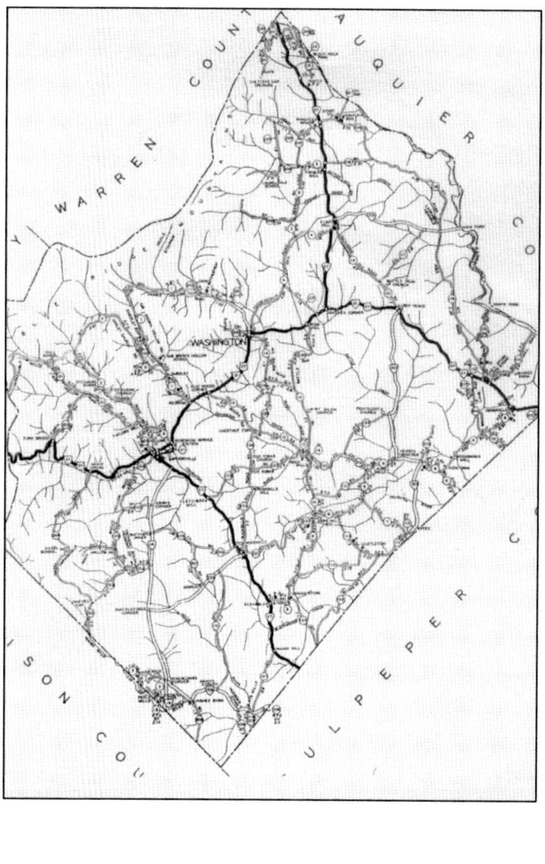

Rappahannock County encompasses 274 square miles in the northern part of the state. It is located approximately 70 miles southwest of Washington, D.C., and 100 miles northwest of Richmond. (Courtesy of the Estes family.)

Contents

ACKNOWLEDGMENTS

It has been a privilege working with coauthor Judy Tole and the Rappahannock Historical Society Board of Directors. This book would not be possible without the generosity and support of many people in the community. Words cannot express our gratitude to everyone who shared their enthusiasm and provided encouragement during the process of researching and writing this book.

This book is not intended to be an exhaustive photographic essay of Rappahannock County's historic past, but rather a broad overview of this rural county. With a rich history that spans more than 200 years, it would be impossible to capture it all in one book.

We would like to acknowledge the following people for their contributions in making this book a reality: Kim Abraham, Ranny Aylor, Wayne Baldwin, Seth Blackwell, Diane Bruce, Sandra Cartwright-Brown, Chris Collins, Bud Corder, Steve and Ann Critzer, Fran Eldred, Reed Engle and the Shenandoah National Park Archives, Betty Estes, Kim Estes-Baader, Mary Frances Fannon, Maybelle Gilkey, Pat Giles, Dr. Charles Henry Harrison, Rachel Hayden, Dan Hitt, Martha Hitt, Mary Jenkins, Aline Johnson, Bob Johnson, Jean Lillard, Todd Lowman, Peter Luke, Chris Lynch, Kimberly Lynch, Jan Hackley Makela, Carolyn and Jim Manwaring, Amy Silver O'Leary, Melbry Paratore, Mary Priest, Nancy Reeve, Katherine Riley, Regina Rush, James Russell, Wallace Russell, Anita Sherman, Lisa Taglauer, John Tole, Stephanie Weakley, Eve Willis, Cheri Woodard, and the Rappahannock Historical Society Board of Directors: Lillian Aylor, Wayne Baldwin, Donna Fisher, Misty Hitt, Lucia Kilby, Richard Lykes, Bob Massie, Jean Morris, Pat Saltonstall, Louise Van Dort, and Arland Welch.

Finally, to our family and friends, we appreciate your patience and understanding.

INTRODUCTION

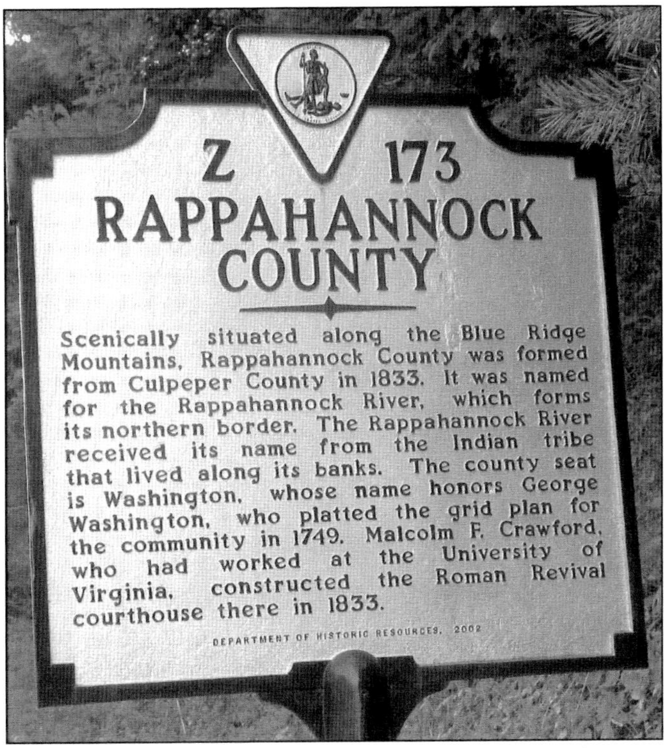

Rappahannock County is located in the Piedmont region of the state. It lies in an area where the coastal flatlands give way to gently rolling hills and then to the magnificent ancient and graceful peaks of the Blue Ridge mountain range.

Humans are known to have lived here for at least 10,000 years. For much of this period, it was mainly nomadic Manohoac Indians, a sub-tribe of the Sioux Nation, which traversed its streams and hollows. When European settlers first came to Virginia, the Blue Ridge Mountains and the surrounding area were far in the distance. It was over 100 years after the settlement of Jamestown before Gov. Alexander Spotswood, who had founded the Germanna Colony along the Rappahannock River, conducted one of the first explorations of the Blue Ridge. Not long thereafter, a number of families from Germanna migrated westward toward the mountains. Other settlers were granted land here for service in the Revolutionary War. These early people established farms, mills, and orchards.

Rappahannock County was established after land was divided with Culpeper County in 1833. The county is comprised entirely of small towns and villages. The oldest of these, Washington, was incorporated in 1796. In 1833, Washington contended with the other major town, Woodville, as the county seat; the former won out due to its more central location. Woodville nonetheless continued to thrive until the 1920s, when a tornado destroyed much of the town. Amissville, settled in 1810, and Sperryville, settled in 1820, lie near the eastern and western boundaries of the county respectively. They were originally important waypoints on the series of turnpikes that ran across the Blue Ridge Mountains and on eastward to the port at Alexandria. Flint Hill, settled in the 1820s, with its north-central location, lies astride the historic Richmond Road, once a major thoroughfare from the mountains to the state capital. On the same road, but at the northern edge of the county, is Chester Gap. Residents have long been attracted to this mountain passageway due to its panoramic vistas, with the Piedmont on one side and the Shenandoah Valley on the other.

The Blue Ridge Mountains have always been an integral part of the county. The natural resources of the region, including the abundance of trees, minerals, and fine highland grazing pastures, provided early settlers with their livelihood. A combination of factors brought about the end of traditional mountain life, including the depletion of natural resources, shifting economic trends, and the establishment of the Shenandoah National Park in the 1930s. Many families were moved involuntarily to resettlement areas along the base of the mountains.

After the Shenandoah National Park opened and automobiles became the primary mode of transportation, Rappahannock County became a tourist destination. Small motels, cabins, and souvenir stands sprang up along the rural roads. Each year, the fall foliage of the Blue Ridge Mountains attracts visitors to Skyline Drive and the surrounding area.

Readers of this book will be able to explore Rappahannock County's rich, historic past through its people, places, architecture, and the natural beauty that has remained largely unchanged for more than 200 years.

—The Rappahannock Historical Society

One

AMISSVILLE

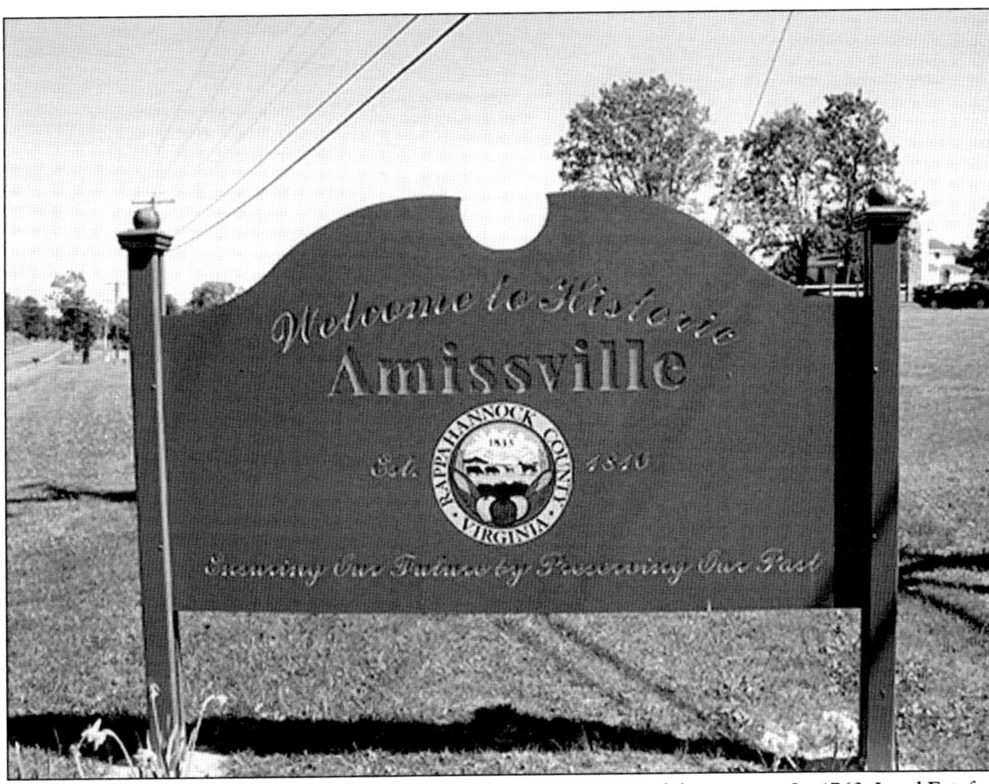

Amissville is situated on Lee Highway at the eastern boundary of the county. In 1763, Lord Fairfax made land grants to Joseph Bayse and Joseph Amiss. Both the Amiss and Bayse families settled in the village and wanted the post office named after them. In 1810, the post office was established. The residents voted to name the post office Amissville. (Courtesy of John Tole.)

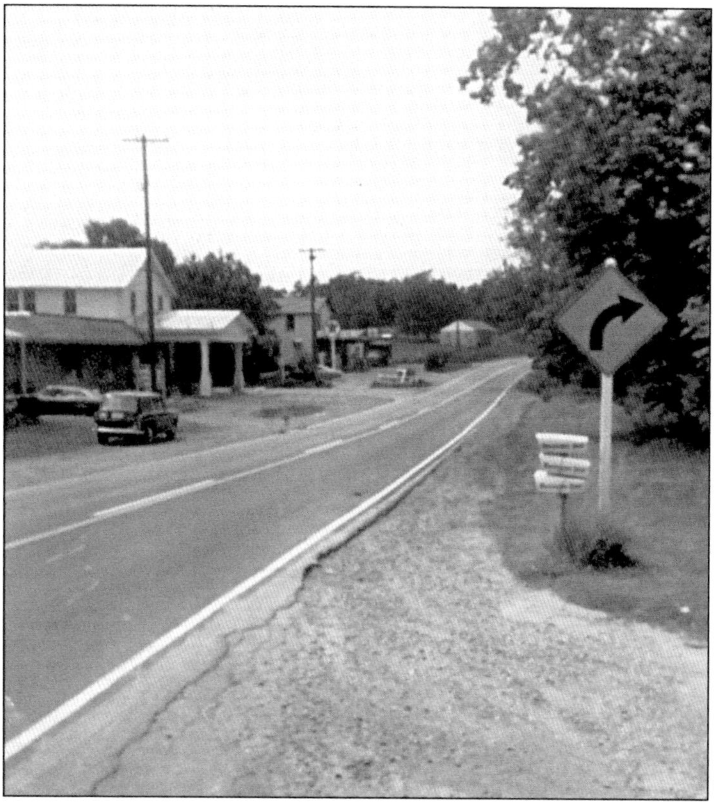

Entering Rappahannock County from the east on Route 211, the old post office and Hackley's Store are visible on the left. This photograph was taken prior to 1972, when the highway was widened to four lanes. (Courtesy of Dan Hitt.)

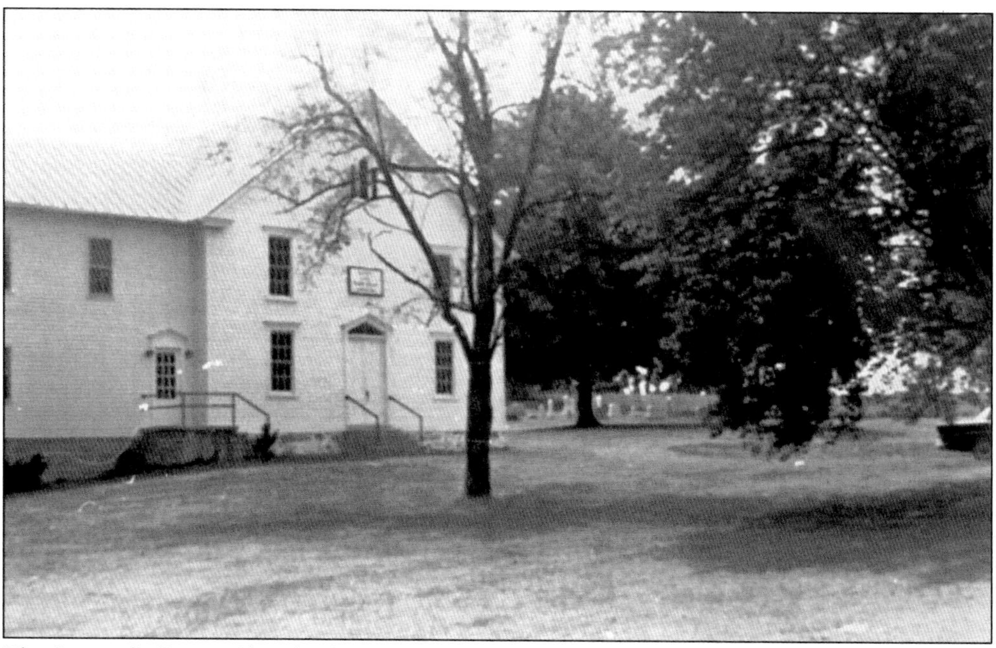

The Amissville Baptist Church is located on Viewtown Road. The church was organized in 1888, and the present building was erected in 1891. (Courtesy of the Rappahannock Historical Society.)

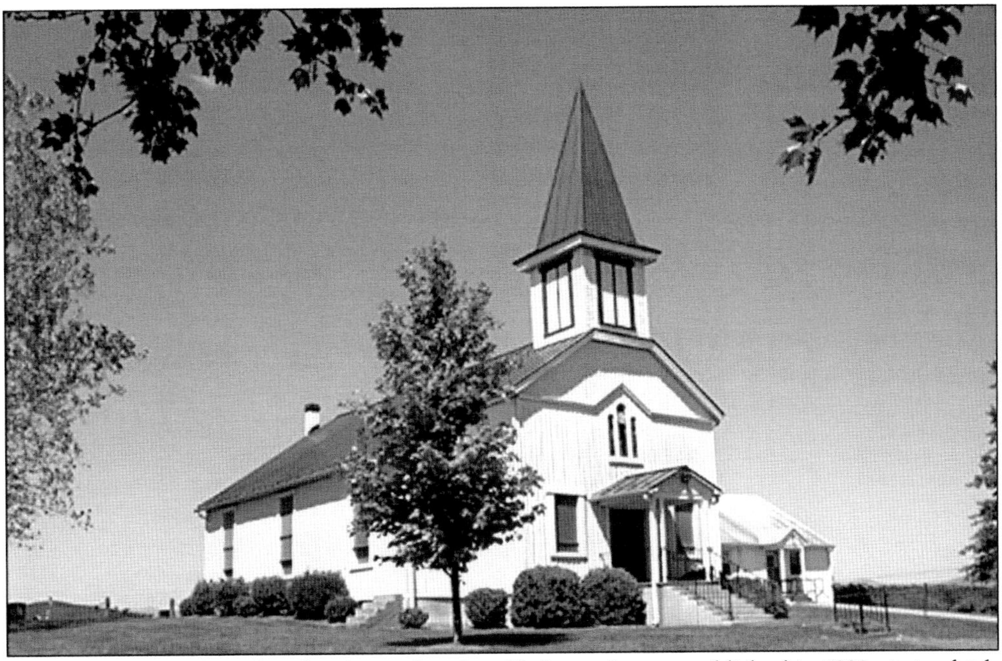

Amissville Methodist Church is located on Lee Highway. It was established in 1829; sitting high on a hill, it looks much the same as it did in the 1860s. The cemetery contains the remains of John Mason Lawrence, one of the last surviving Confederate soldiers of the Civil War. (Courtesy of John Tole.)

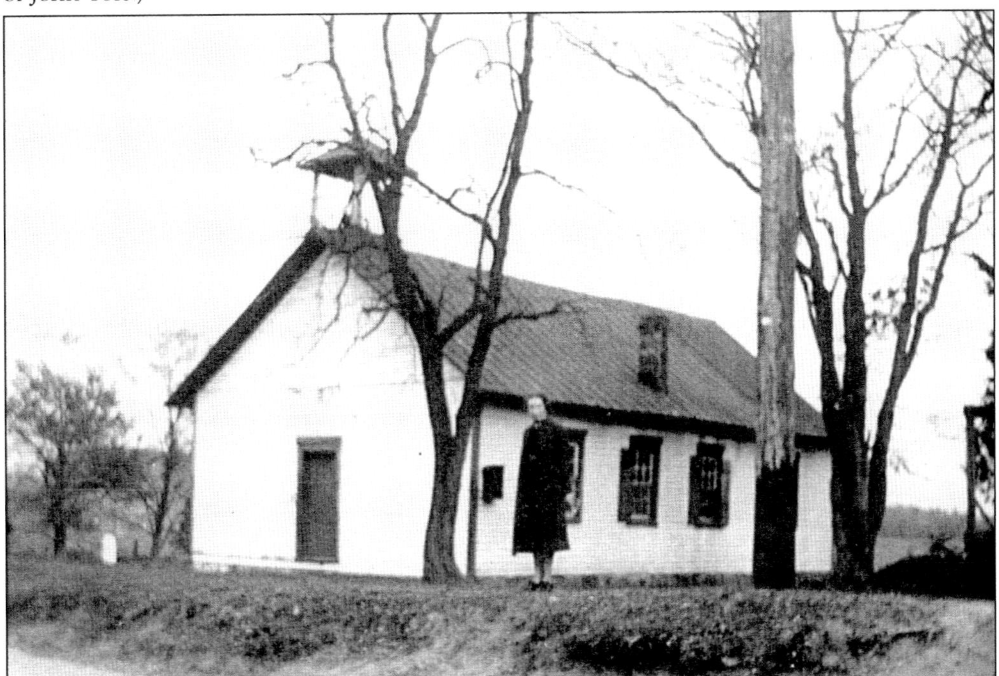

The old Bethel Church was organized by African Americans in the area in the 1870s. The old church and cemetery were located on the east side of Viewtown Road. A new Bethel Church was built in 1937 on the west side of the road. (Courtesy of Mary Priest.)

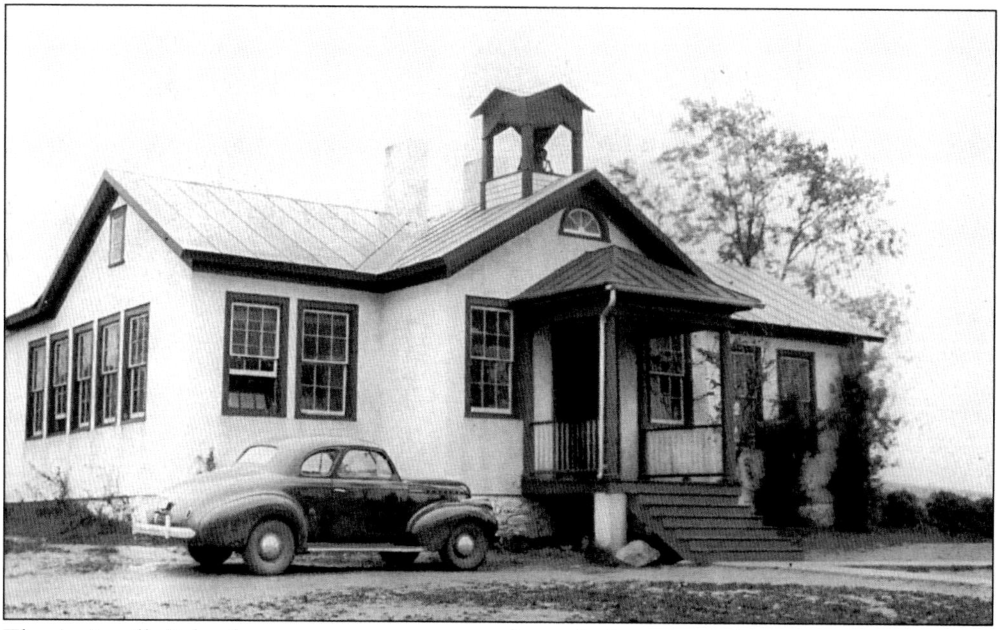

The Amissville School was a one-story structure. It was built in the early 1900s on Lee Highway, directly across from the Amissville Methodist Church. The school closed in 1960 and was razed in the 1970s when the highway was expanded. (Courtesy of the Rappahannock Historical Society.)

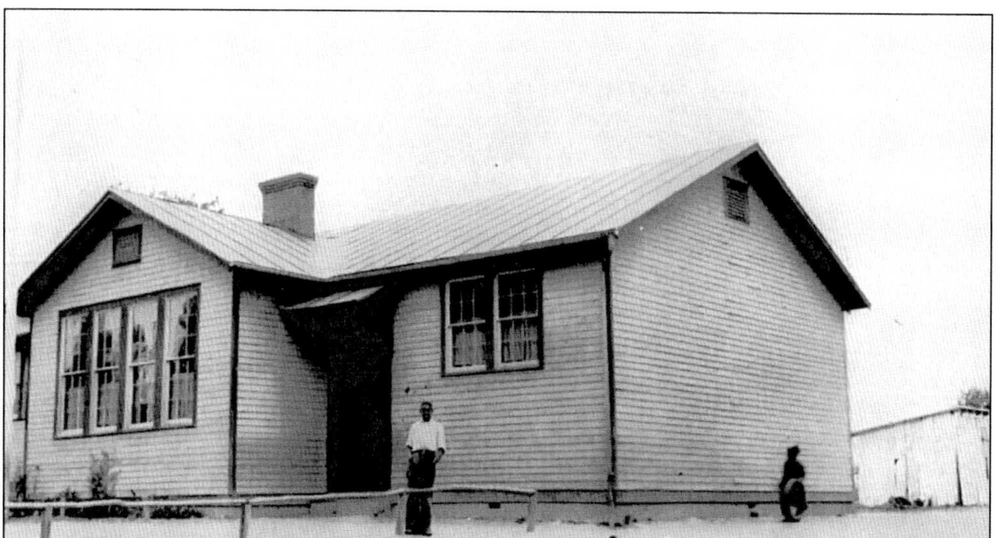

The Amissville Graded School on Poe's Road was built in 1927 with the help of the Rosenwald Fund. It was a two-room elementary school. (Courtesy of the Rappahannock Historical Society.)

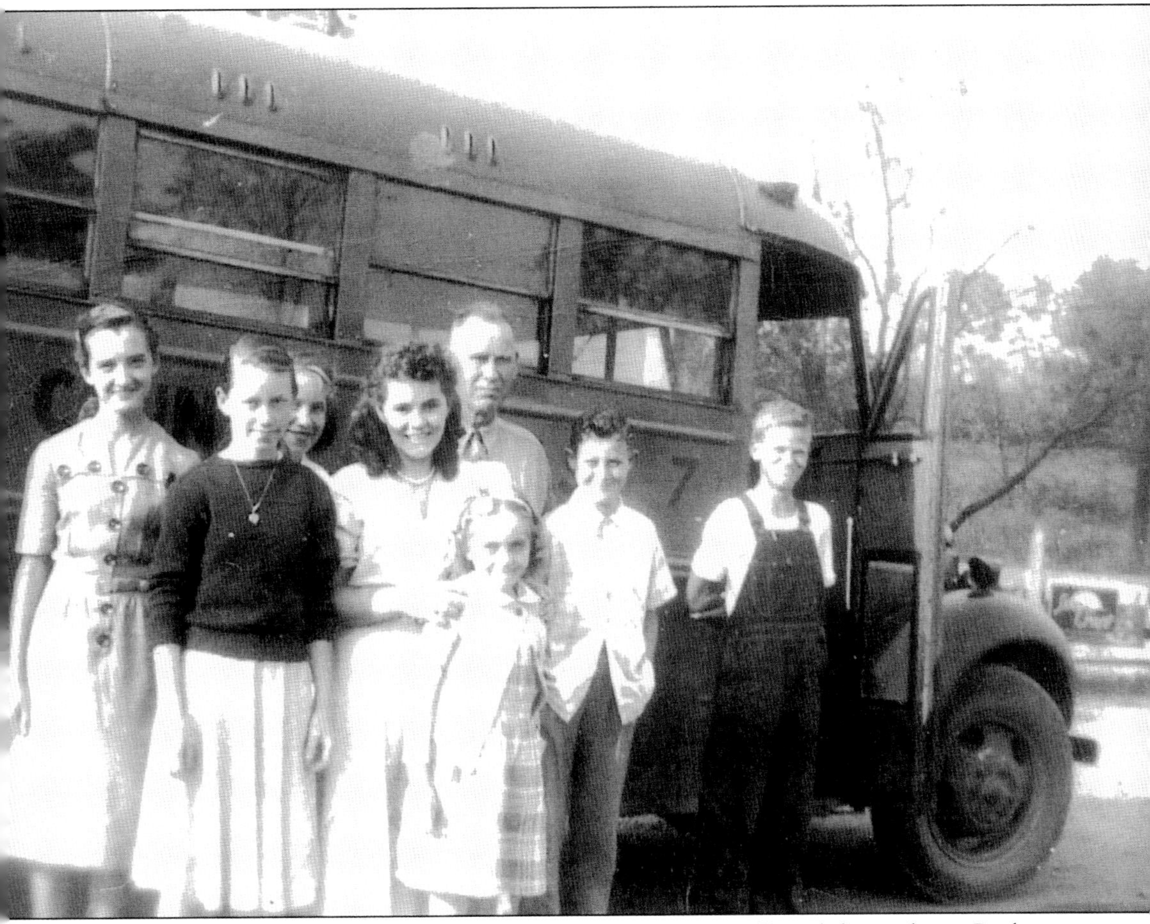

Eddie Martin, a school bus driver, poses with some of his passengers. From left to right are Pauline Newcomer, Hazel Spicer, Joyce Spicer, Dorothy Printz, Elizabeth Printz, Richard Woodward, and Jim Corbin. (Courtesy of Dan Hitt.)

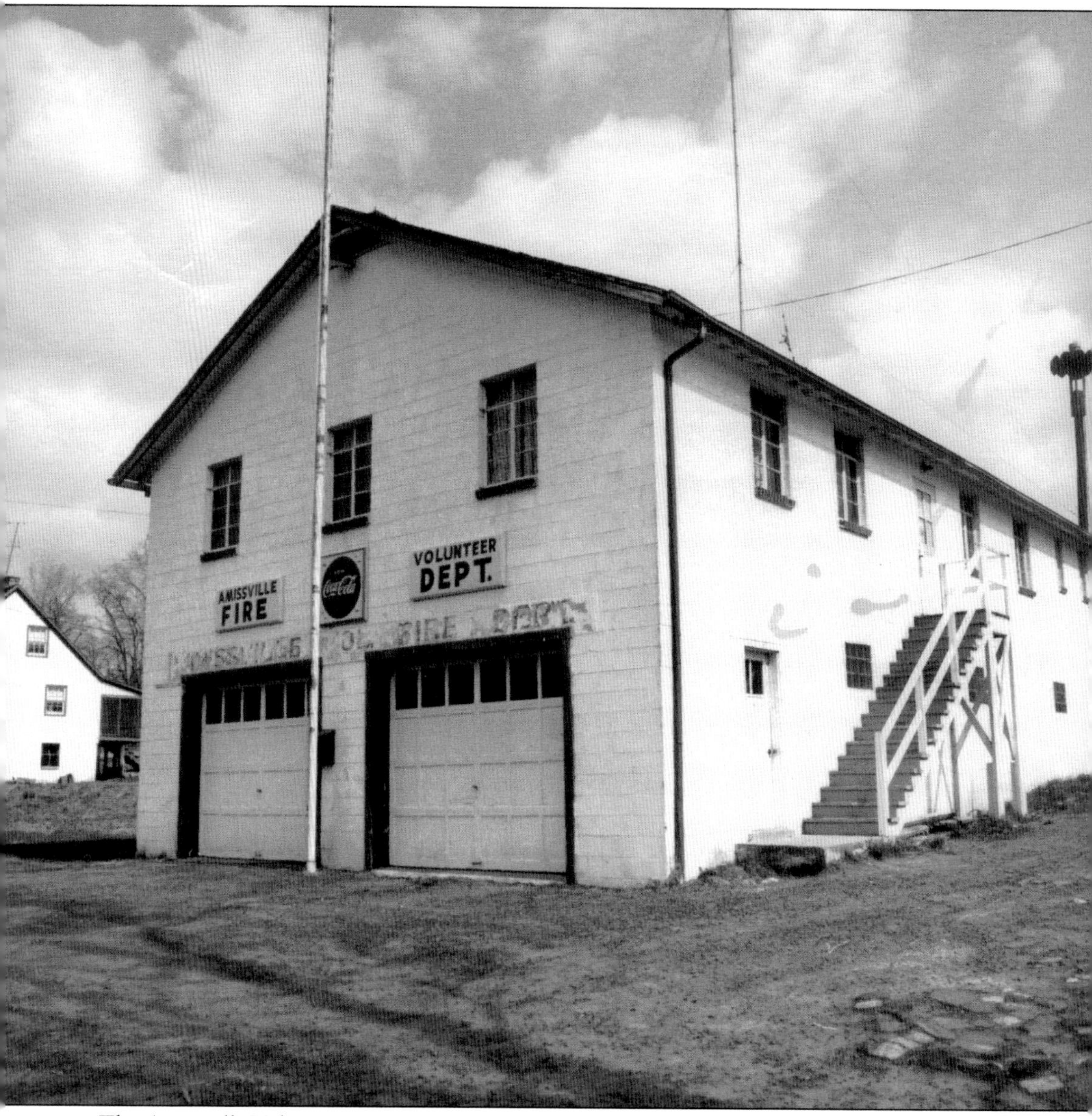

The Amissville Volunteer Fire Department was organized in 1952. This building sat in the median strip and was razed in 1974 when Lee Highway was widened. The present fire department building was erected in 1974. Jimmy Dean, of sausage fame, performed along with a band at the grand opening of the new firehouse. (Courtesy of Mary Priest.)

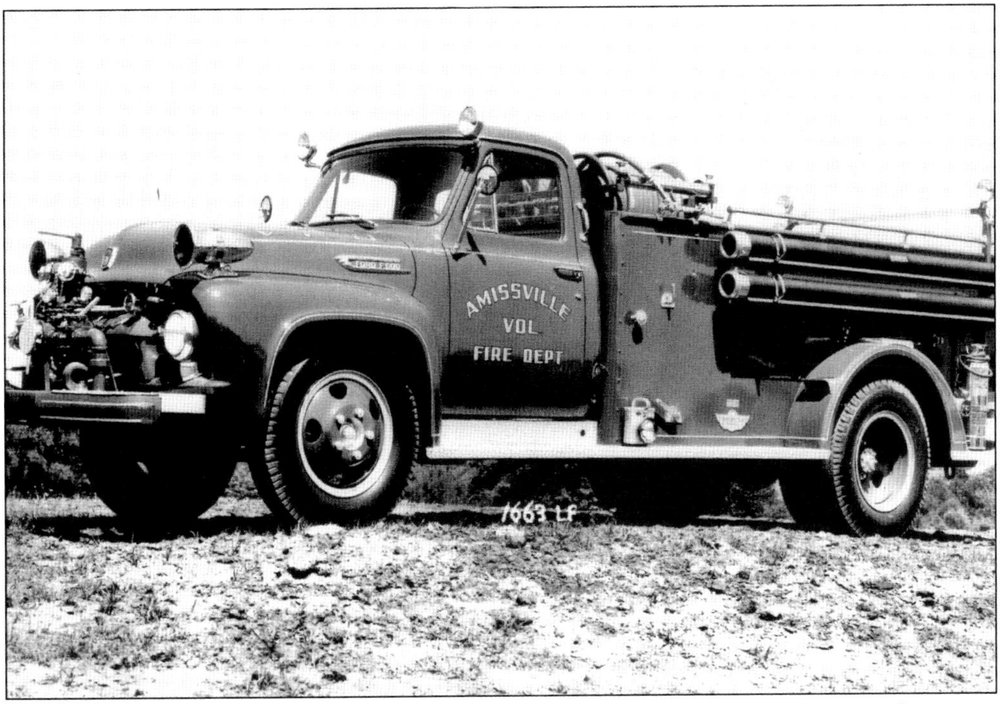

This fire truck was featured in an advertisement for the American Fire Apparatus Company. (Courtesy of Dan Hitt.)

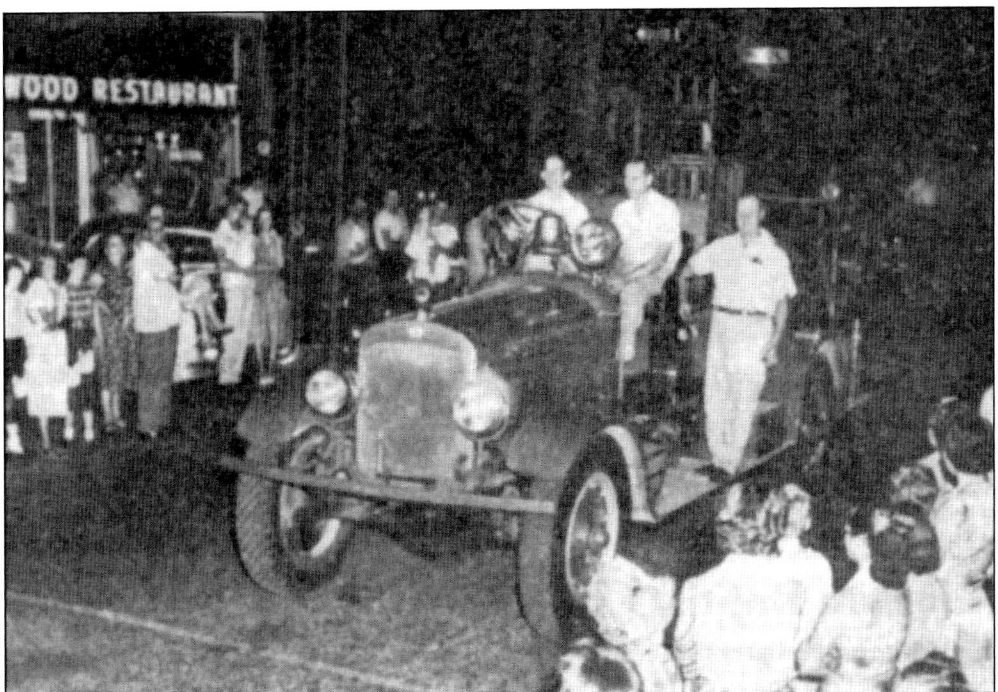

Proud volunteers of the Amissville Fire Department appear in a parade in 1952, the year the company was founded. (Courtesy of the Rappahannock Historical Society.)

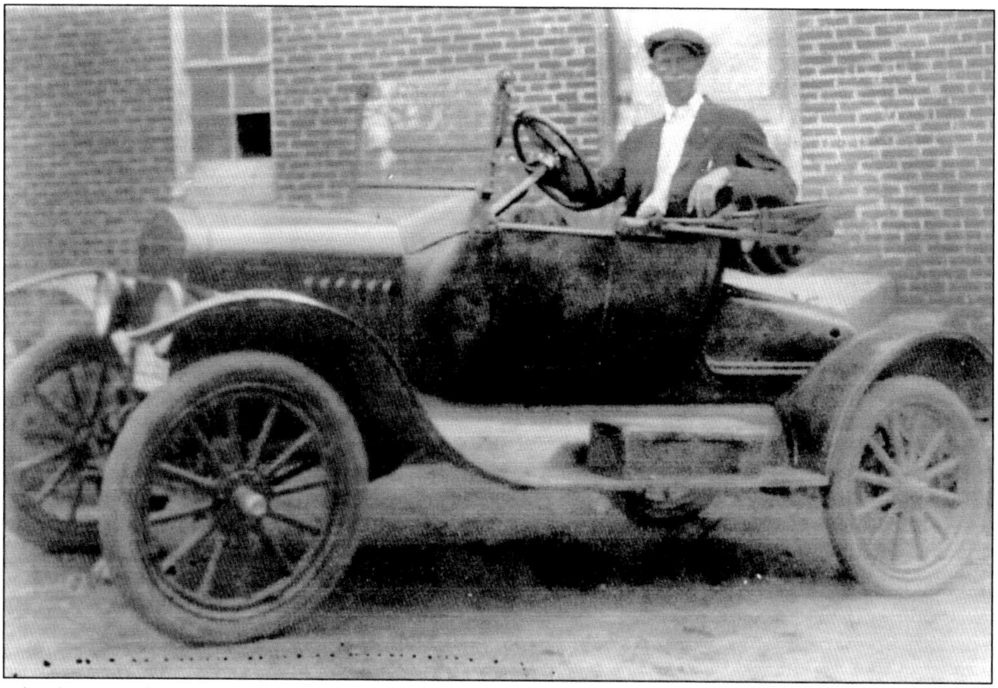

Charlie Cloud is shown behind the wheel of his new 1923 car. (Courtesy of Dan Hitt.)

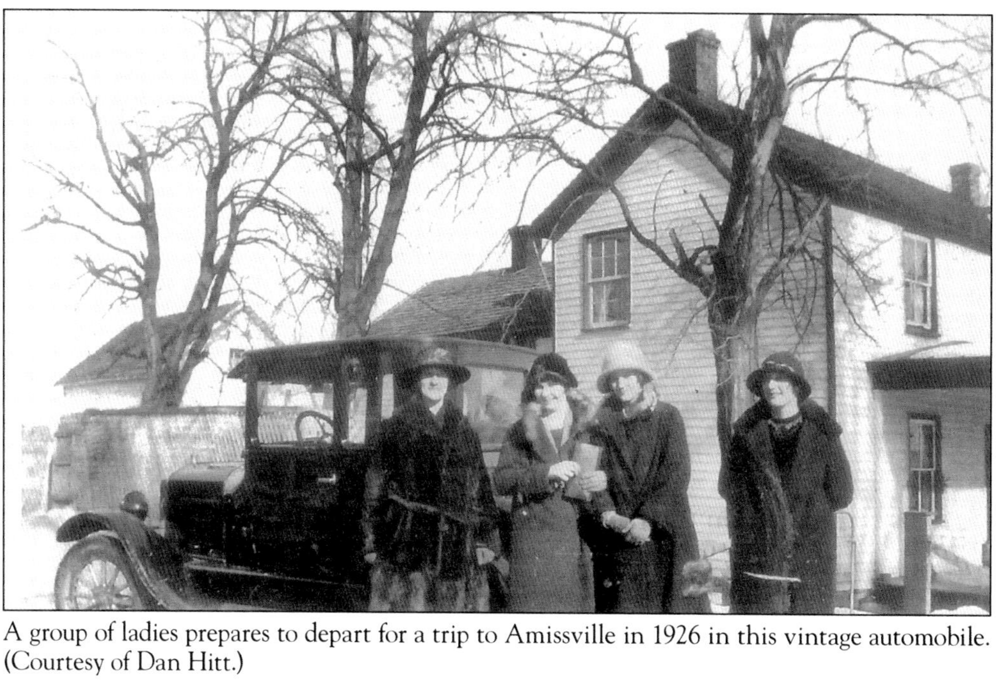

A group of ladies prepares to depart for a trip to Amissville in 1926 in this vintage automobile. (Courtesy of Dan Hitt.)

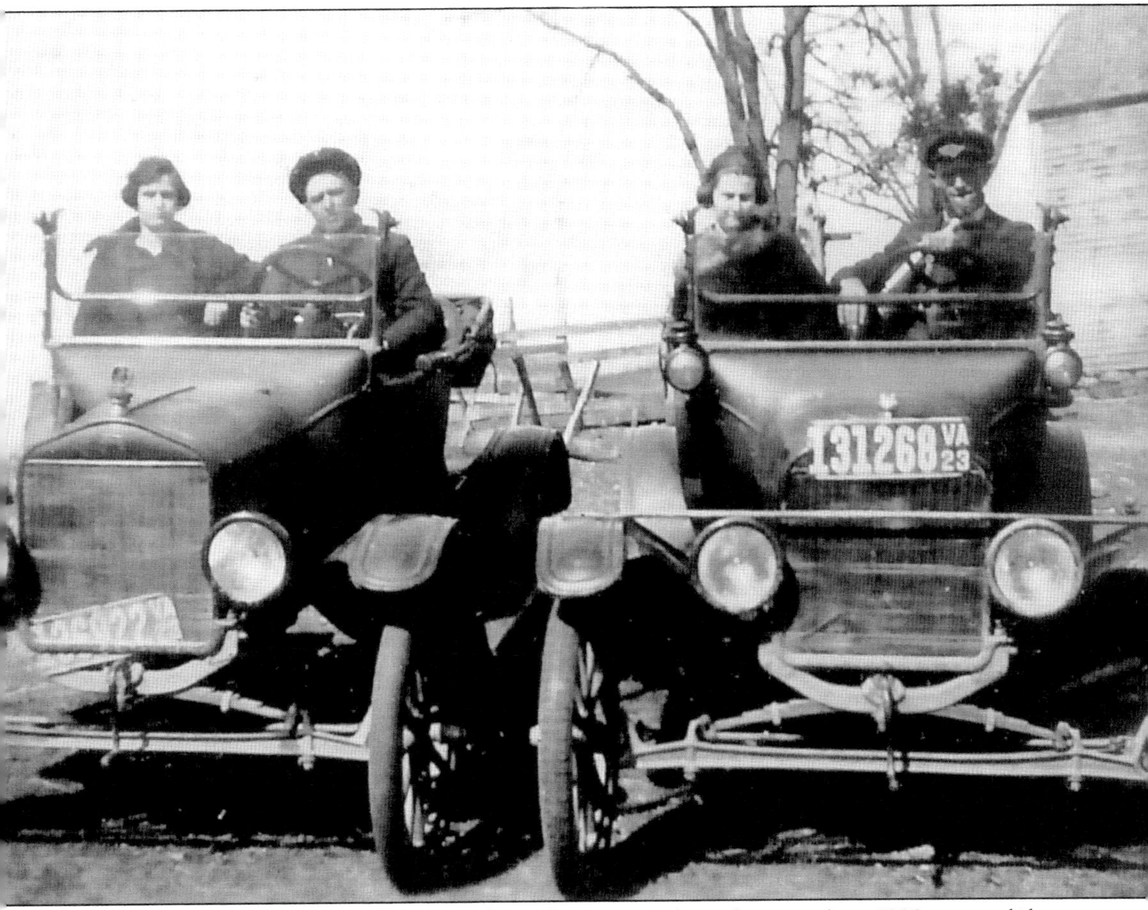

Addie Wharton and Charlie Cloud, on the right, prepare for a drive in their 1923 automobile along with some friends. (Courtesy of Dan Hitt.)

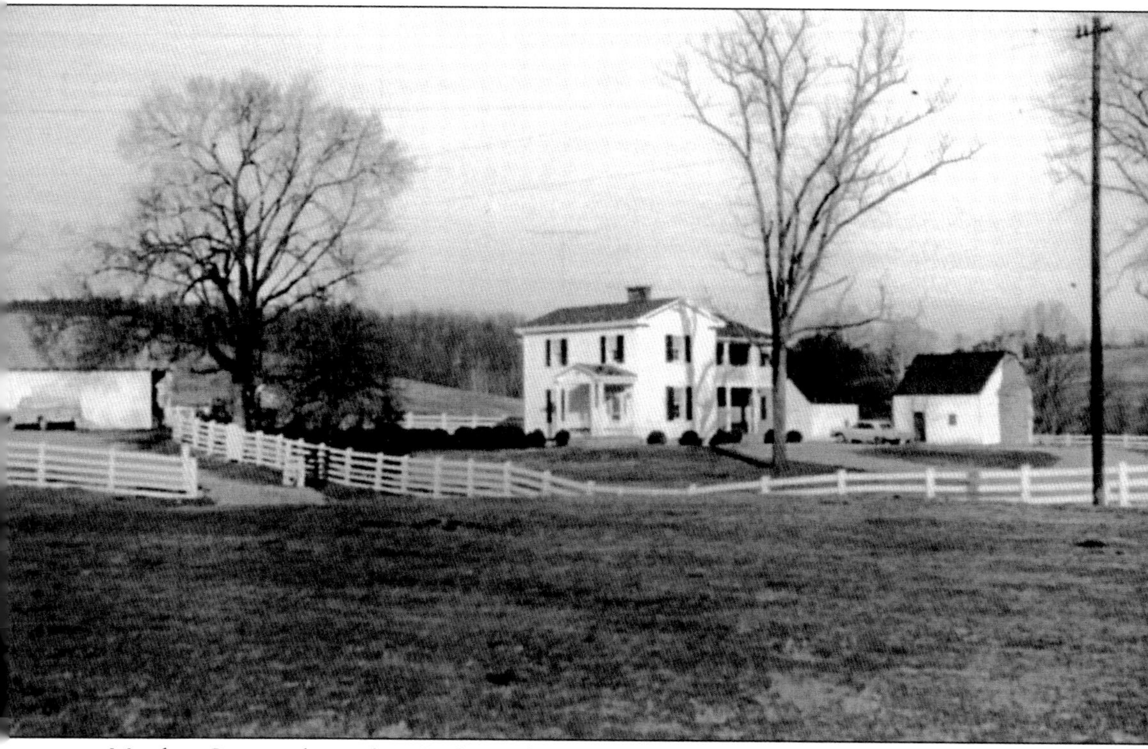

Meadow Grove is located on Richmond Road, three miles south of Ben Venue. This historic house was built in four distinct phases beginning with a one-and-a-half-story log structure c. 1820. In 1880, Col. Thomas Benjamin Massie, a Civil War veteran, and his wife, Elizabeth Anderson Foushee, niece of one of the first owners of the property, established residence there. Meadow Grove has been in the Massie family for six generations and is listed on the National Register of Historic Places and the Virginia Landmarks Registry. (Courtesy of the Rappahannock Historical Society.)

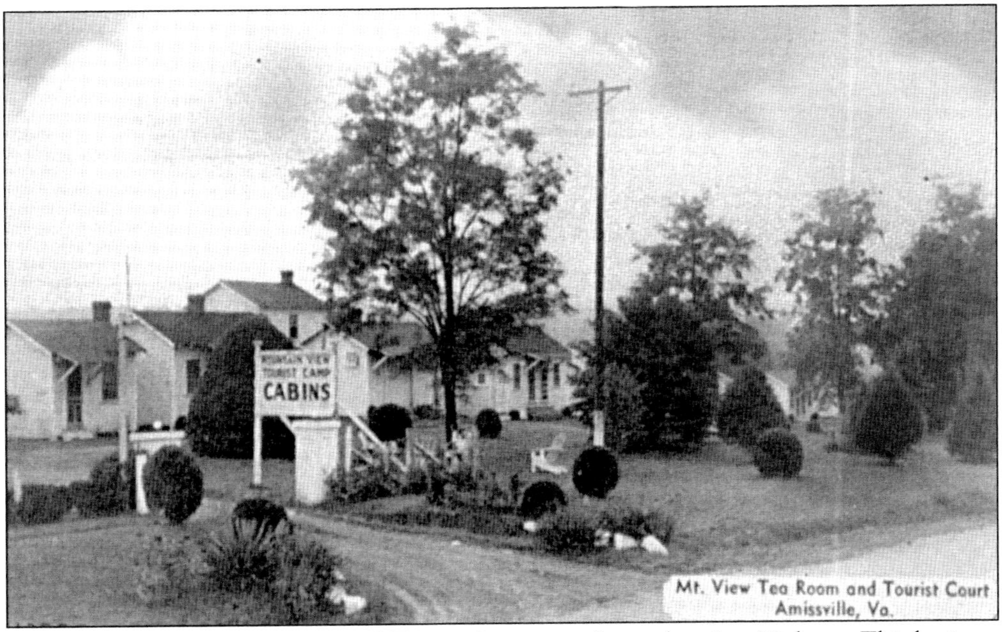

The Mountain View Tea Room and Tourist Court were located on Lee Highway. This business operated from the 1930s until the late 1950s, serving the tourist trade traveling to visit the mountains. (Courtesy of Dan Hitt.)

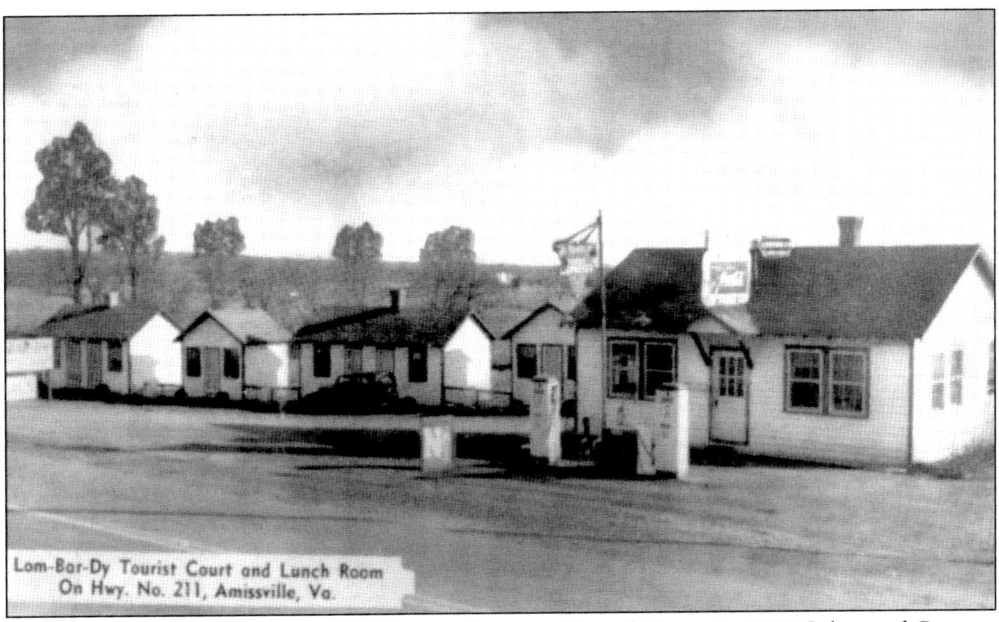

Irva M. Poe owned the Lom-Bar-Dy Tourist Court and Lunch Room in 1940. It boasted Conoco products, lunches and cold drinks, and modern cabins. (Courtesy of Dan Hitt.)

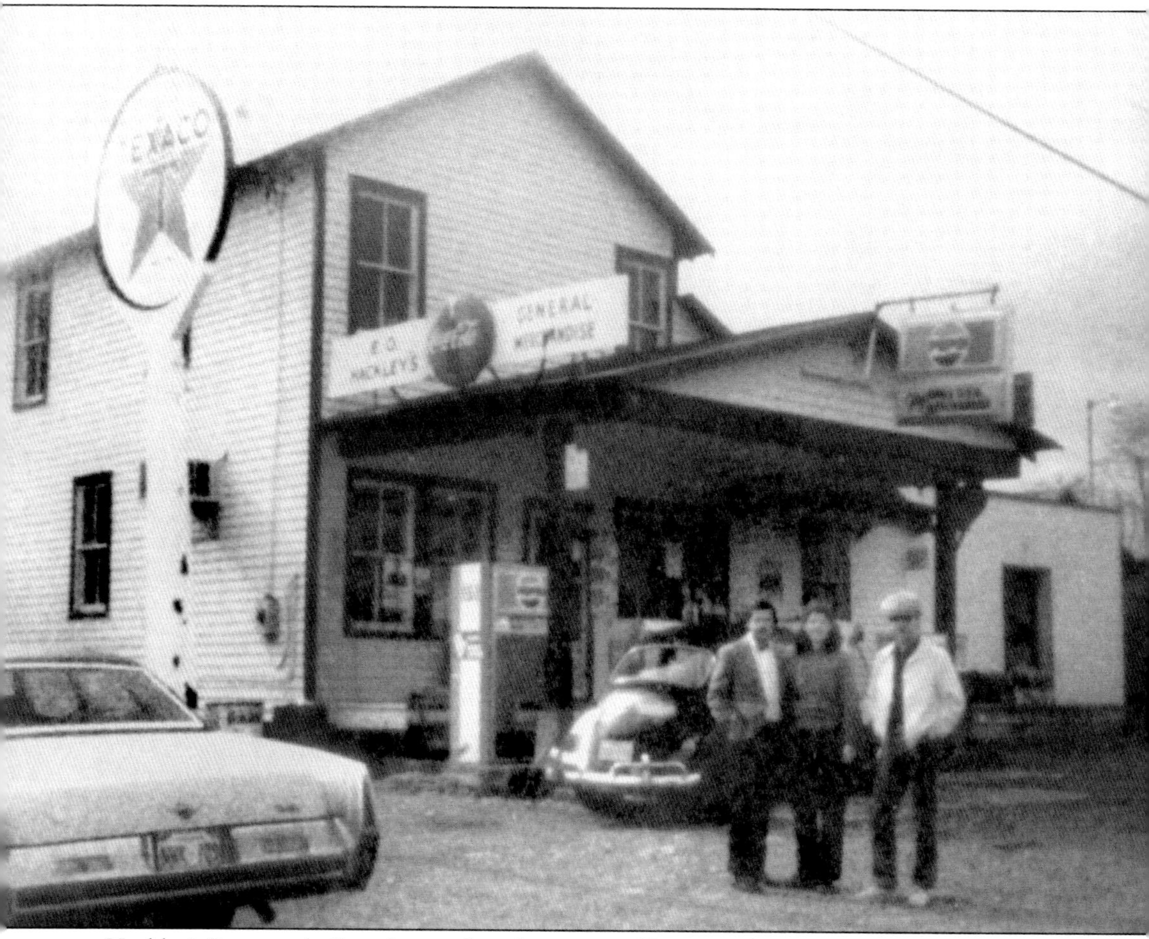

Hackley's Store was built and opened on the corner of Route 642/Viewtown Road and Lee Highway by L. E. and Rosalie Hackley. The store burned and a new general merchandise store was built in its present location in 1934. After the deaths of the original owners, their son Graham Hackley and his wife, Dorothy Zinn, ran the store for 57 years. Daughter Jan and her husband, Ron Makela, continued the family business from 1991 to 2000. The building is currently owned by Dorothy Hackley and is run by her nephew, Brad Nicholas. (Courtesy of Jan and Ron Makela.)

Two

CHESTER GAP

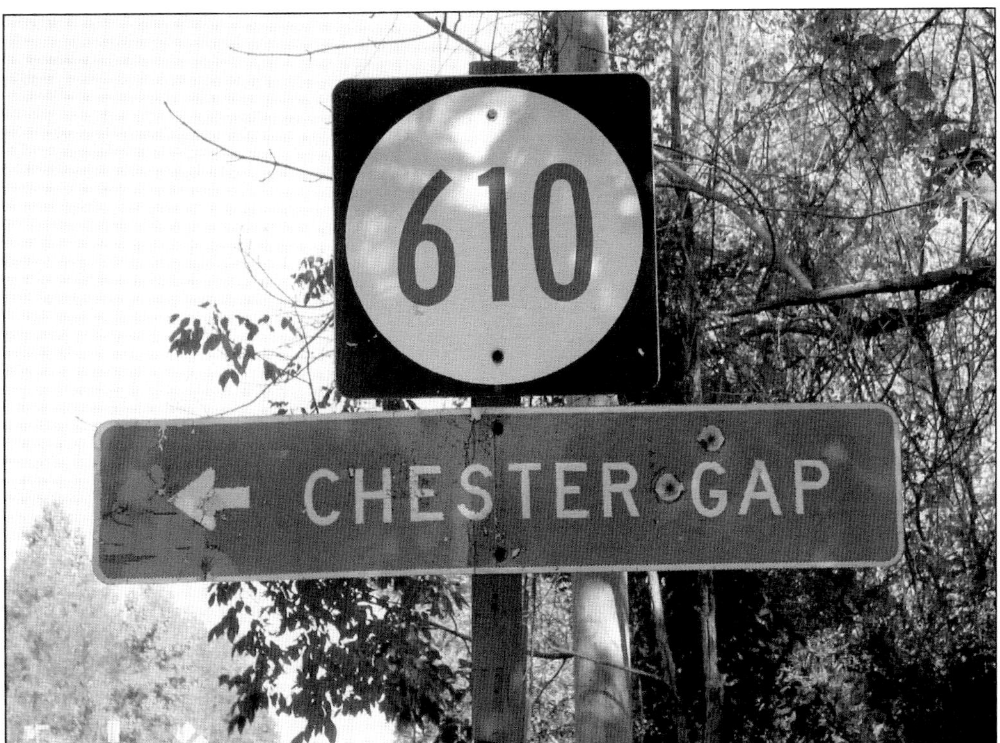

Rising to an elevation of 1,670 feet above sea level, Chester Gap was settled along Routes 610 and 660 west of Route 522. Once known as Happy Creek Gap, it was renamed after Capt. Thomas Chester, who owned land in the area in the 1700s. (Courtesy of John Tole.)

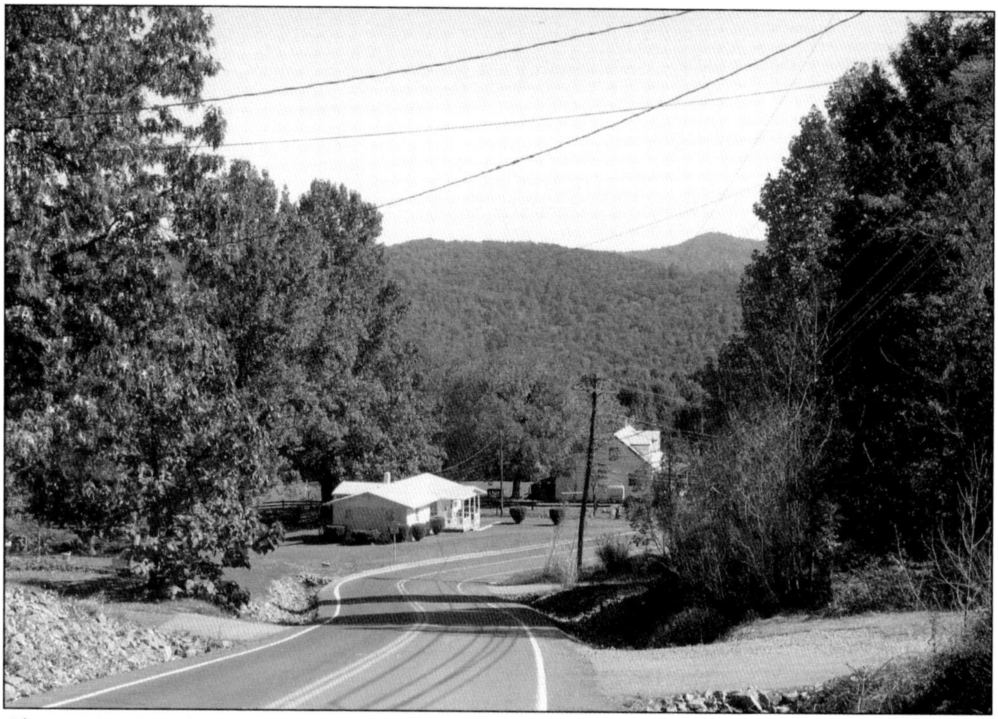

Chester Gap Road was once the main road from Richmond to Culpeper. It was also known as the Richmond/Falmouth Road and runs across the mountains at Chester Gap toward Front Royal. (Courtesy of John Tole.)

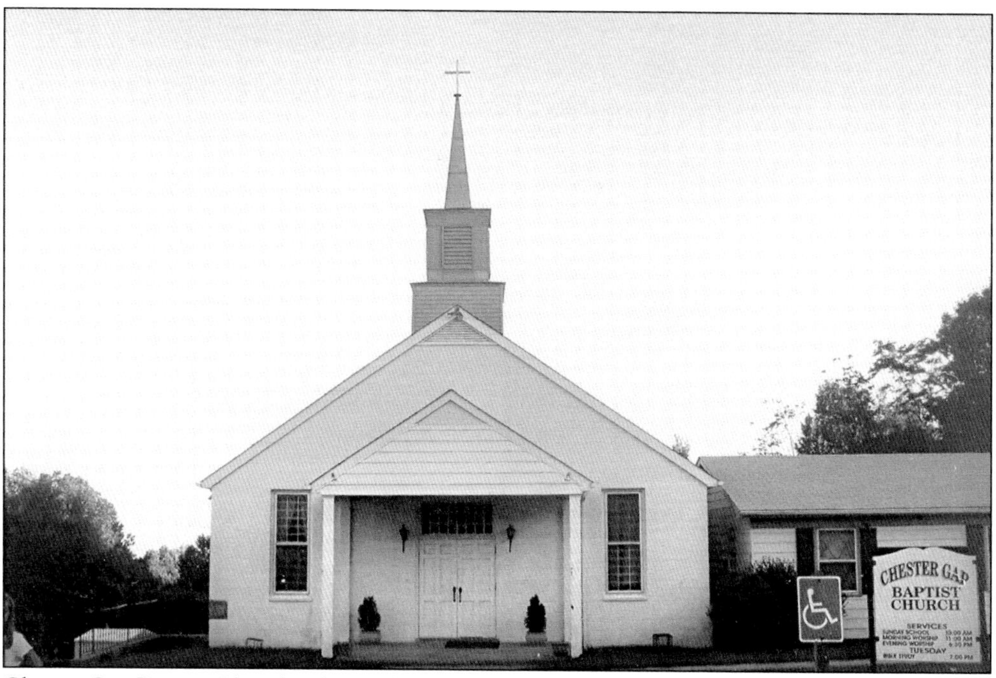

Chester Gap Baptist Church is located on Waterfall Road. It was started as a mission in 1957 and was constituted as a church in 1987. (Courtesy of Maybelle Gilkey.)

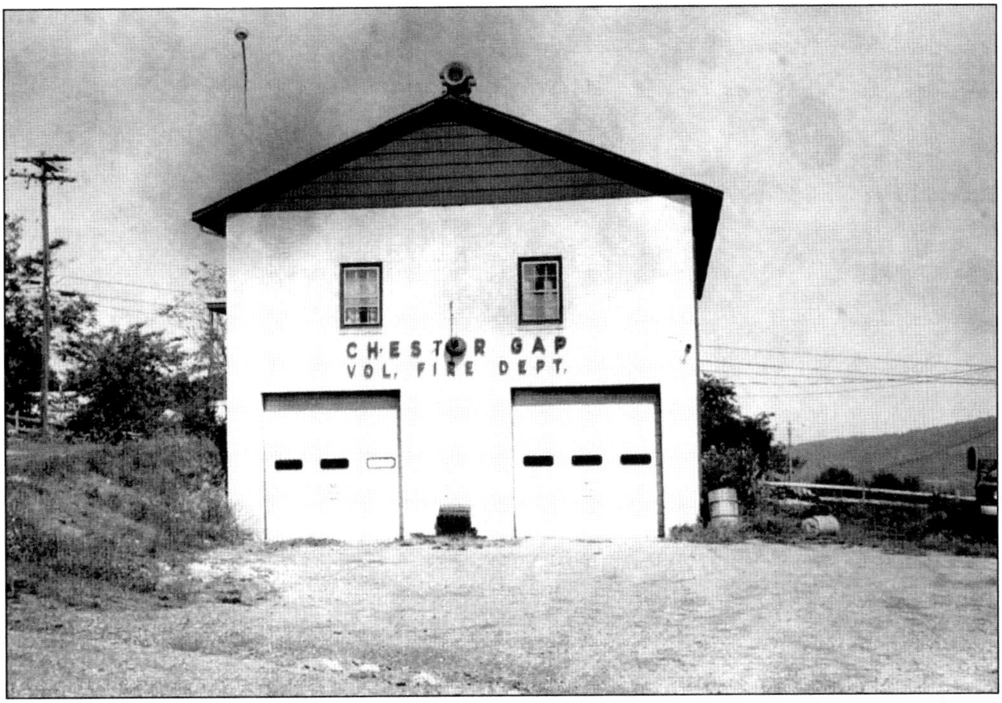

The Chester Gap Volunteer Fire Department was organized in 1960 with Merritt Greeley as president. Built almost entirely by volunteers, the building was completed in 1961. (Courtesy of Maybelle Gilkey.)

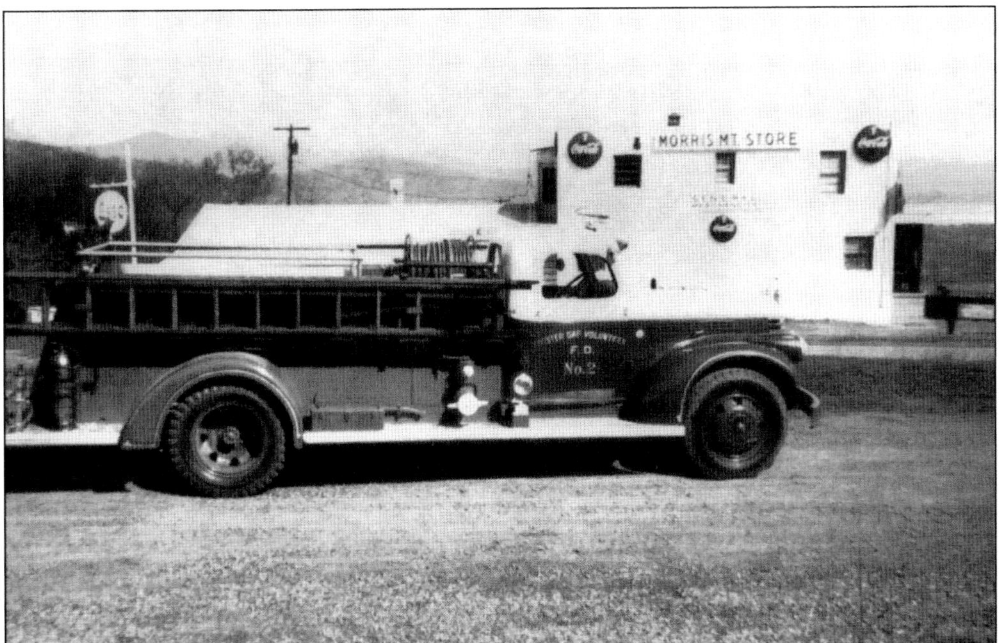

This is one of Chester Gap Volunteer Fire Department's fire trucks in 1964. The fire department was equipped with a 500-gallon Chevrolet-Maxim pumper, an old 250-gallon pumper, and a well-equipped ambulance. (Courtesy of Maybelle Gilkey.)

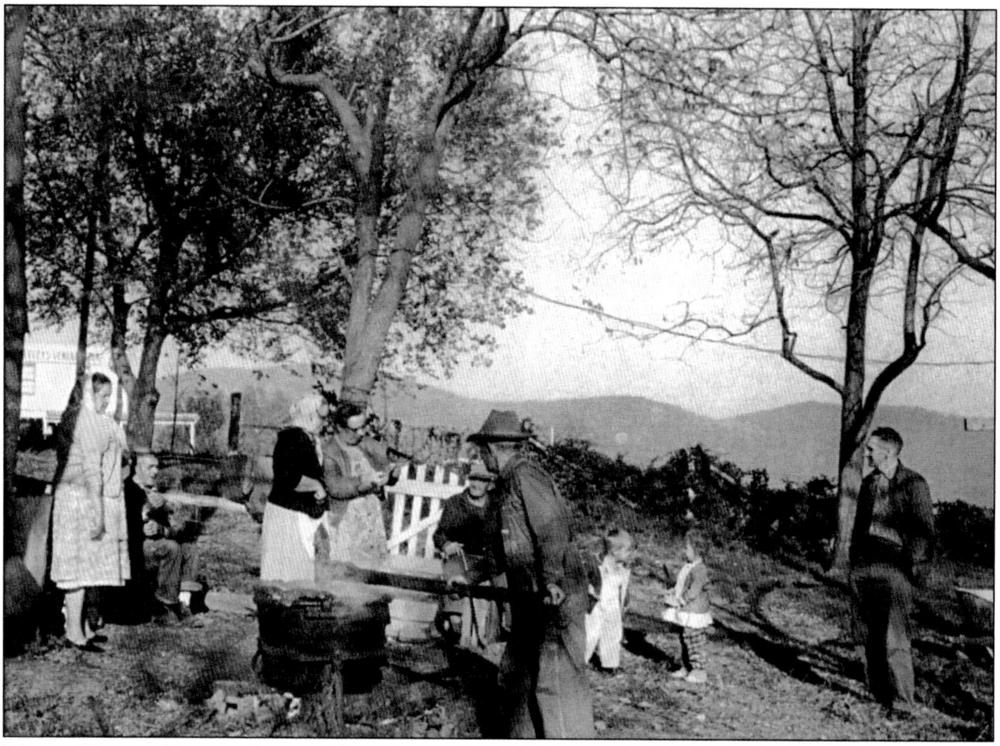

These Chester Gap residents gathered to make apple butter in the 1950s. Beginning the process with cider, sliced apples were added along with spices and sugar for seasoning. The sauce simmered for hours until the contents cooked down to the right consistency. (Courtesy of Bob Johnson.)

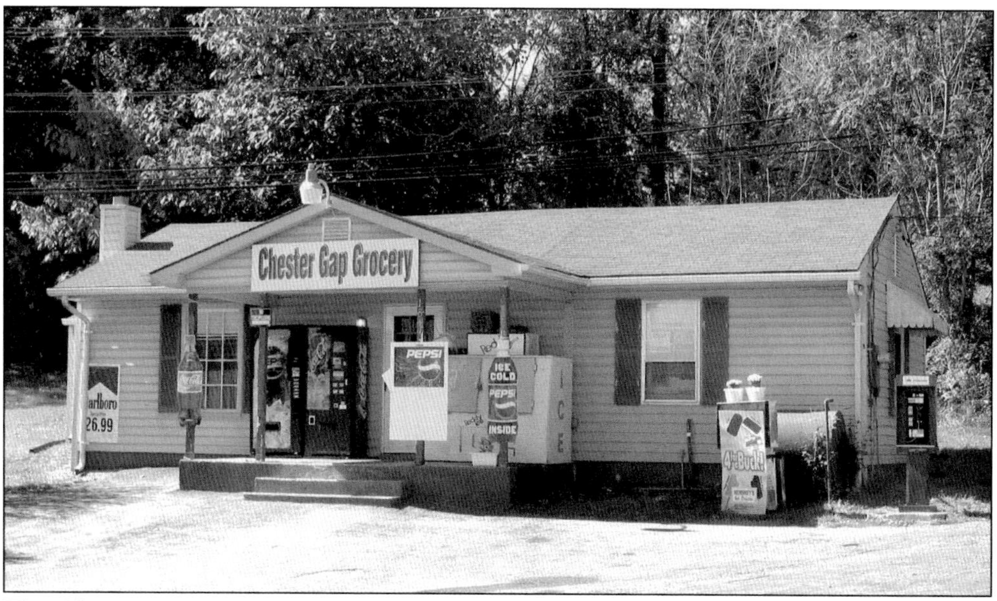

The Chester Gap Grocery on Chester Gap Road was built in the 1950s. It carries general merchandise for nearby residents and serves as a social meeting place. A post office is also housed in the store. (Courtesy of John Tole.)

Three

Flint Hill

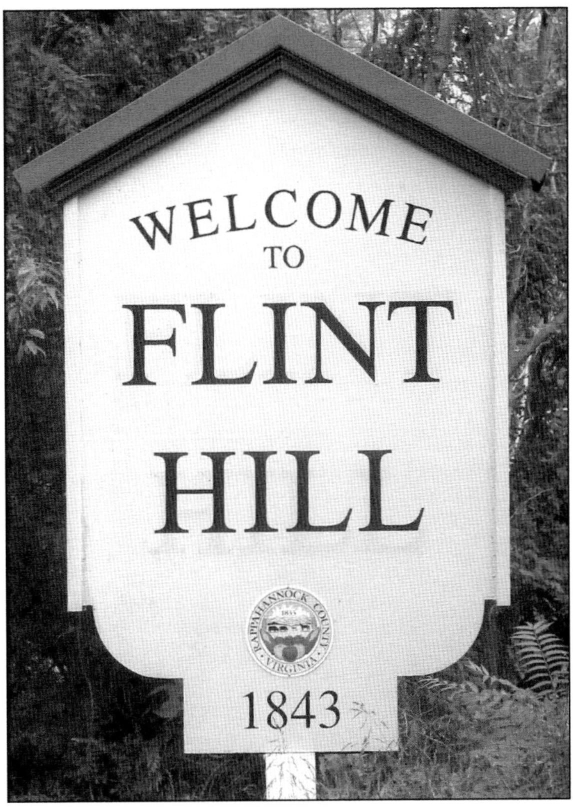

The Hickmans and the Thorntons settled Flint Hill in the early 1800s. The town appeared on a map drawn by John Wood as early as 1821. There is speculation that a family named Flinn or another family named Flynt may have been the source of the town's name. Another possibility is that the name came from the flint rocks or quartz found in the nearby hills. The post office was established in 1823, and the village was established in 1843. (Courtesy of John Tole.)

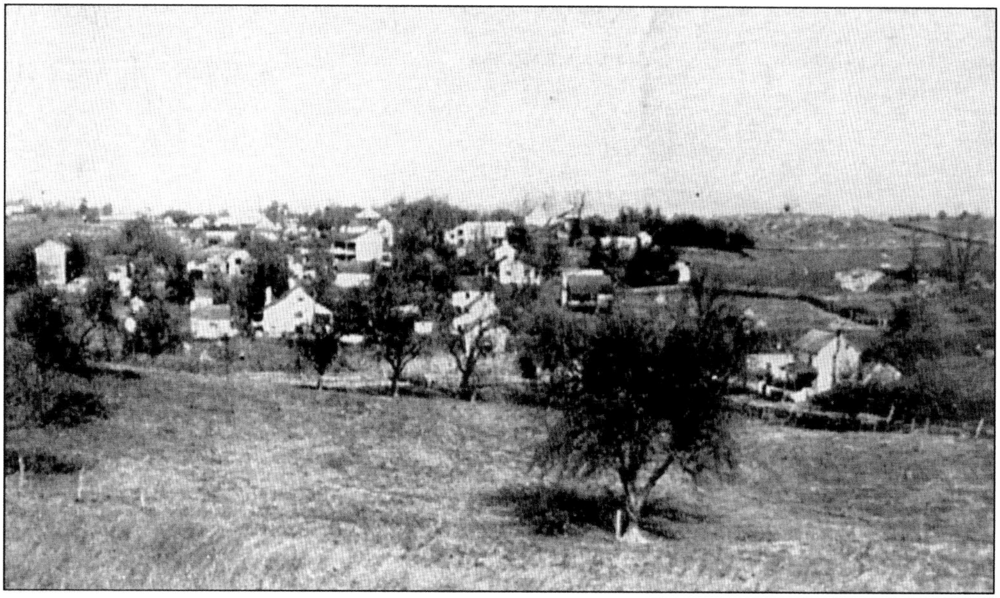

This is Flint Hill as it appeared in 1932, looking north on the old Chester's Road. (Courtesy of Arland Welch.)

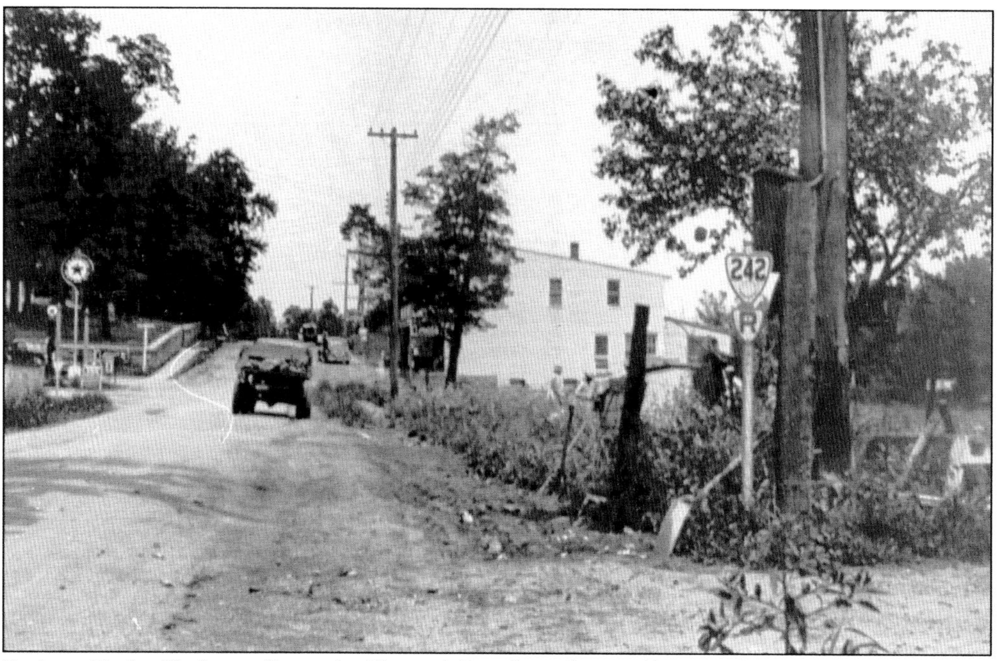

Zachary Taylor Highway (formerly Chester's Road) in Flint Hill proceeds north through Huntly to the top of the mountain at Chester Gap. The road was widened in the 1930s, leaving many homes sitting directly on the road. (Courtesy of Arland Welch.)

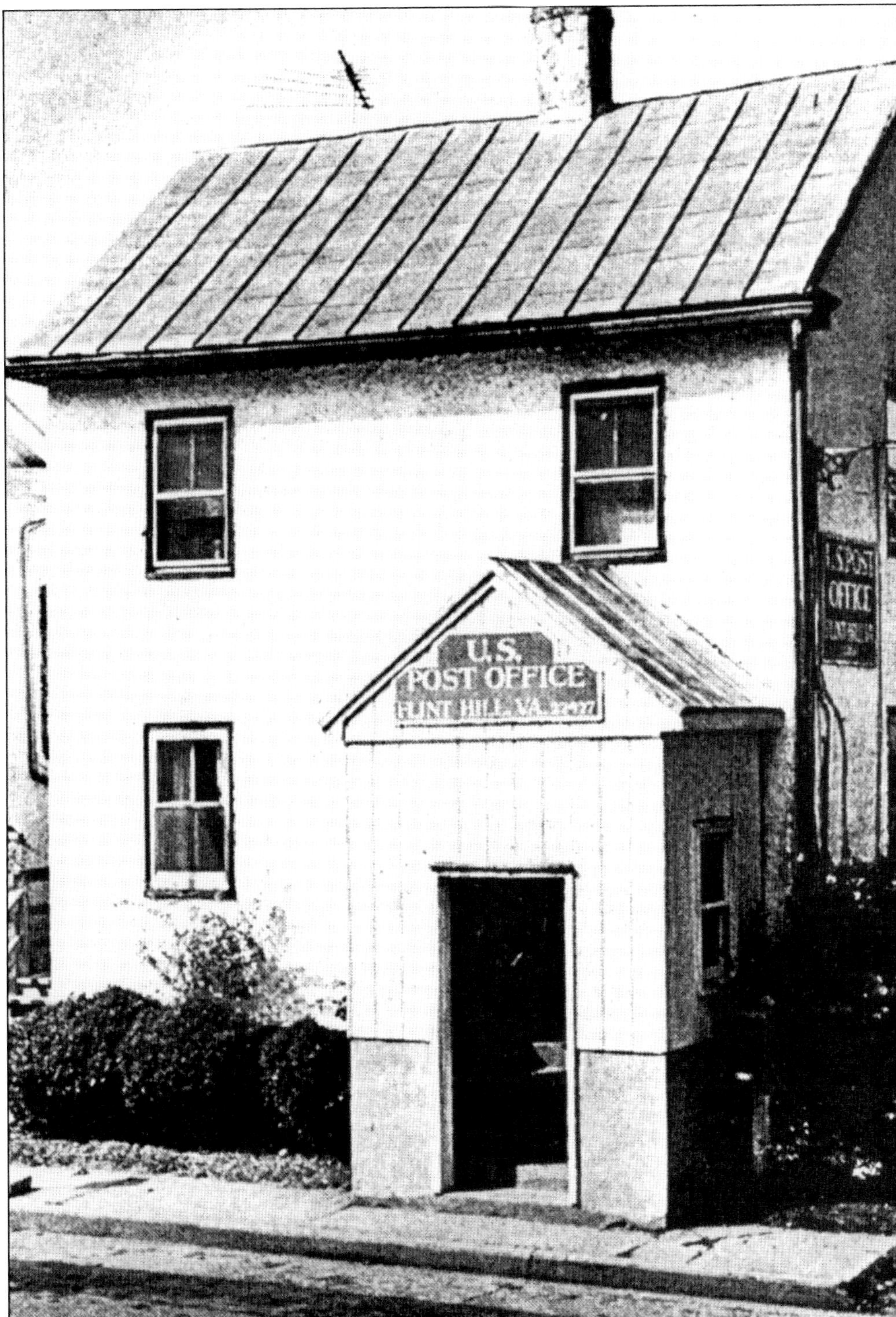

This small building on the Zachary Taylor Highway served as the post office from 1962 until the late 1980s. (Courtesy of Arland Welch.)

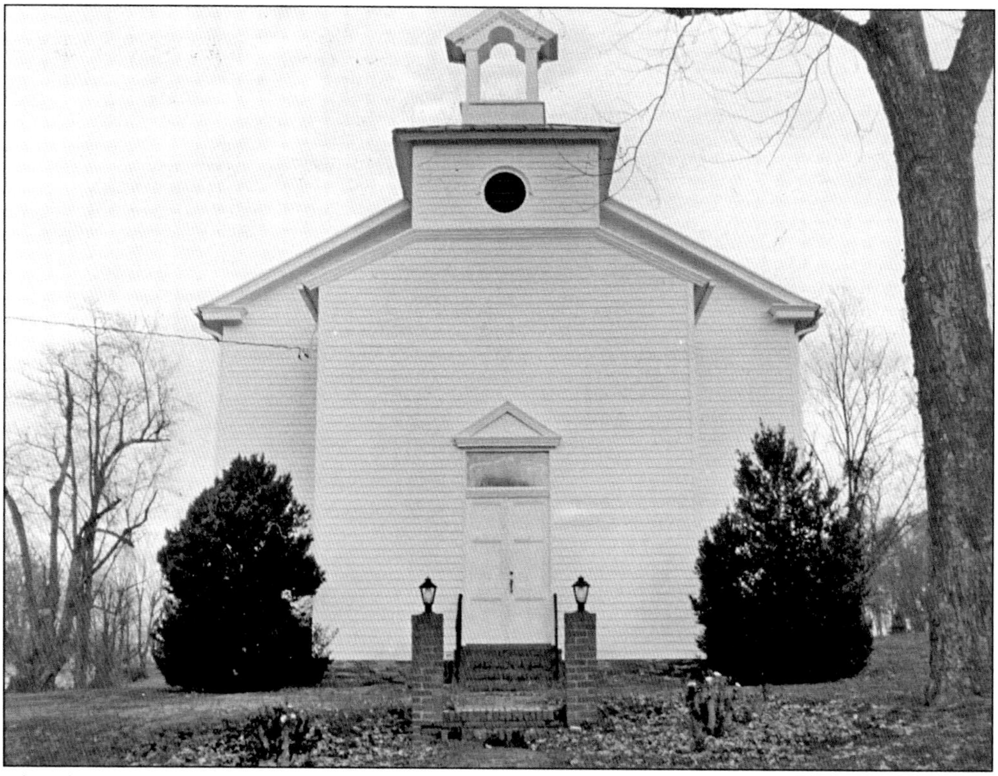

The Flint Hill Baptist Church was built in 1854. The cemetery behind the church includes the grave of Albert Gallitin Willis, a Mosby Ranger who was hanged by Union forces in retaliation for a Union soldier having been killed by Mosby's men. The church is on the National Register of Historic Places and the Virginia Landmarks Registry. (Courtesy of Arland Welch.)

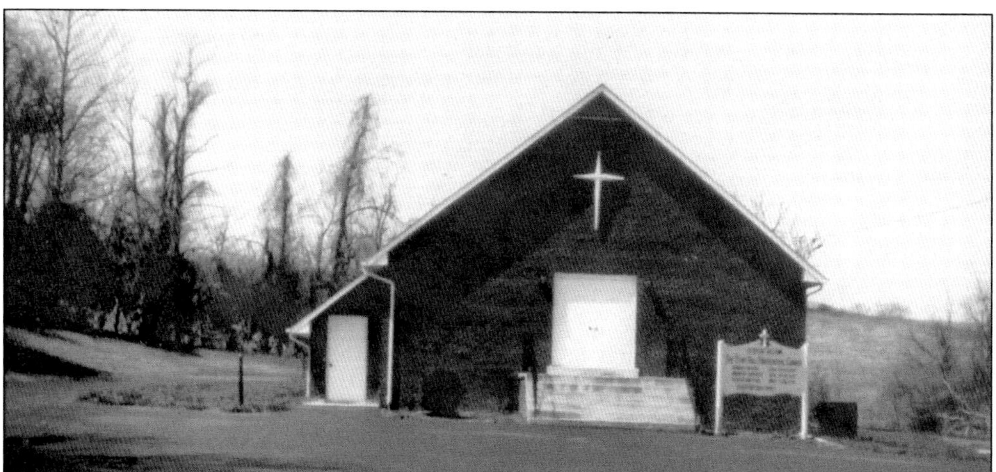

The Flint Hill Pentecostal Church was built in 11 days in 1943 on donated land on Aileen Road. The original church was destroyed by fire in 1986 and rebuilt within the year. (Courtesy of Arland Welch.)

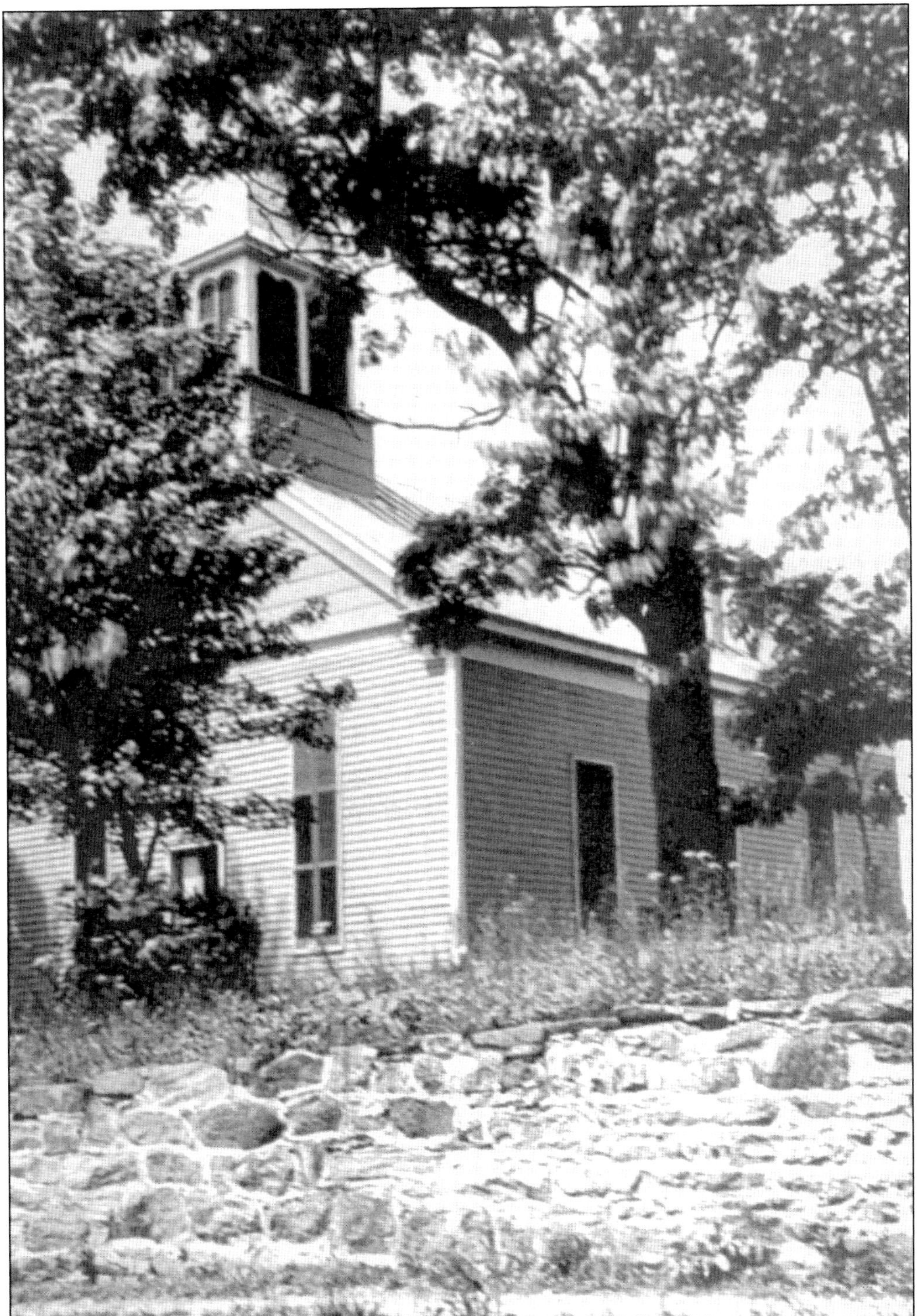

The Flint Hill Methodist Church was organized in 1832. The church building was constructed in 1847 and had a Masonic Lodge chapel on the upper floor. It is said that local people hid their meats upstairs during the Civil War. (Courtesy of Arland Welch.)

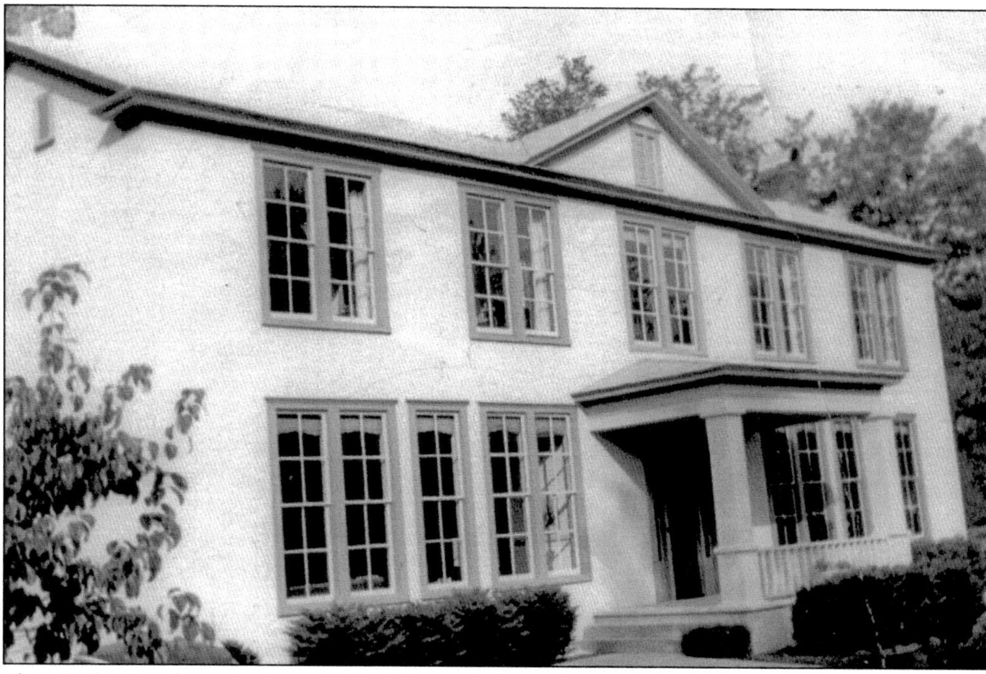

Flint Hill School was built in 1908. It housed three classrooms and an auditorium, with a rear classroom added at a later date. Students from elementary through third-year high school attended. (Courtesy of Arland Welch.)

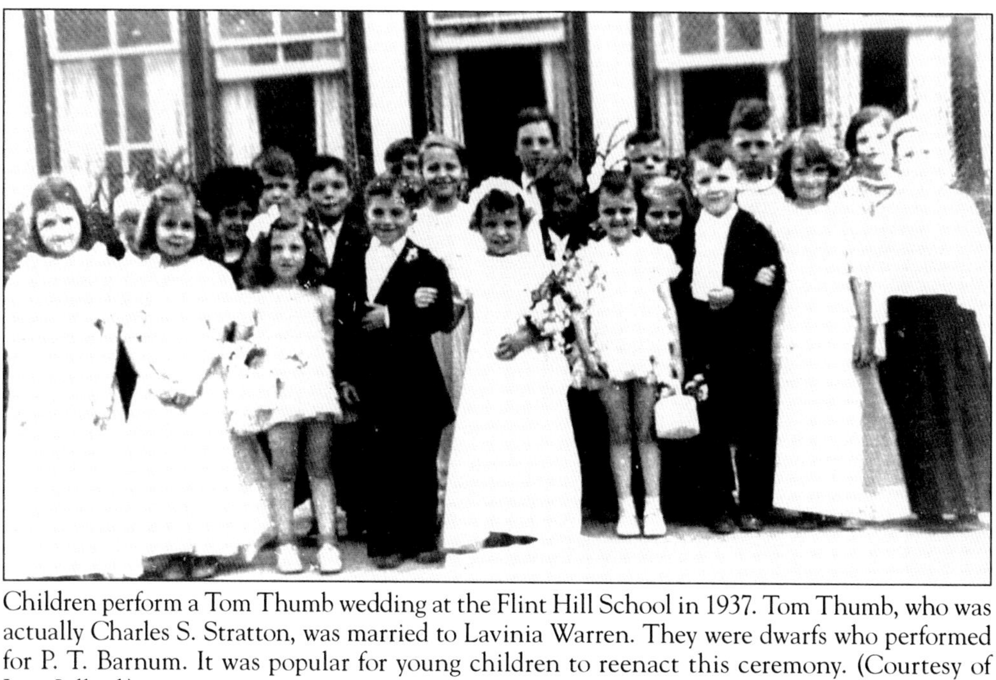

Children perform a Tom Thumb wedding at the Flint Hill School in 1937. Tom Thumb, who was actually Charles S. Stratton, was married to Lavinia Warren. They were dwarfs who performed for P. T. Barnum. It was popular for young children to reenact this ceremony. (Courtesy of Jean Lillard.)

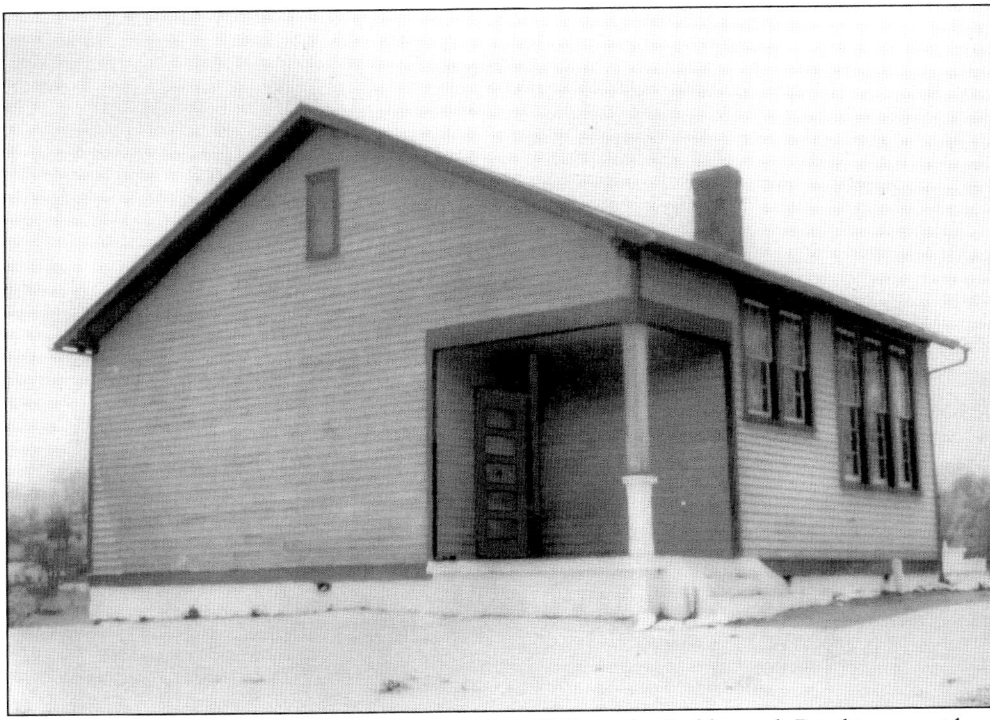

The Flint Hill Graded School was constructed in 1925 on the Fodderstack Road just outside of Flint Hill. It housed African American students from grades one through five until 1966. This school was one of four Rosenwald schools in Rappahannock County. Julius Rosenwald, then president of Sears, Roebuck, and Company, established a foundation to erect schools for African American students. (Courtesy of the Rappahannock Historical Society.)

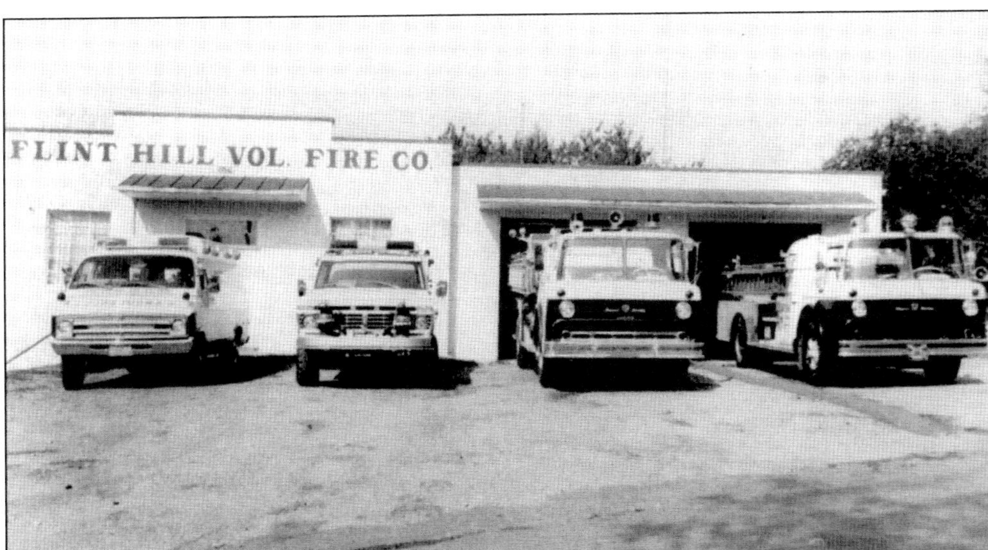

The Flint Hill Volunteer Fire Company, located on Fodderstack Road, was organized in 1954. The fire station is situated on land donated by Roberta K. Massie Spalding, who lived beside it. (Courtesy of Arland Welch.)

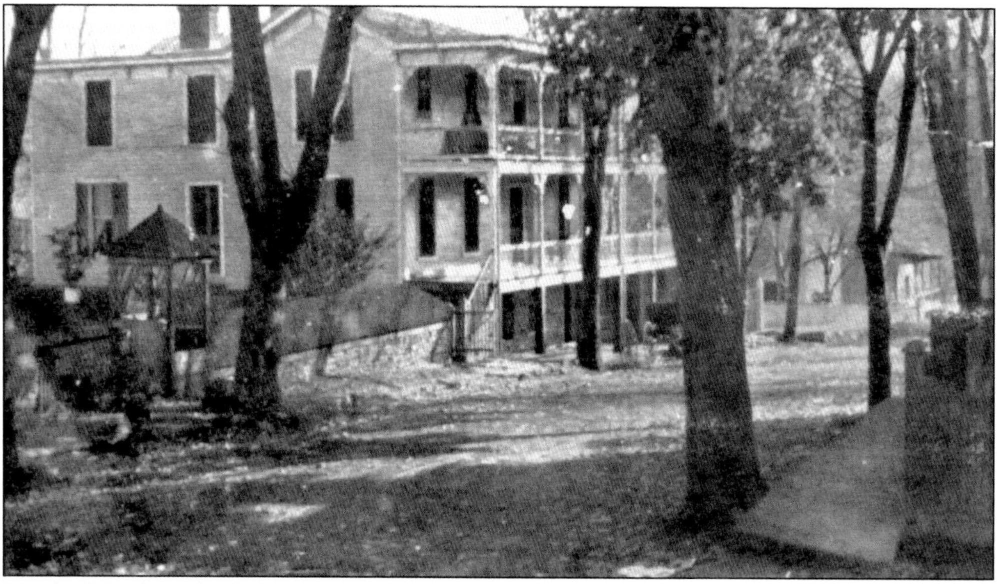

Hezekiah Ricketts built the Ricketts Hotel in 1869. The Ricketts Hotel was more like a rooming house with permanent roomers most of the time. Two doctors were known to have had their medical practices there at one time. (Courtesy of Arland Welch.)

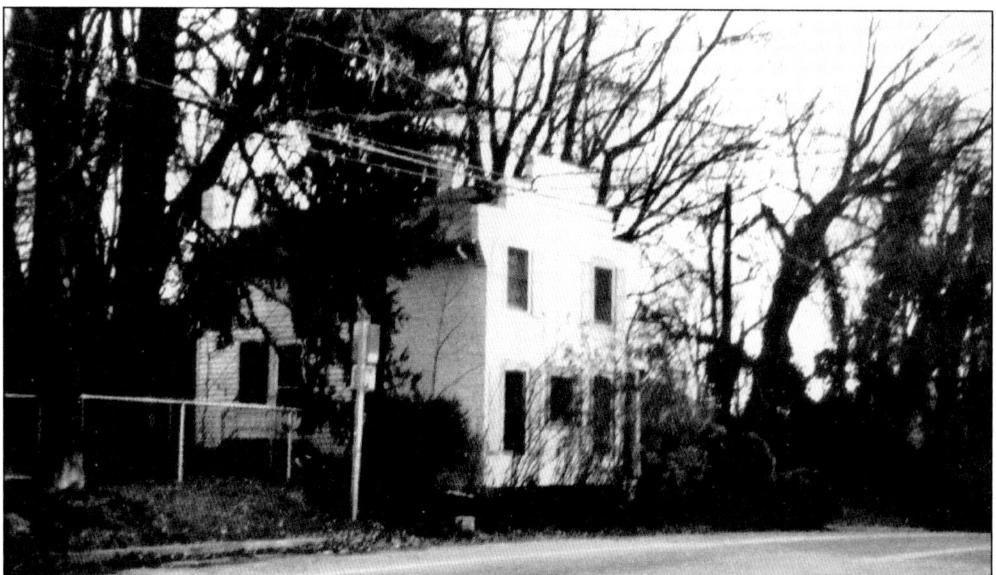

The Ricketts Tavern and Saddle Shop was established in the 1830s. It was located on Zachary Taylor Highway at the intersection of Fodderstack Road. The building served as the Flint Hill Post Office from 1916 to 1962. (Courtesy of Arland Welch.)

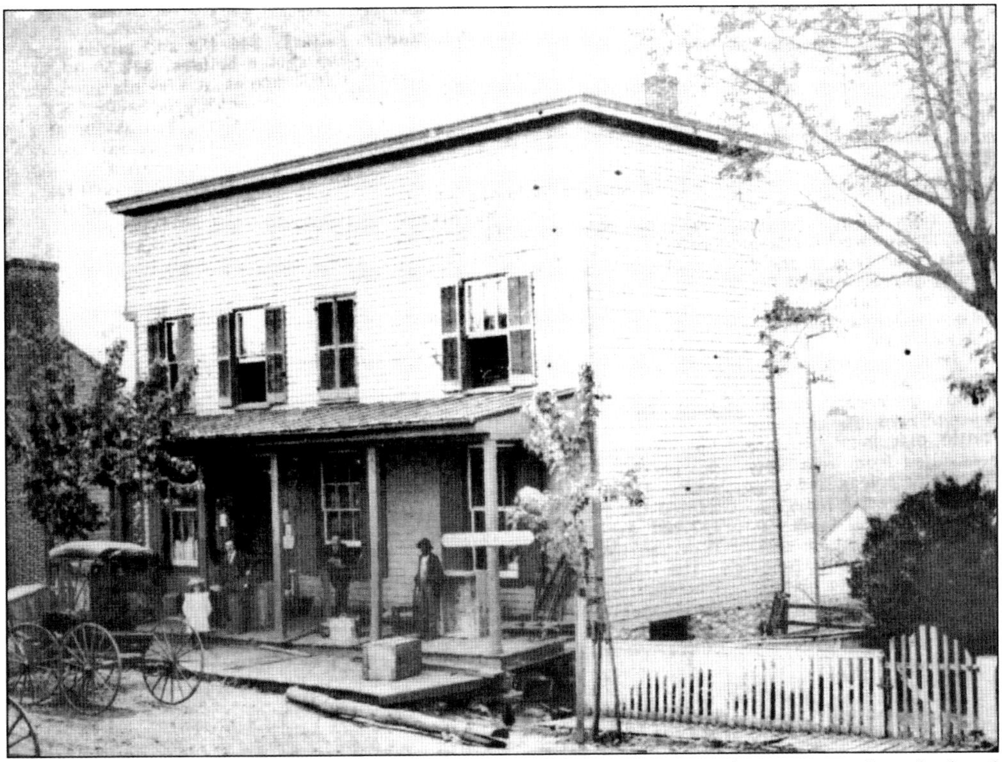

The Flint Hill Store, located on Zachary Taylor Highway, was a popular meeting place for local residents in the late 1800s. (Courtesy of Arland Welch.)

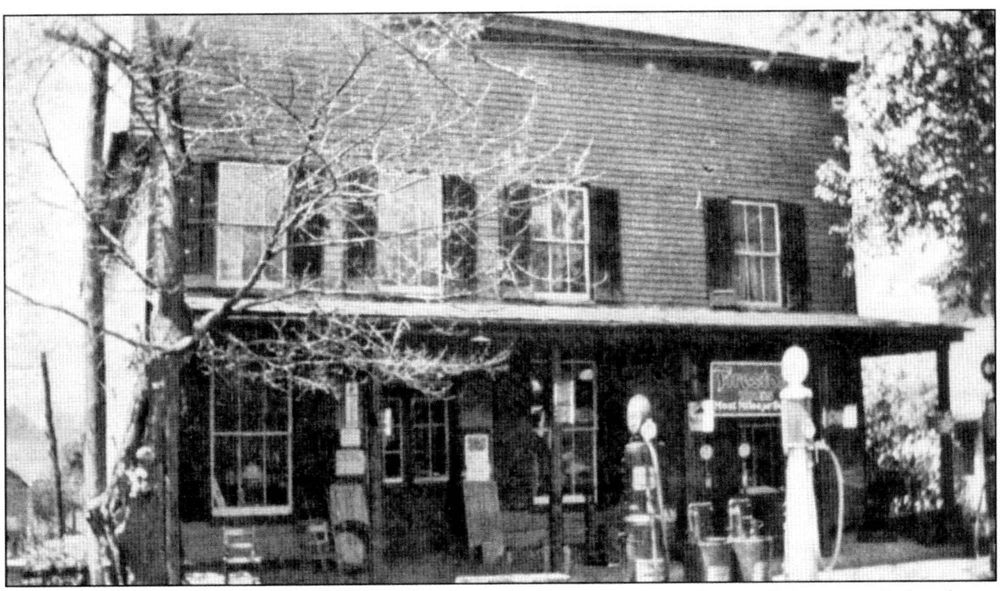

By the early 1930s, the Flint Hill Store had installed gas pumps in front of the store. It has been said that you could find just about anything that you needed at this store. (Courtesy of the Rappahannock Historical Society.)

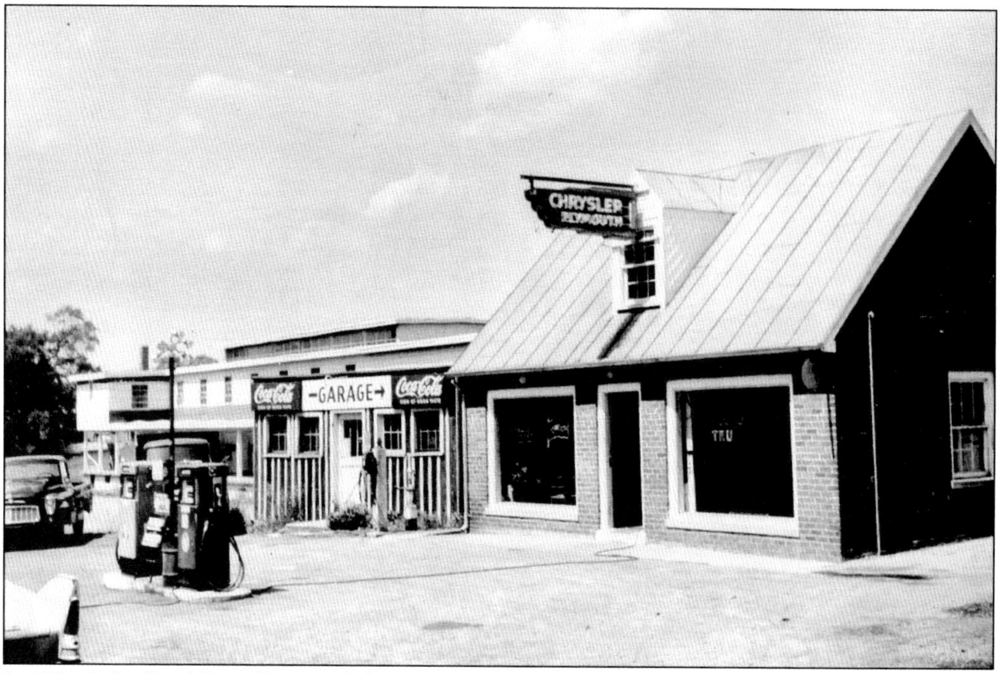

In 1939, J. Garland Russell opened the Russell Brothers Garage and Chrysler dealership on Route 522. The dealership closed in 1971. (Courtesy of Wallace Russell.)

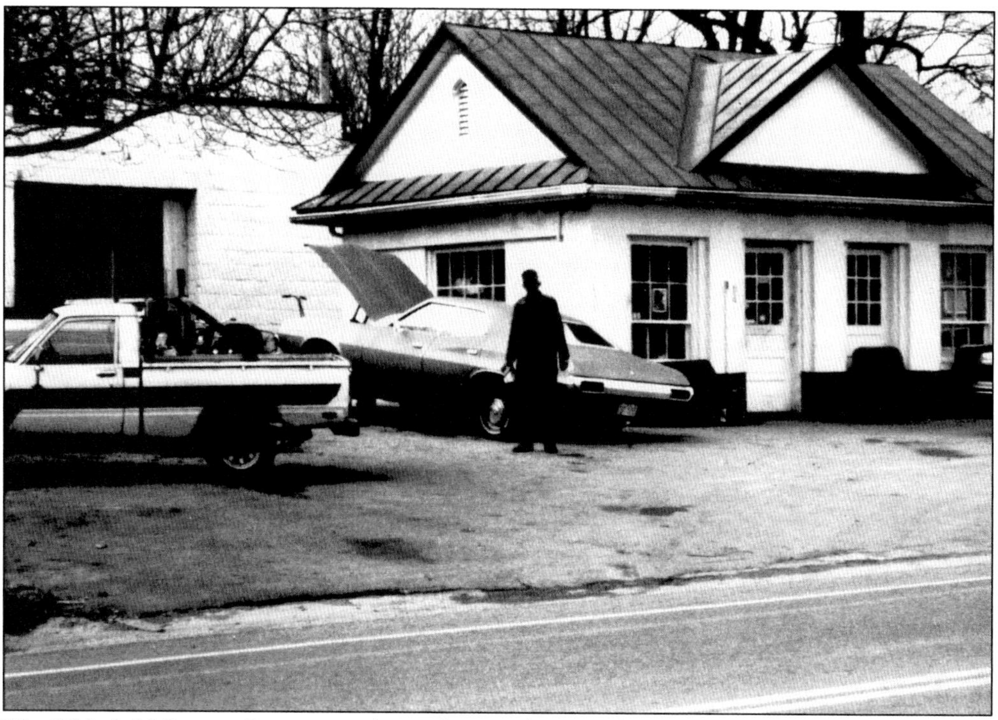

The Wakefield Service Station was located on Zachary Taylor Highway. This location has been the site of various local businesses since the 1840s. This building was constructed in the late 1930s. (Courtesy of Arland Welch.)

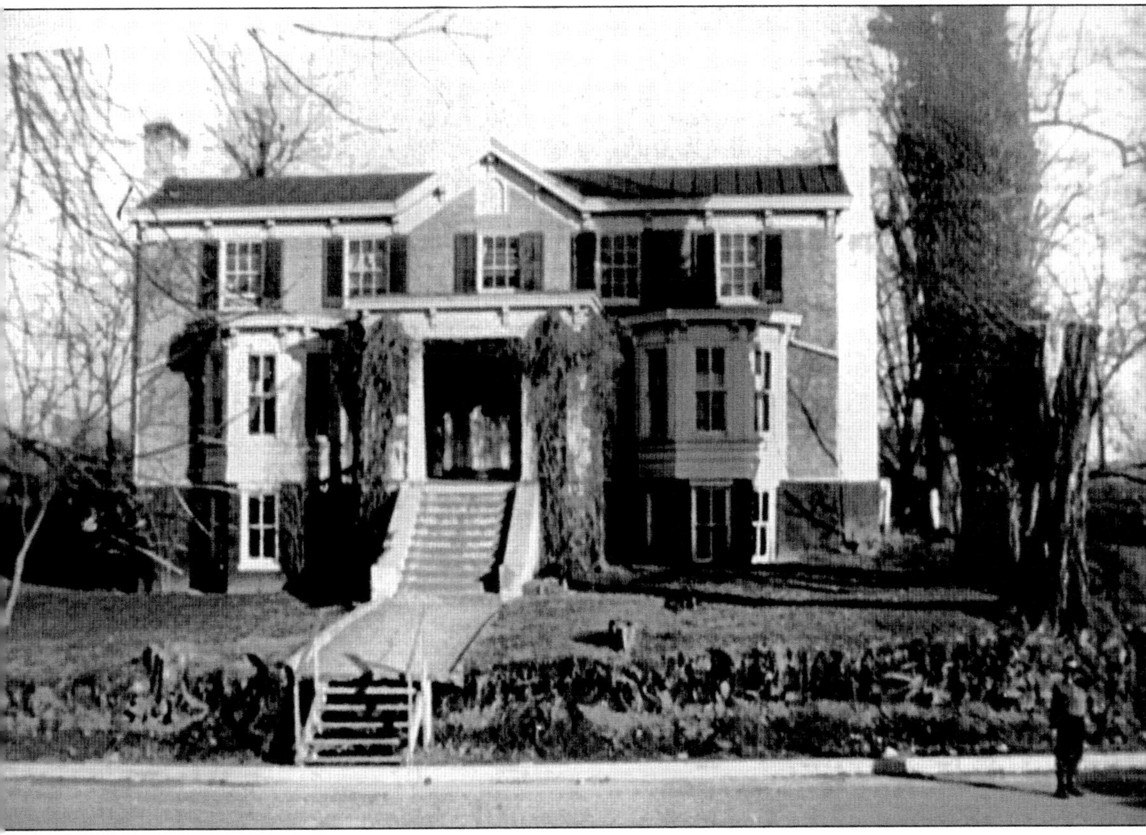

Edward Moore; his wife, Ida Lippett Yates; and their five children lived in this imposing Victorian house known as the Yates/Settle House during the winter months so their children could attend school in town. In 1923, the Yates family sold the house to James Minor Settle. (Courtesy of Arland Welch.)

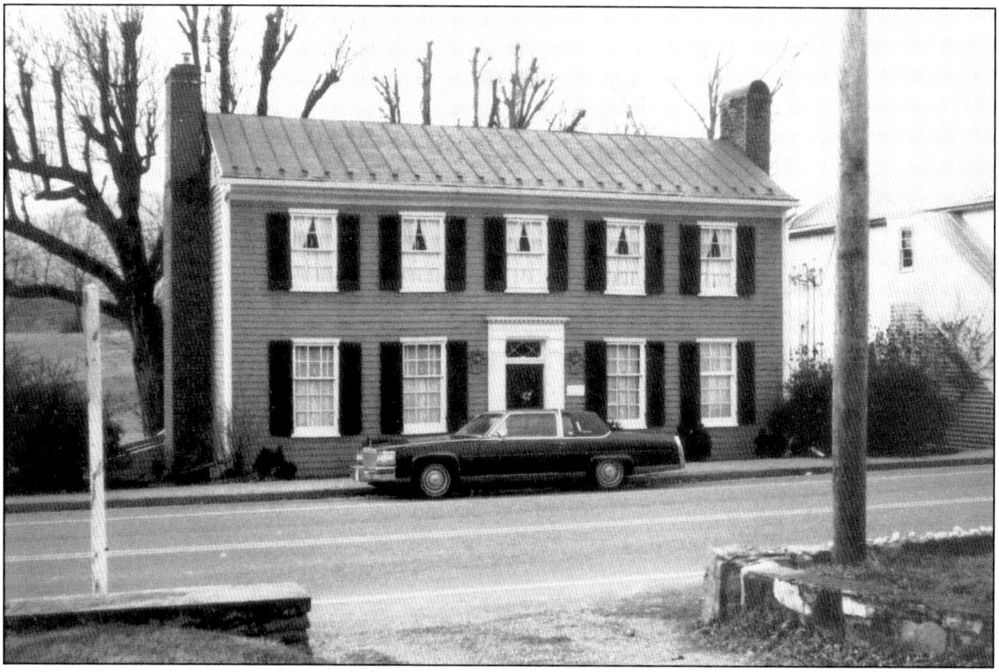

Althea Terrace occupies three of the original lots in the center of Flint Hill. The house was initially a one-story log structure dating to the 1750s. Over the years, the house took on the Colonial Federal appearance it has today. The house was named for the Althea bushes, or Rose of Sharon, that were plentiful here. (Courtesy of Arland Welch.)

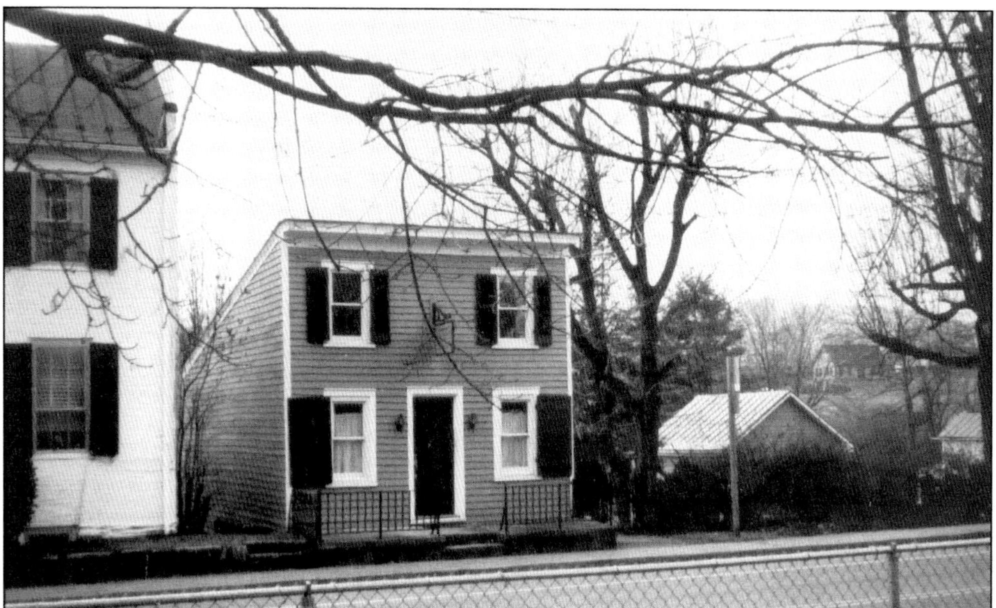

The small building next to Althea Terrace was a dependency used for many purposes. The building has been used as a saddler's shop, blacksmith shop, carriage house, dry good store, hardware store, and a Red Cross center where bandages were rolled during World War I. (Courtesy of Arland Welch.)

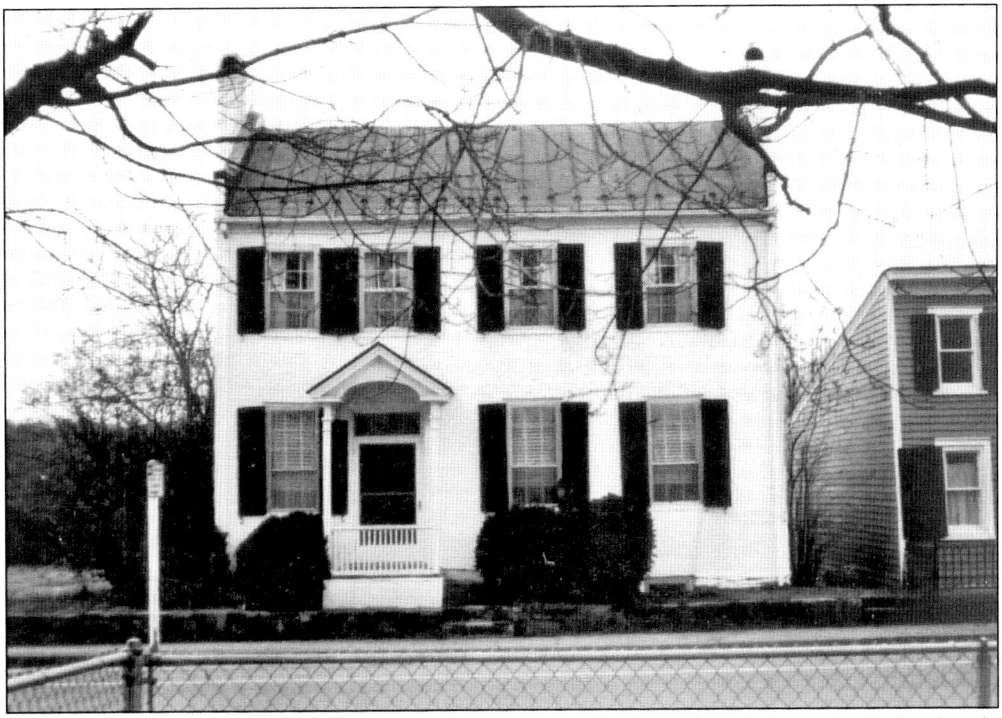

The Spalding House, on Zachary Taylor Highway, was built in the 1820s in the Federal style of soft-gray brick painted white. The house was used for a time as the Blue Ridge Institute, a private school where music and languages were taught. The school closed in 1908. (Courtesy of Arland Welch.)

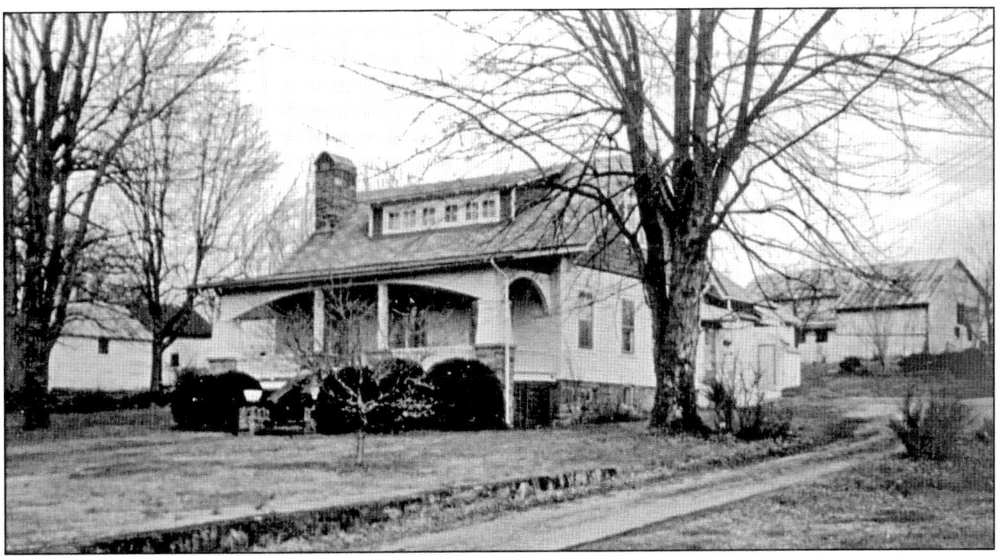

The Brady House on Zachary Taylor Highway was built in the 1920s. The house is an American bungalow with elements of a Craftsman house. Unlike other homes in the village, this home stands some distance from the road. (Courtesy of Arland Welch.)

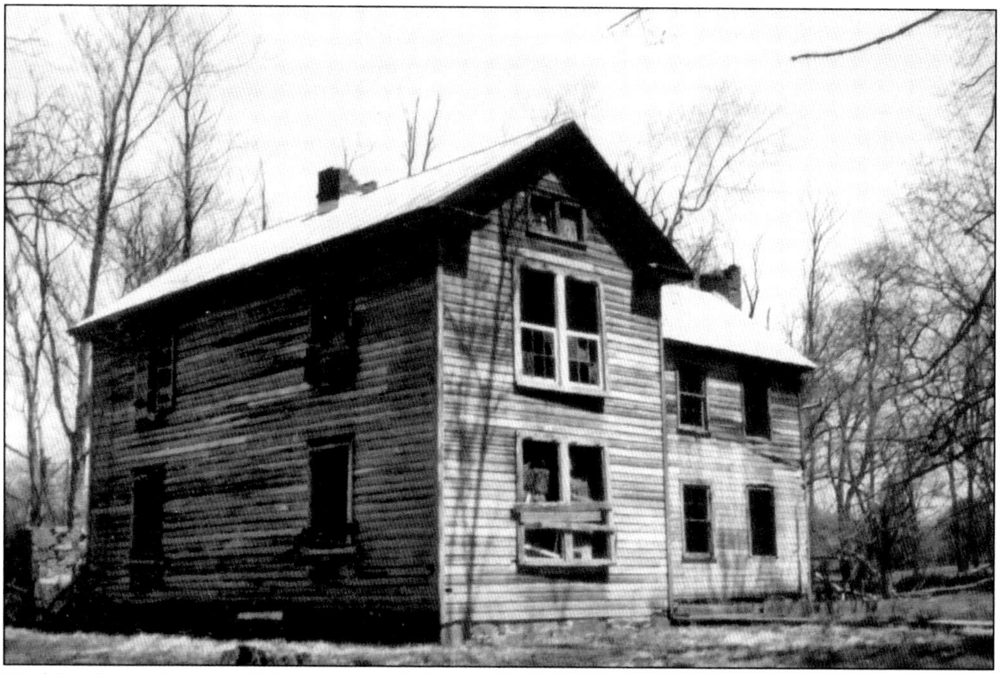

Bird Eastham, born in 1762, purchased this land in 1802 and built Glen Ayre on Shiloh Road. He and his wife, Lucy Chapman, had 11 children. Many of these children and their descendants helped develop the Flint Hill community. After falling into disrepair, the house was purchased in 1960 and restored. (Courtesy of Arland Welch.)

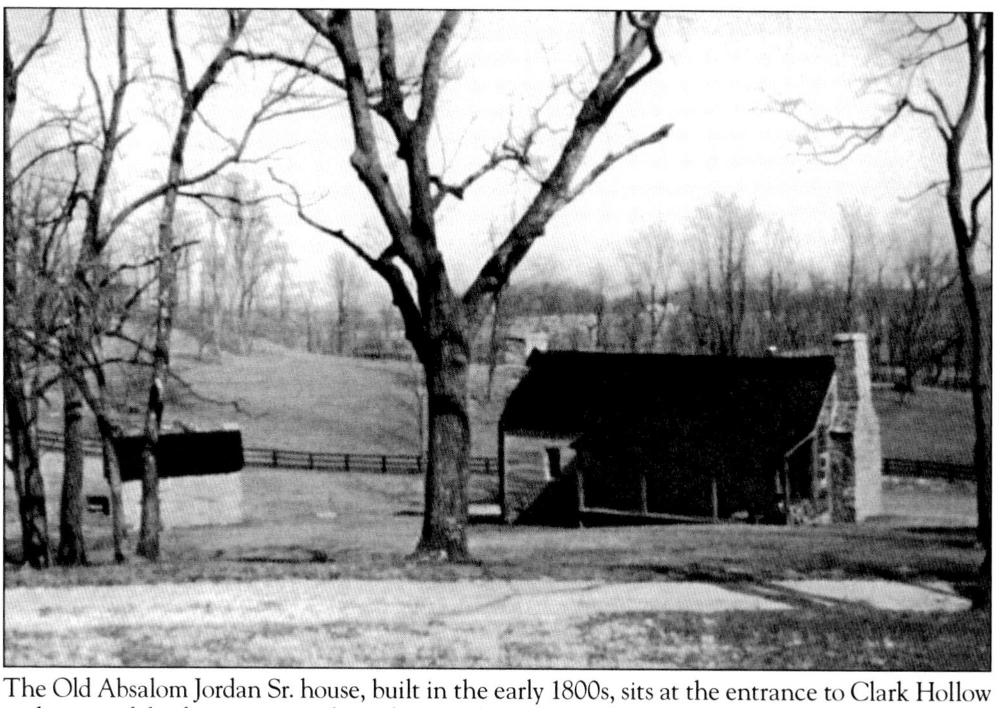

The Old Absalom Jordan Sr. house, built in the early 1800s, sits at the entrance to Clark Hollow and is one of the few remaining log cabins in the area. The home remained in the Jordan family for 146 years before being sold in 1948. (Courtesy of Arland Welch.)

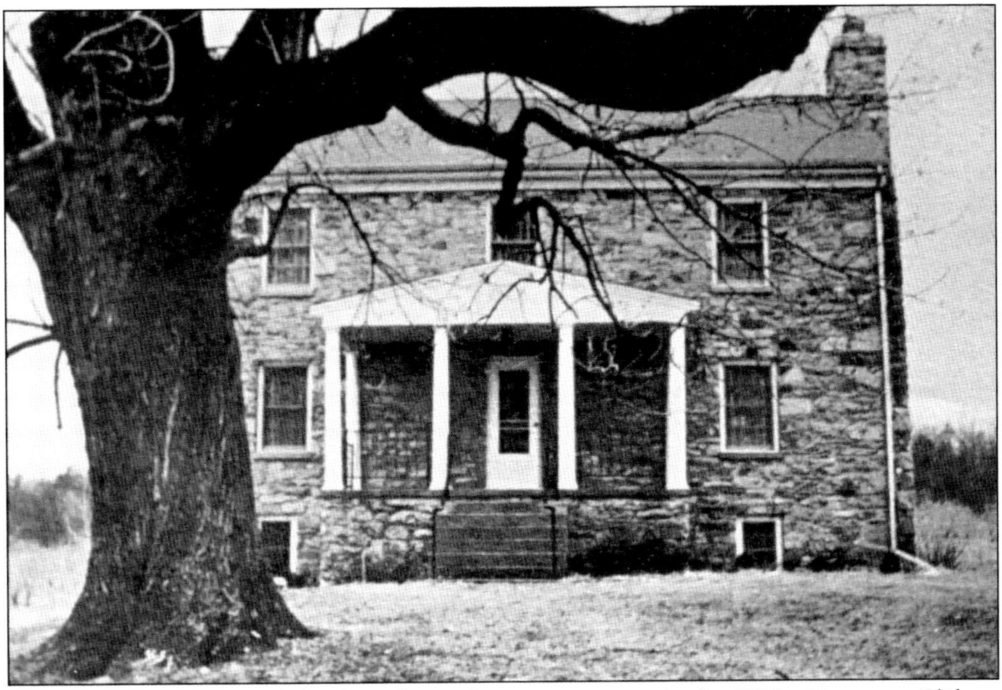

Elias Chelf Jr. constructed this large house from native stone in the 1820s. Known as Clifton, the house was sold to Dr. Robert H. Sears in 1854. During the Civil War, the house was used as a hospital. (Courtesy of Arland Welch.)

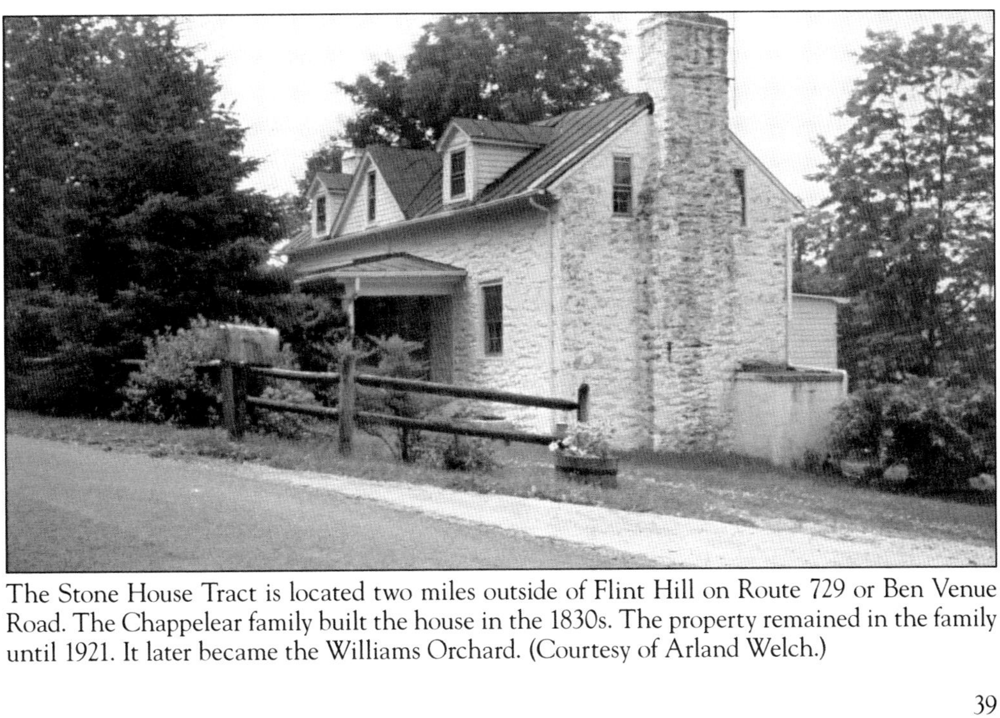

The Stone House Tract is located two miles outside of Flint Hill on Route 729 or Ben Venue Road. The Chappelear family built the house in the 1830s. The property remained in the family until 1921. It later became the Williams Orchard. (Courtesy of Arland Welch.)

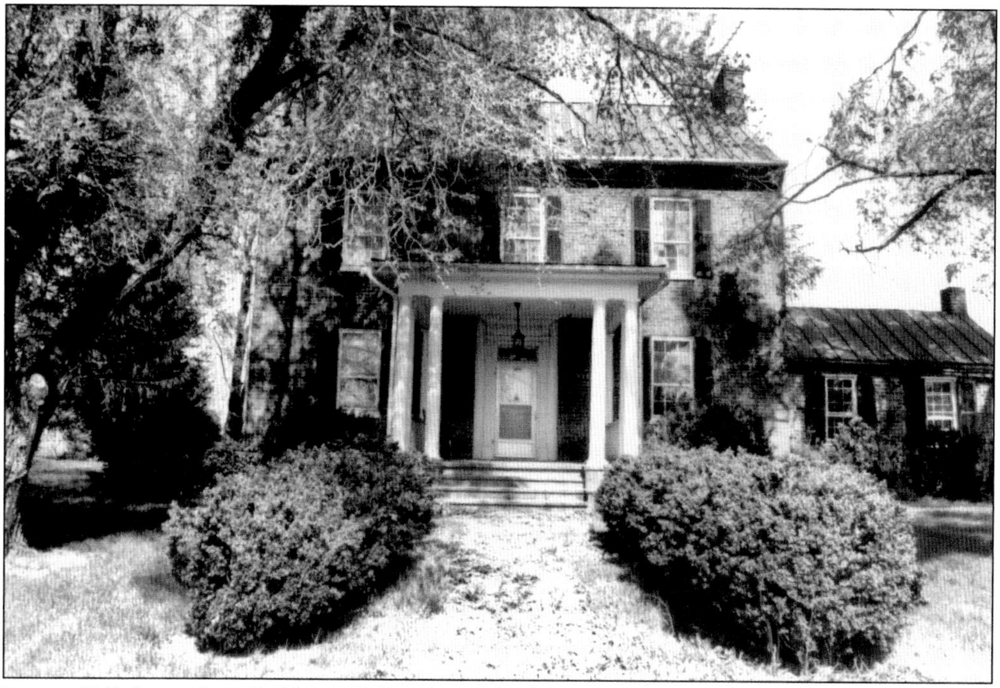

Locust Hill, located on Fodderstack Road, was built between 1812 and 1825. The property was conveyed to Robert and Frances Fisher Eastham in 1839. The Eastham family retained ownership of the property for 138 years before selling it in 1977. (Courtesy of Arland Welch.)

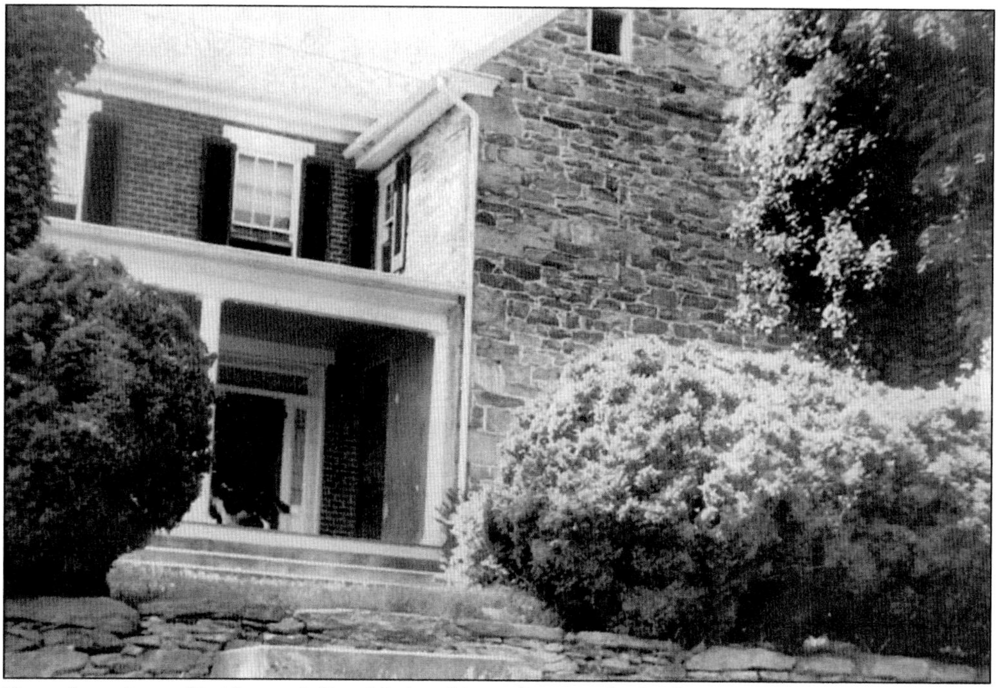

Horseshoe sits on Fodderstack Road behind huge boxwoods. Built in 1770 by George and Ann Crupper Calvert on thousands of acres below Fodderstack Mountain, the original home was constructed of stone. (Courtesy of Arland Welch.)

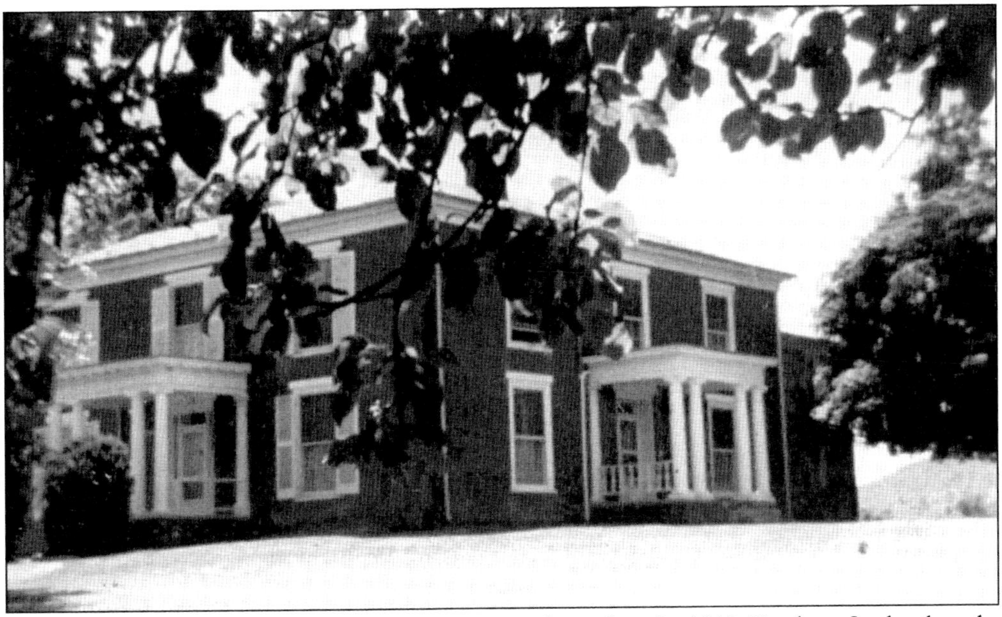

Bowling Green began as a 12-by-12-foot one-room log cabin. In 1840, Eastham Jordan bought the property and added the brick part to the house. All the material used in the construction of the house came directly from the farm. Bowling Green was saved from demolition in the 1930s when the government acquired the land for the resettlement of some families who were displaced when the Shenandoah National Park was established. (Courtesy of Arland Welch.)

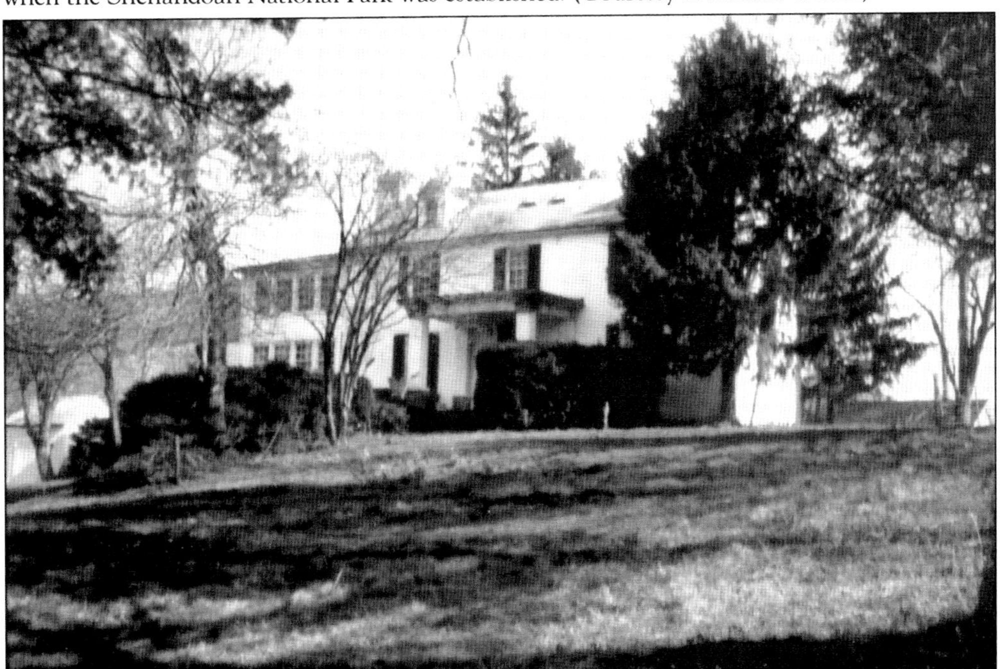

Buena Vista was built between 1839 and 1840 of native stone with a plaster facade. Robert Woodford "Bob Ridley" Eastham, an infamous member of Mosby's Rangers, was born and raised here. This property is located almost at Massie's Corner on Route 522. (Courtesy of Arland Welch.)

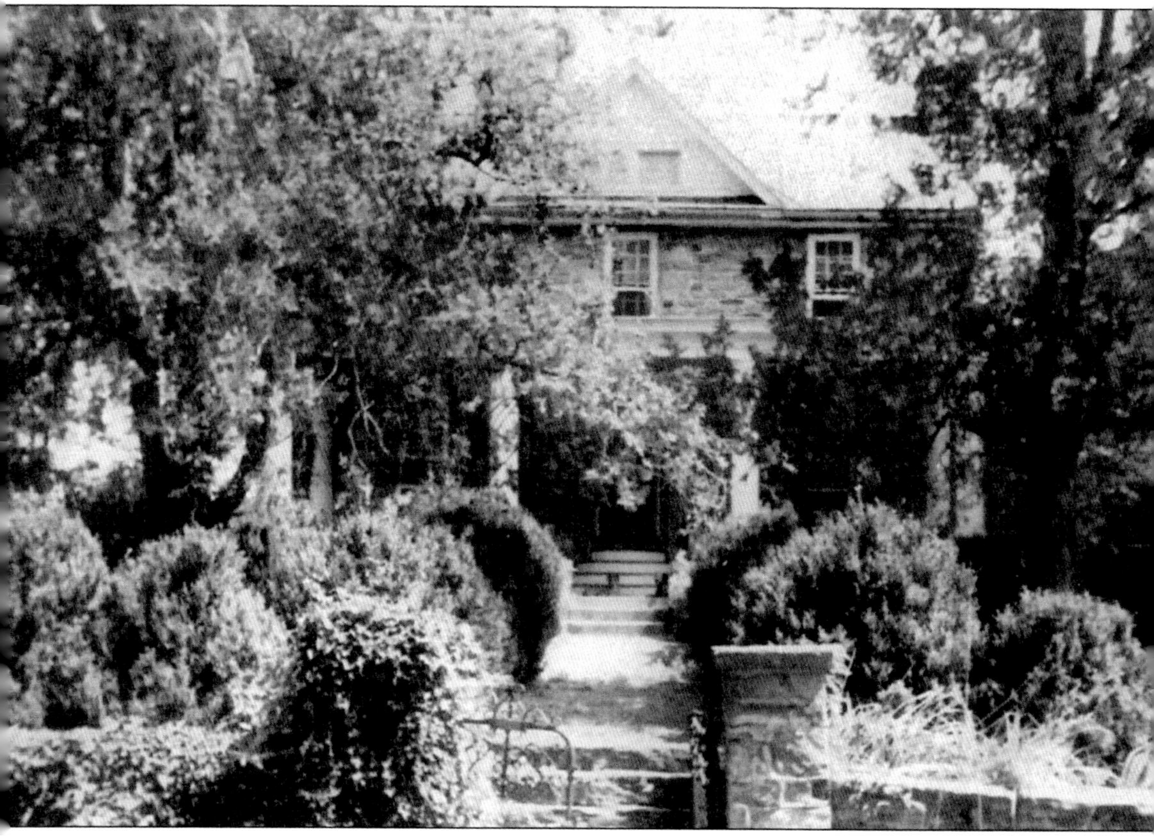

James and Lucy Deatherage Moore built Rock Hill in the early 1830s where they raised 11 children. The property is located on Fodderstack Road. (Courtesy of Arland Welch.)

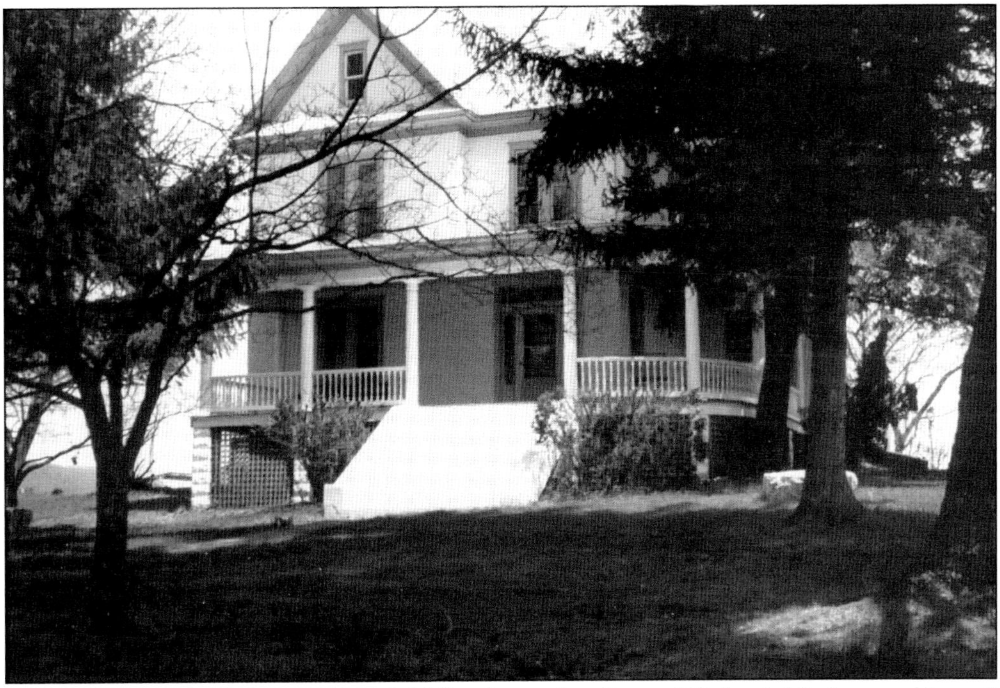

Germany Mills, also known as Hittle's Mill, is located on Route 522. Jacob Hittle owned it until 1836, when he sold it to Addison Turner. It remained in the Turner family for 110 years until 1947, when it was sold to the Foster brothers. (Courtesy of Arland Welch.)

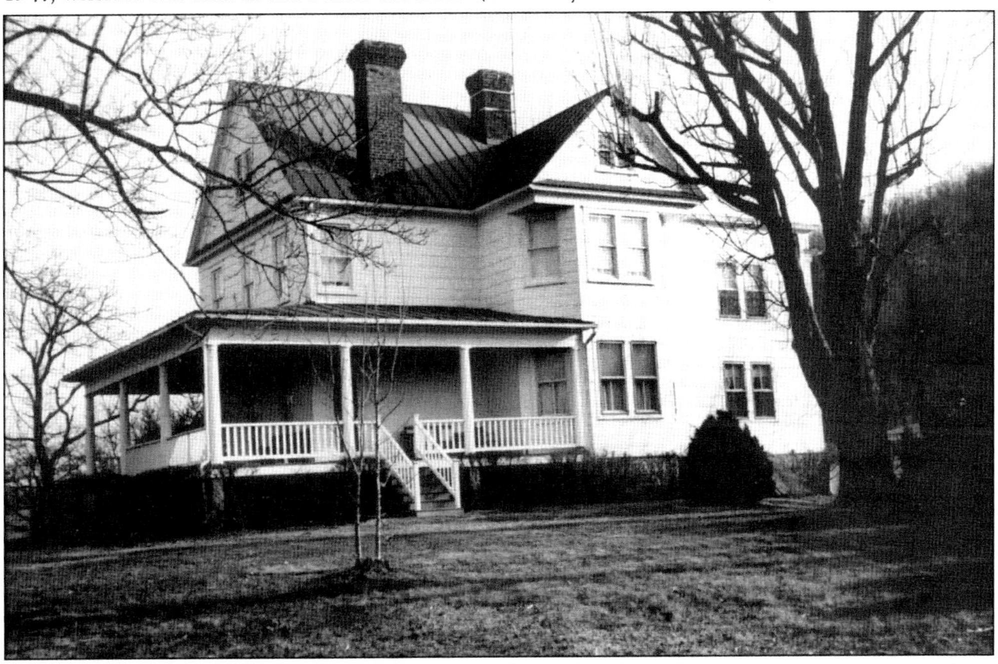

The Mountain View Farm house was built in 1890. The Eastham family owned the property from 1890 until 1945, when the farm was sold to brothers William Roland Welch and Elwood Welch. William Roland Welch and his wife, Arland, assumed ownership of the farm in 1952. (Courtesy of Arland Welch.)

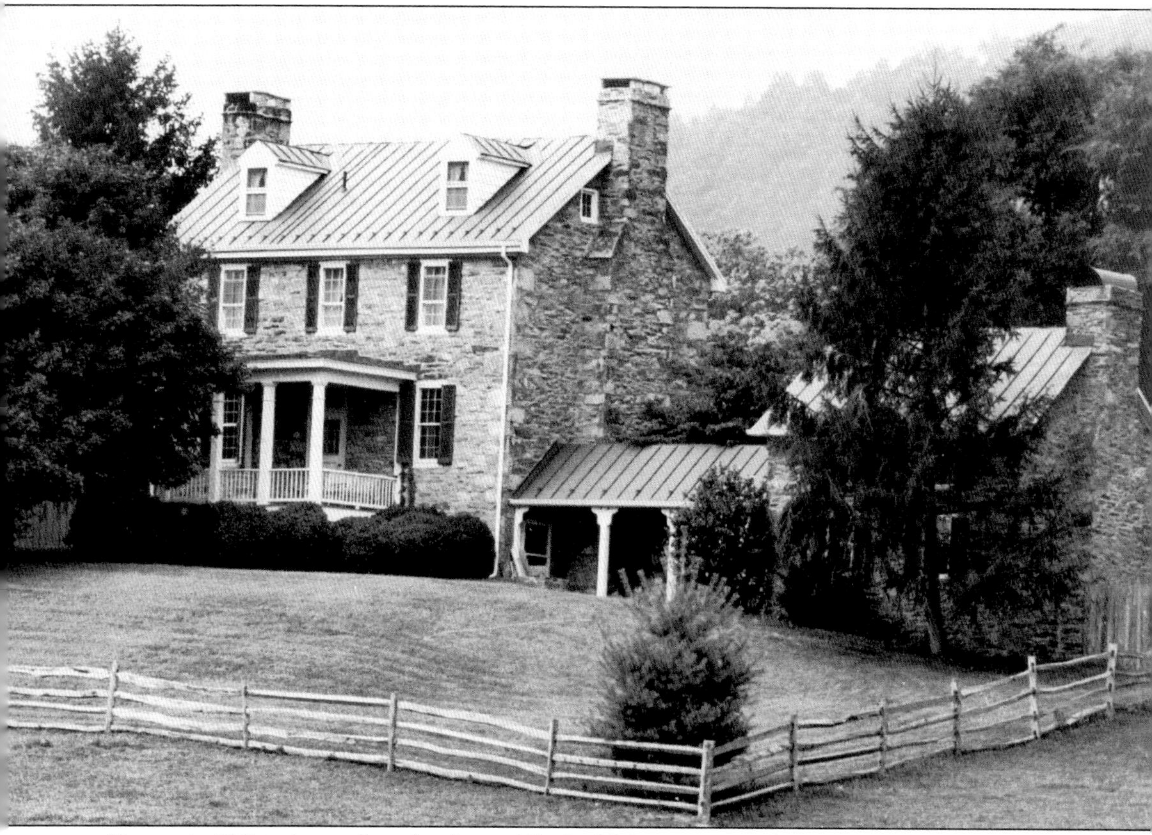

Fountain Hill is located at the foot of Peaked Mountain on Dearing Road. This house was built by John Dearing in 1812 and constructed of local fieldstone. The farm was later renamed Caledonia Farm. This property is listed on the National Register of Historic Places and the Virginia Landmarks Registry. (Courtesy of Arland Welch.)

Four

SPERRYVILLE

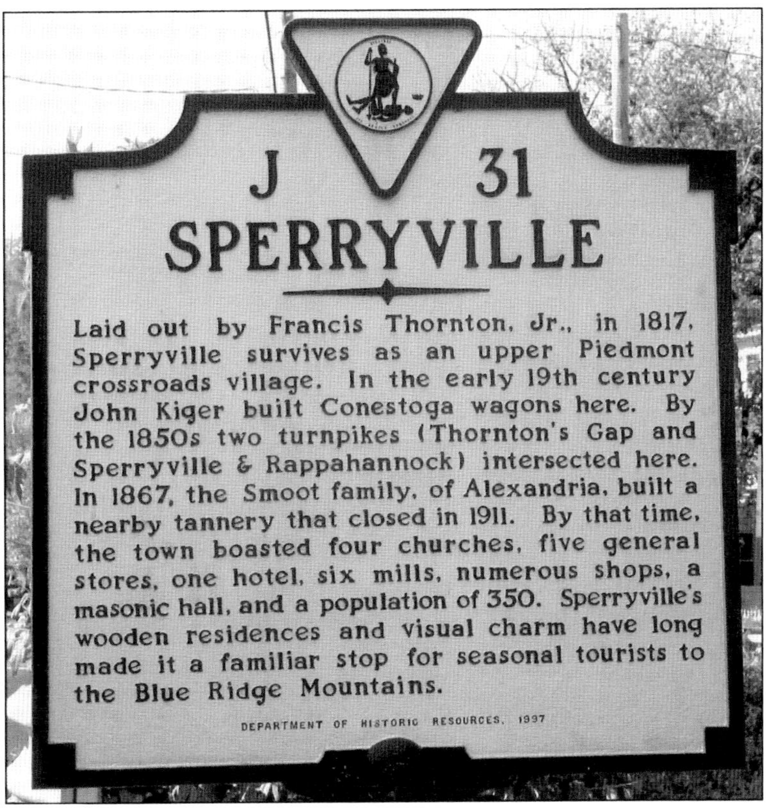

A Virginia Department of Historic Resources sign details the early years of the village of Sperryville. This sign is located on Route 211. The Sperryville Historic District is listed on the National Register of Historic Places and the Virginia Landmarks Registry. (Courtesy of John Tole.)

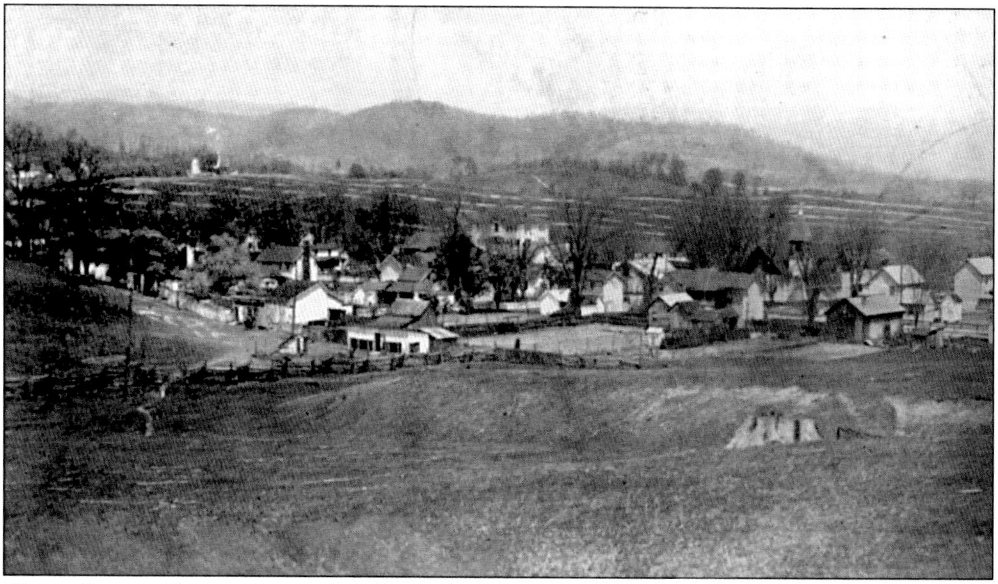

This is Sperryville as it appeared in the early 1900s. Notice the church surrounded by a group of houses in the distance. (Courtesy of the Estes family.)

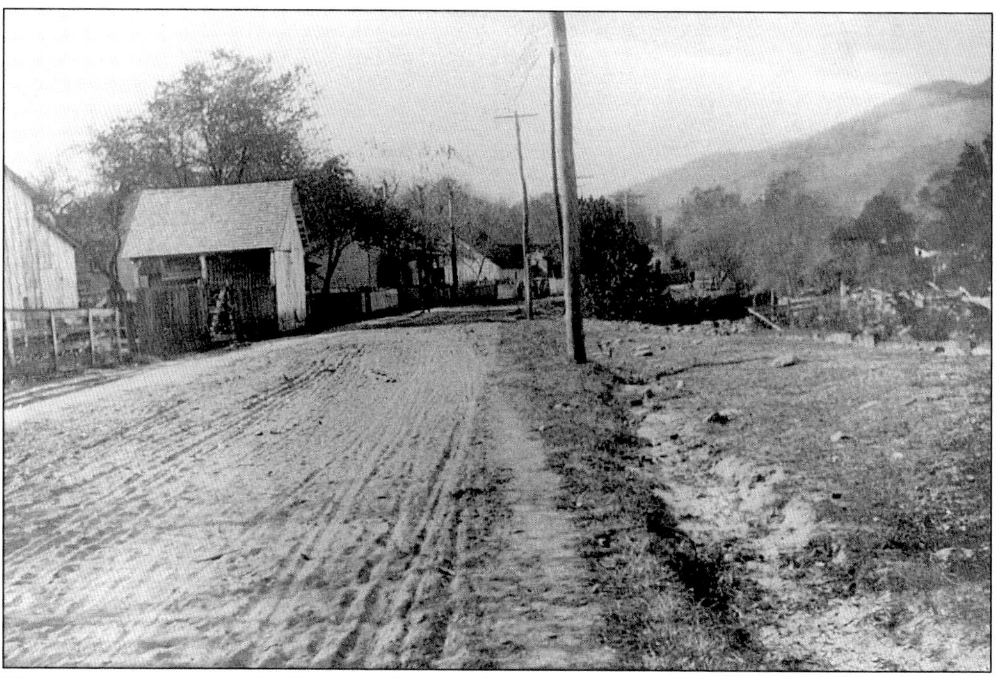

Water Street runs along the Thornton River and was Lee Highway prior to 1929, when the present Route 211 bypassed it. (Courtesy of the Estes family.)

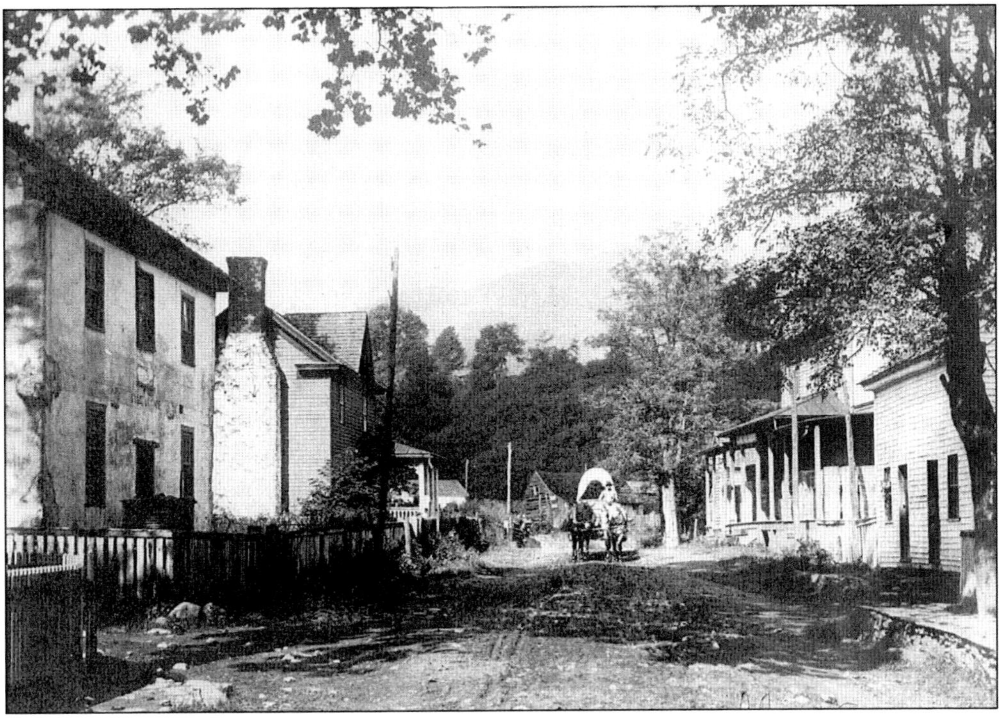

Covered wagons were common sights on Main Street in the early 1800s. The stage office on the left served as a stage stop for the route between Culpeper Courthouse and New Market. (Courtesy of the Estes family.)

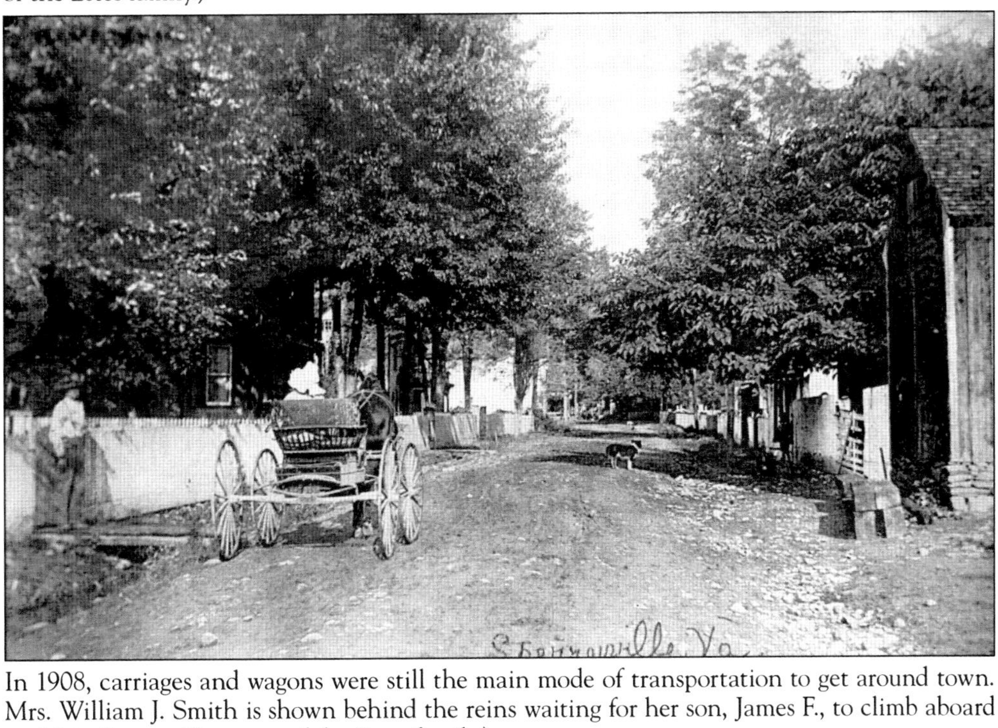

In 1908, carriages and wagons were still the main mode of transportation to get around town. Mrs. William J. Smith is shown behind the reins waiting for her son, James F., to climb aboard on Main Street. (Courtesy of the Estes family.)

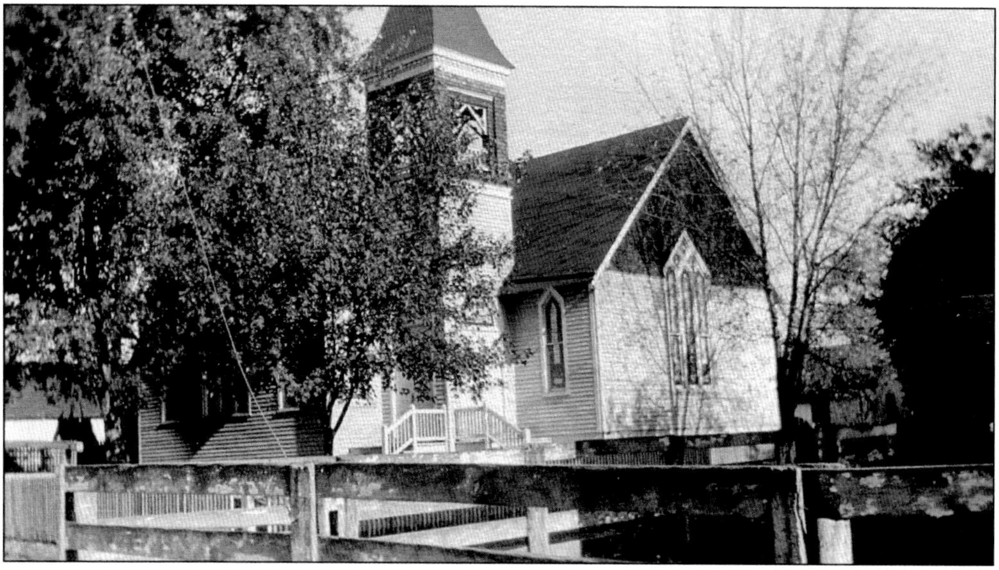

The first Sperryville Methodist Church was built in the early 1850s. Structural damage to the church building necessitated tearing it down. The new church was completed in 1915. (Courtesy of the Estes family.)

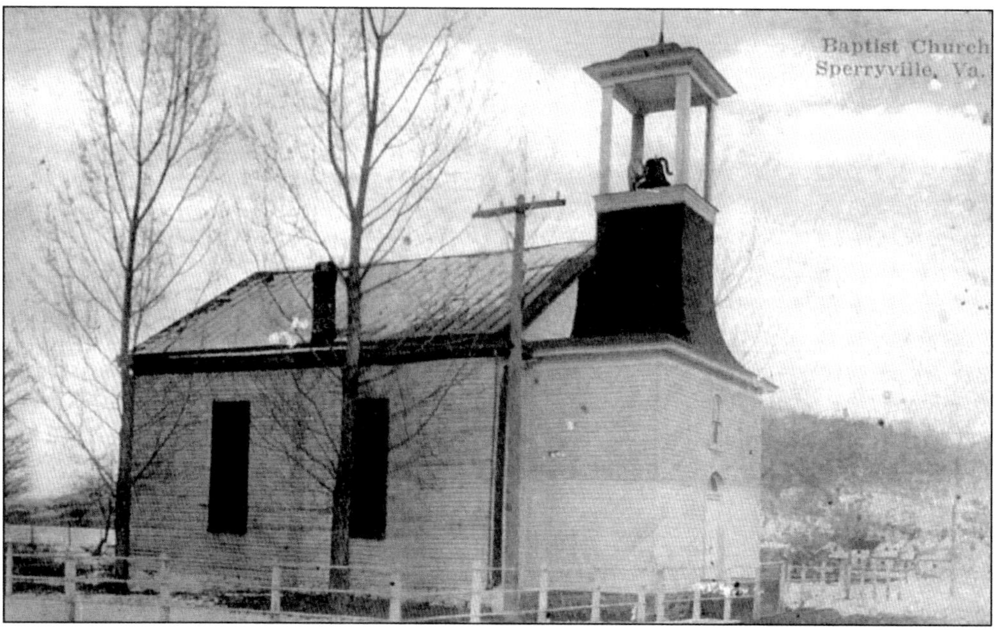

The Sperryville Meeting House was built in 1852. The church building is believed to have been used as a hospital during the Civil War. The building was sold in 1925. (Courtesy of the Estes family.)

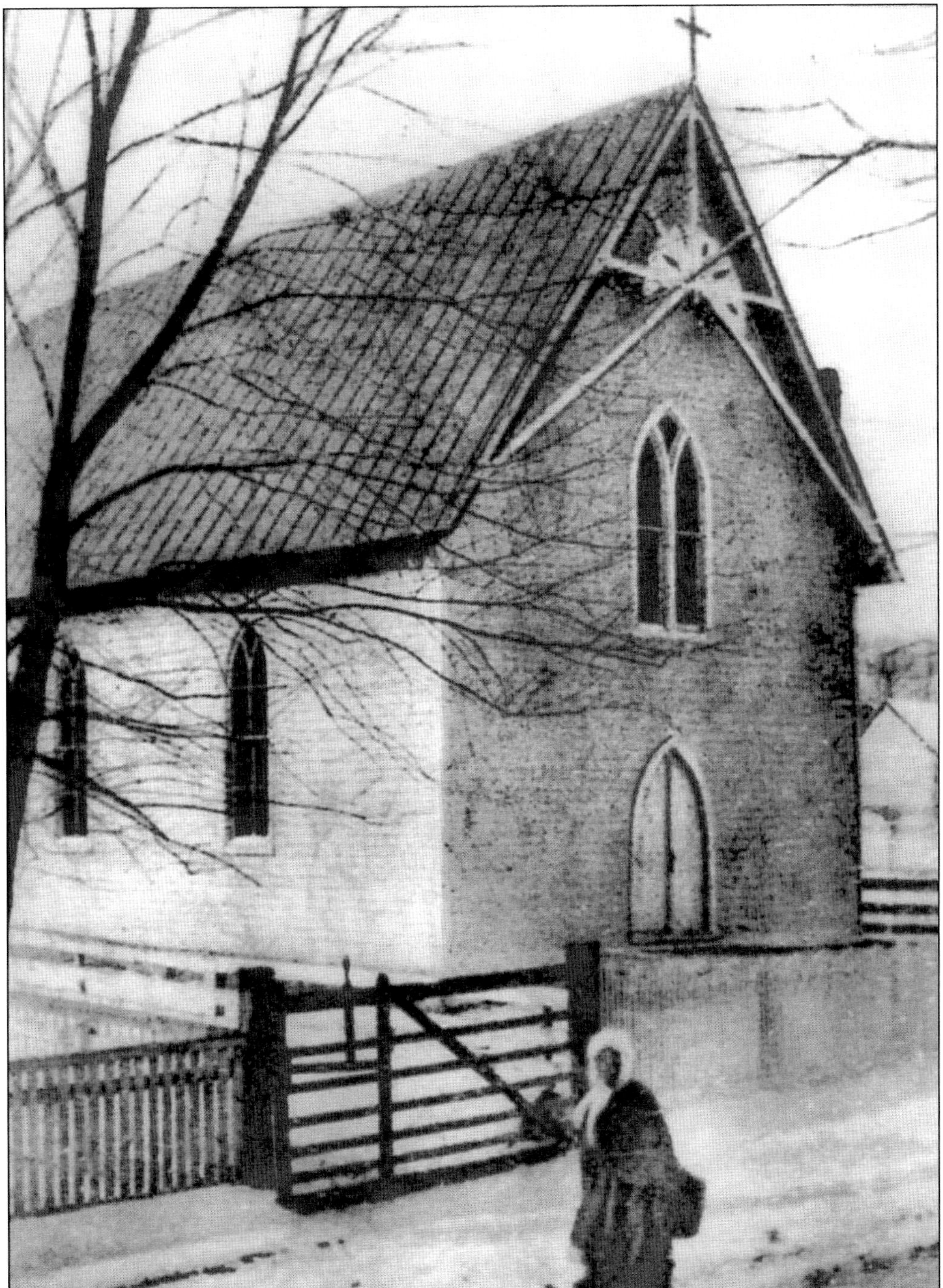

Emmanuel Episcopal Church was built in 1902. It was located on Main Street and served the village of Sperryville until 1955, when the Diocese of Virginia decided it couldn't support two churches in Rappahannock County. The members moved to Trinity Episcopal Church in Washington. In 1988, the building was formally deconsecrated and sold. (Courtesy of the Estes family.)

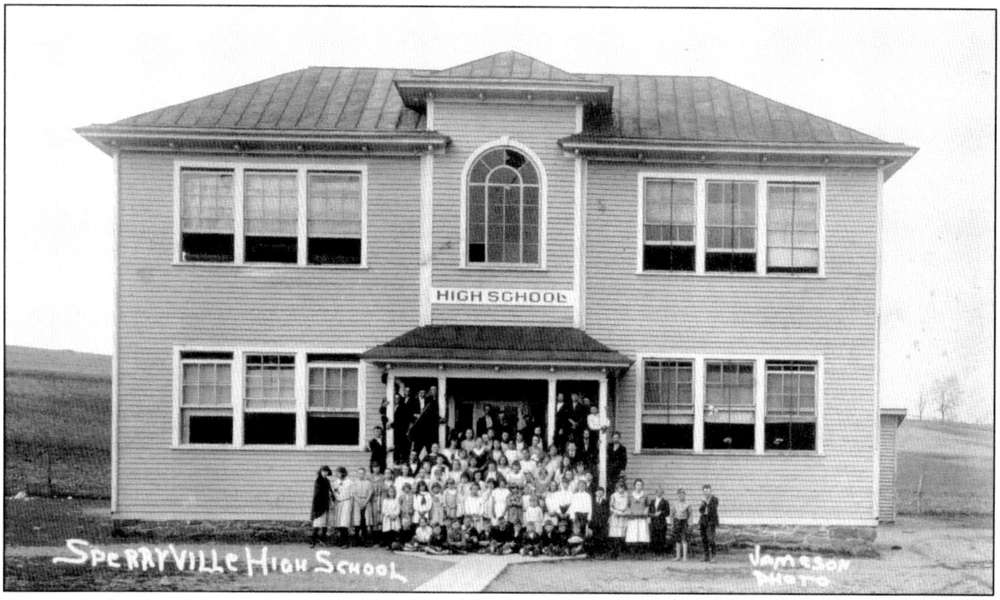

A group of students gather at the entrance of Sperryville High School in 1929. The school closed in 1968, when the new Rappahannock County High School was completed. (Courtesy of the Rappahannock Historical Society.)

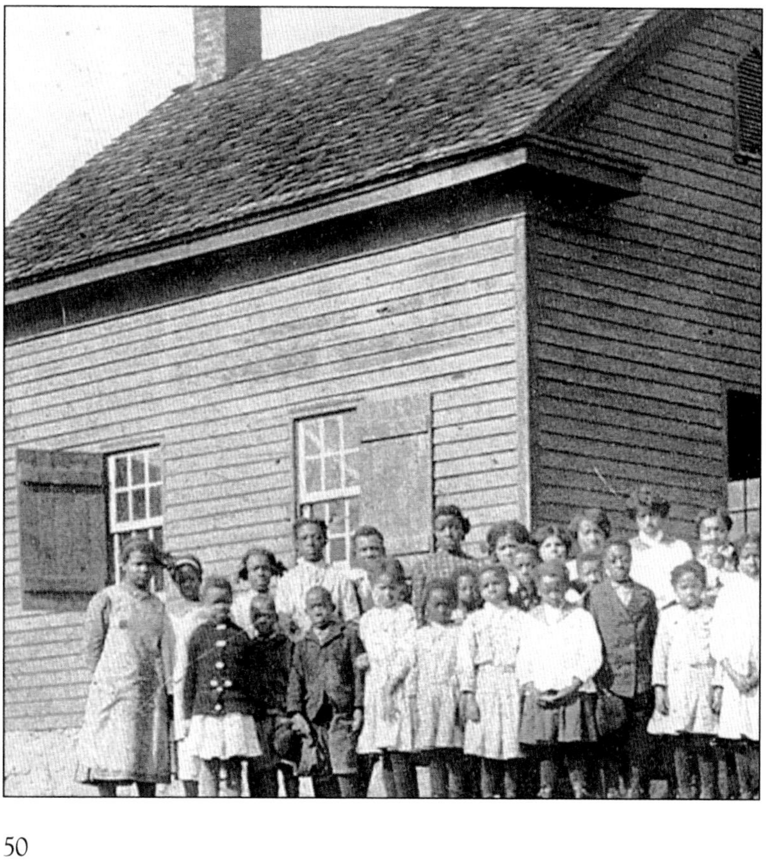
Students gather for a photograph in front of Sperryville Graded School. The school was built in 1916. (Courtesy of James Russell.)

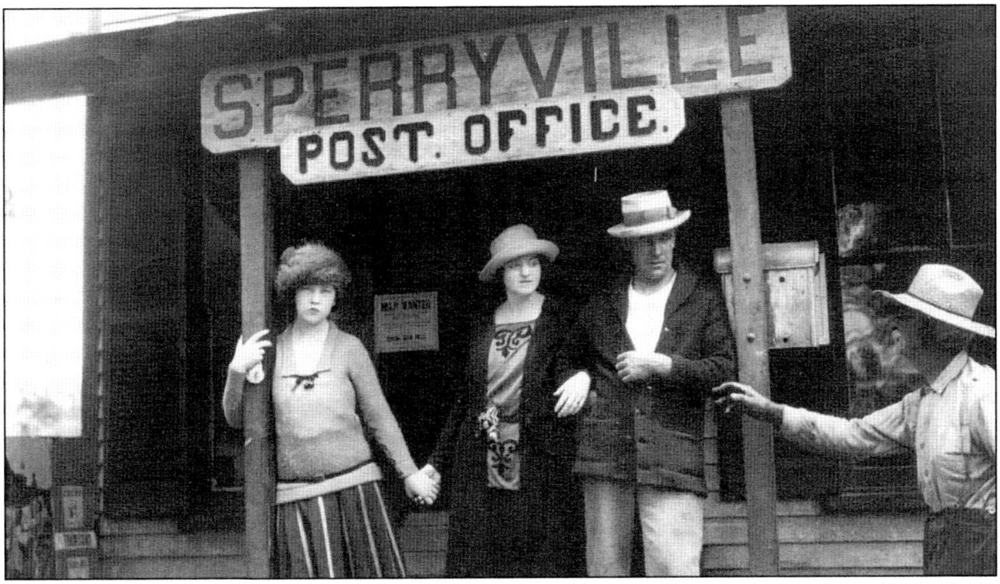

The Sperryville Post Office was a popular meeting place. It was once located inside the J. A. Estes Store. (Courtesy of the Estes family.)

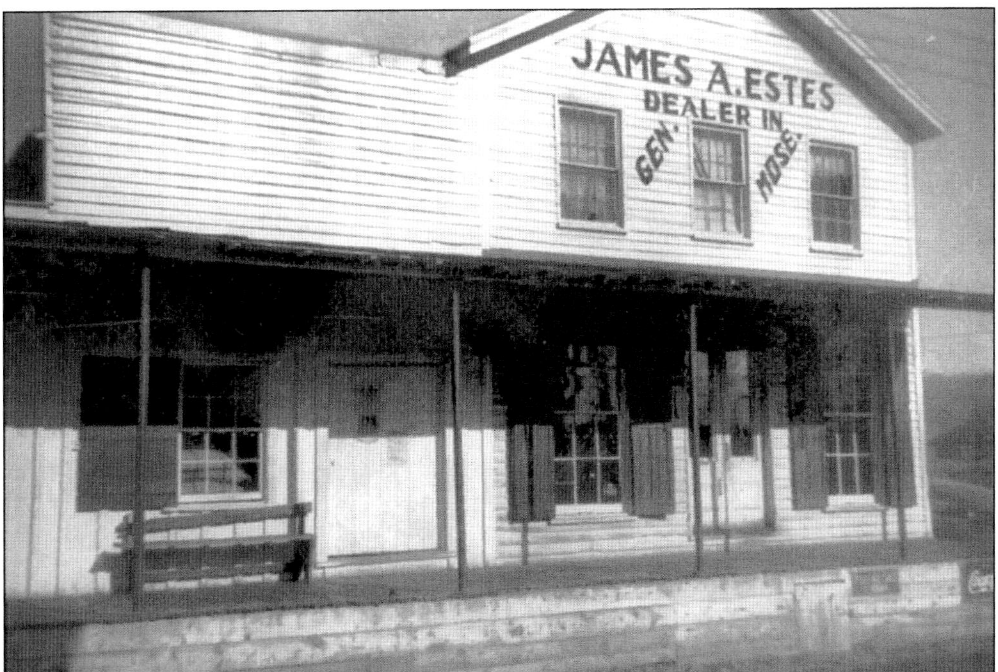

This store was owned and operated by James A. and Edward Estes. Known as the "middle store" because there were two stores to its left and two to its right, it was one of five general stores in town. The store was razed in 1966 to make way for a post office. (Courtesy of the Estes family.)

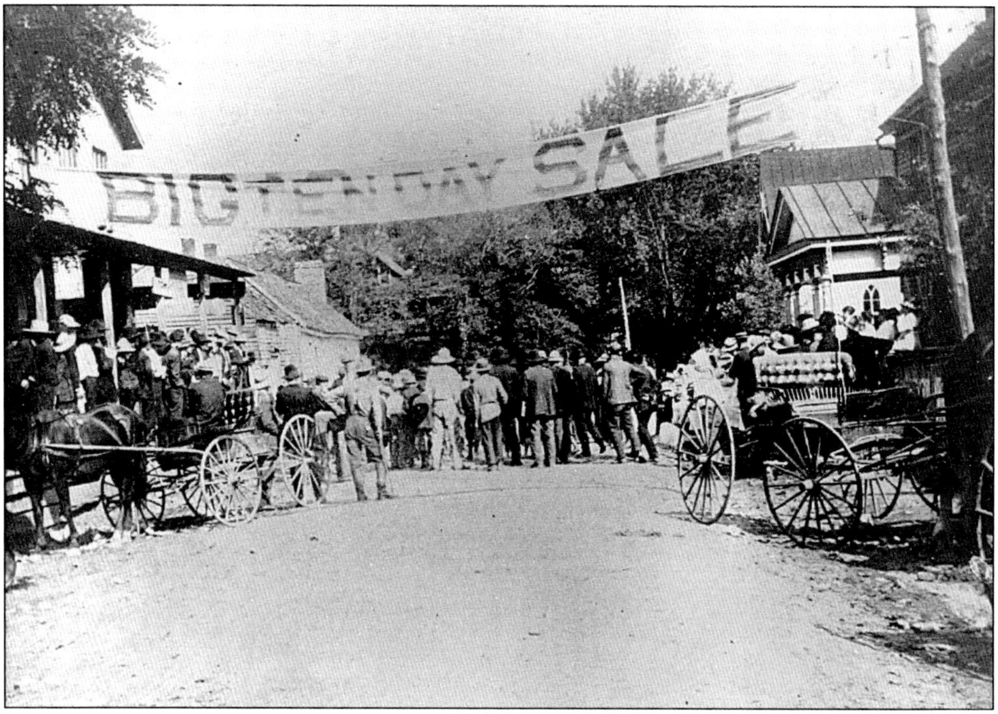

An auction drew quite a crowd on Main Street in 1918. (Courtesy of the Estes family.)

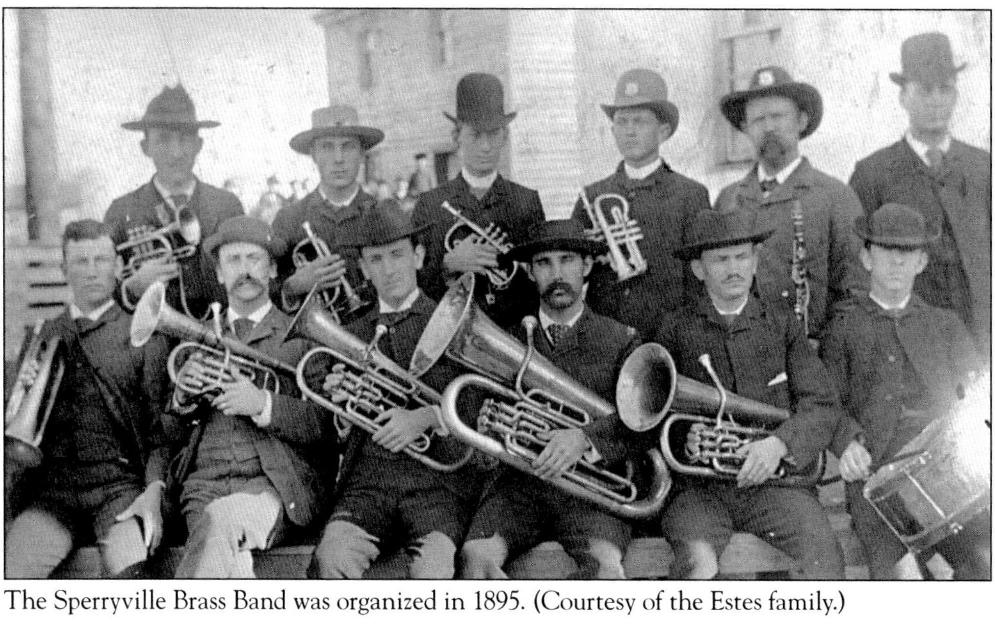

The Sperryville Brass Band was organized in 1895. (Courtesy of the Estes family.)

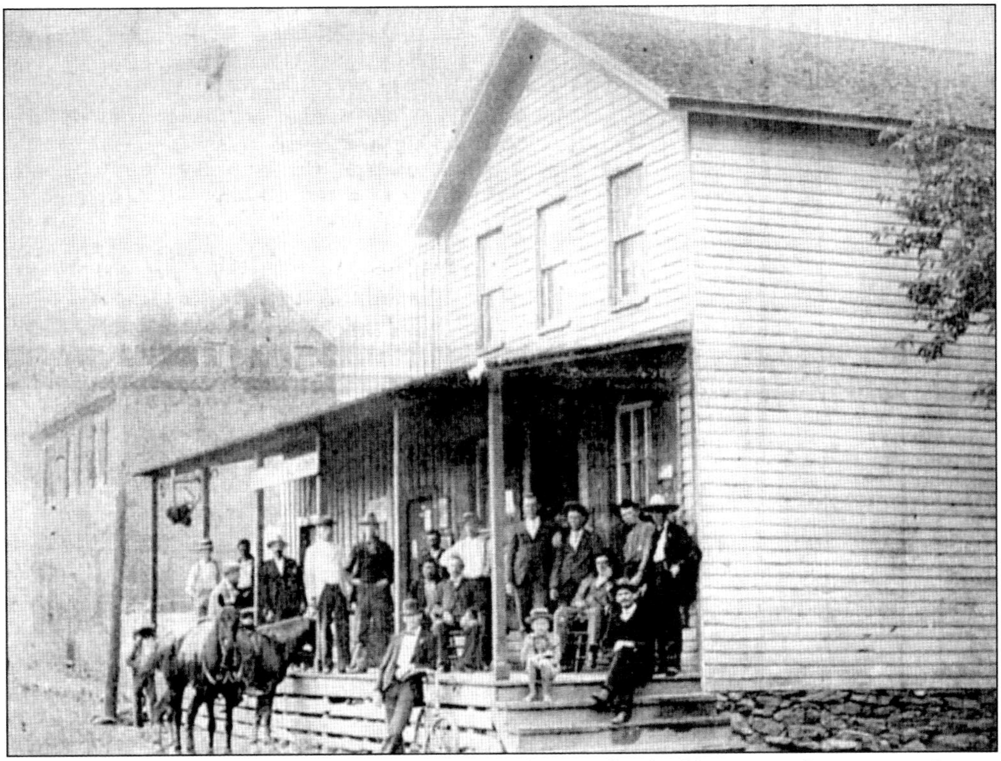

Believed to have been built just prior to the Civil War, this building served as a general store under various owners for more than 100 years. Notice the gentlemen gathered on the porch. (Courtesy of the Estes family.)

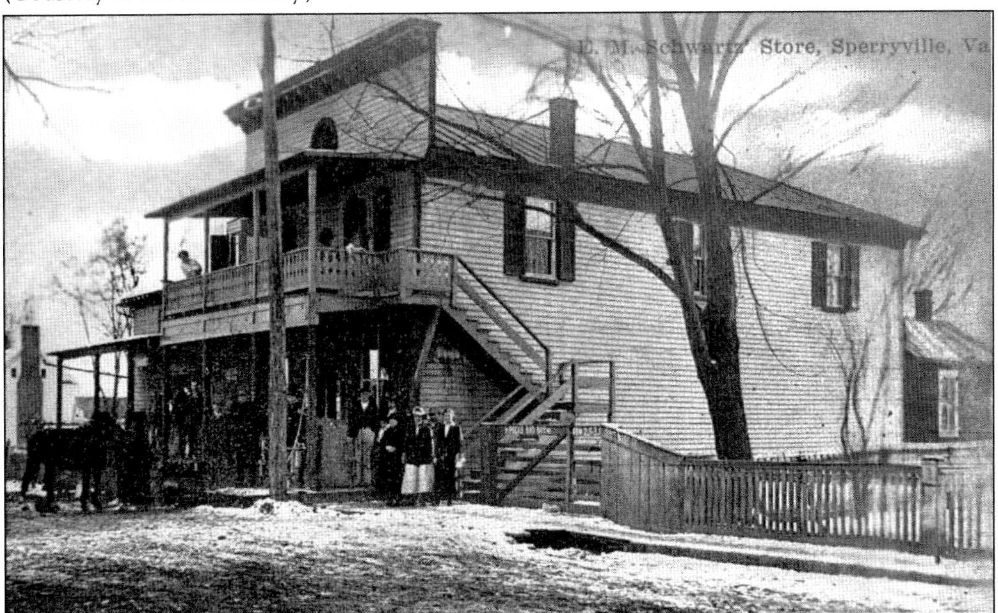

Owned by E. M. Schwartz in the early 1900s, this store sold general merchandise. (Courtesy of the Estes family.)

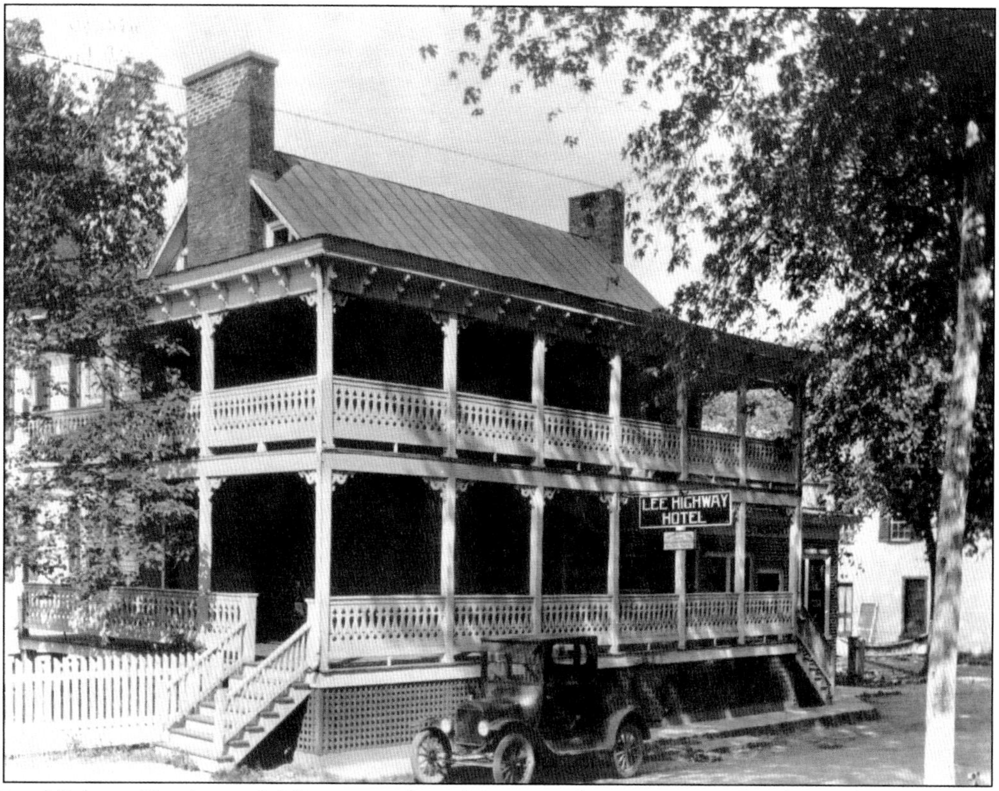

Lee Highway Hotel served delicious meals with homemade ice cream on Sunday in the mid-1920s. The building was constructed on Main Street in 1820.

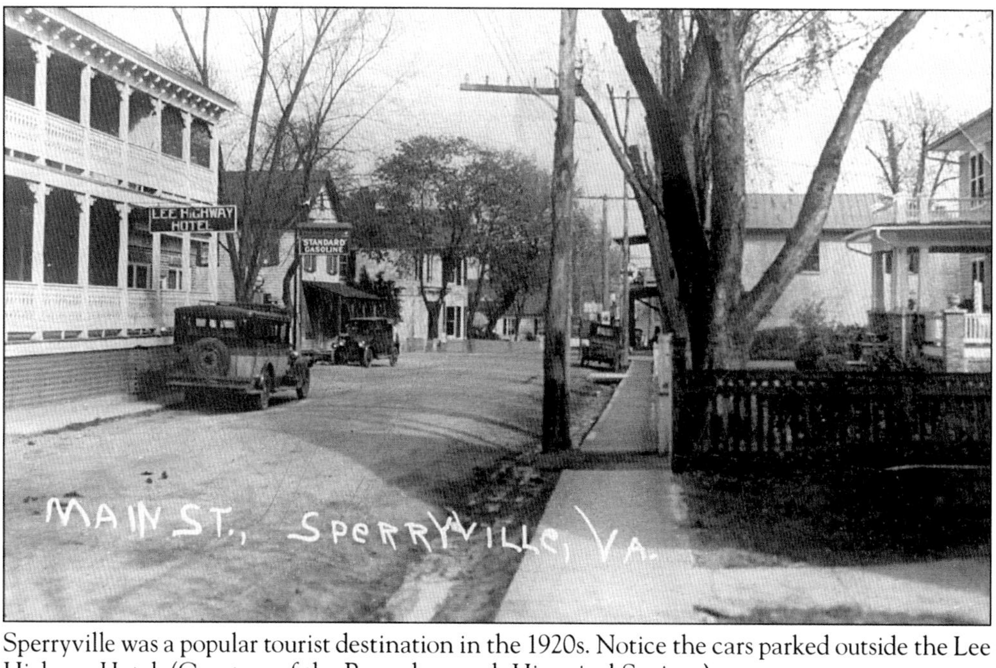

Sperryville was a popular tourist destination in the 1920s. Notice the cars parked outside the Lee Highway Hotel. (Courtesy of the Rappahannock Historical Society.)

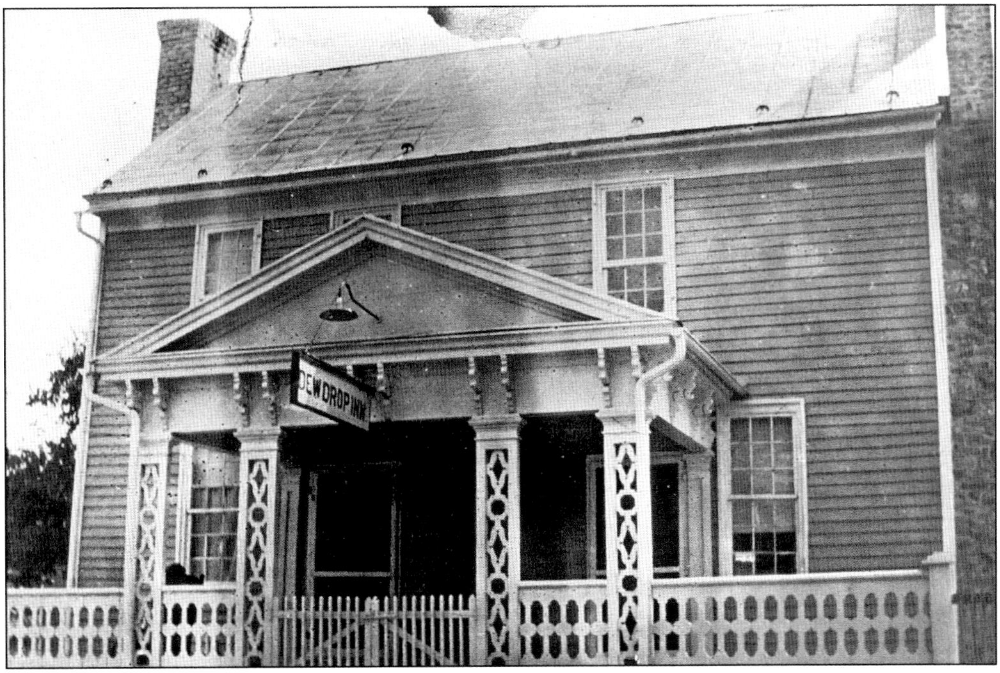

During the 1930s, Mr. Broy served delicious home-cooked meals at the Dew Drop Inn. Built in the 1830s, this late Federal/Victorian wood-frame shingle house is two-and-a-half stories with a metal gable roof. It was once the home of Dr. William H. Amiss, a Civil War surgeon. (Courtesy of the Estes family.)

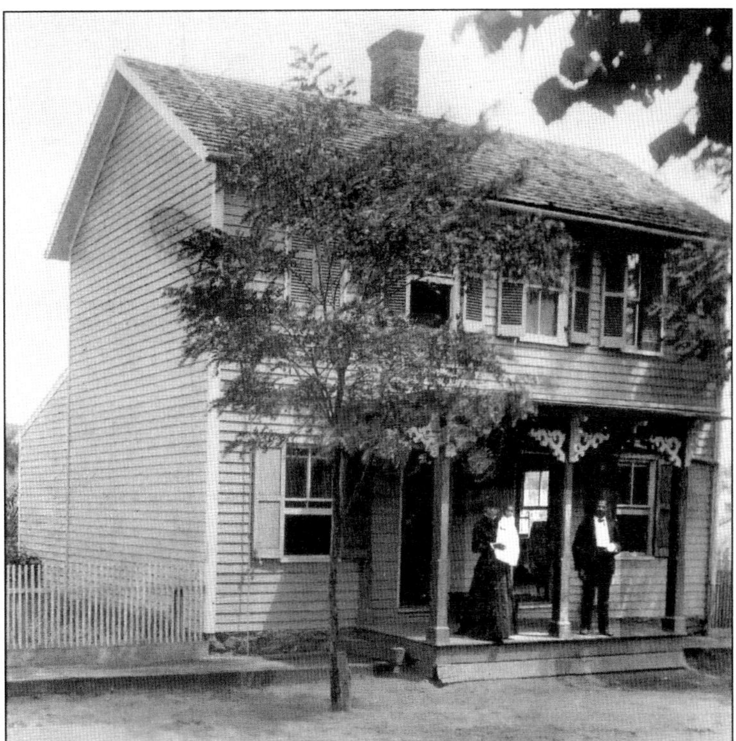

James Arthur Engham, a barber, dentist, jeweler, and watch repairer, owned the Engham House. It was built in 1904. A west wing was added in 1928. It was known as a "Sunday House," meaning those from out of town could come here and stay to attend church on Sunday. (Courtesy of James Russell.)

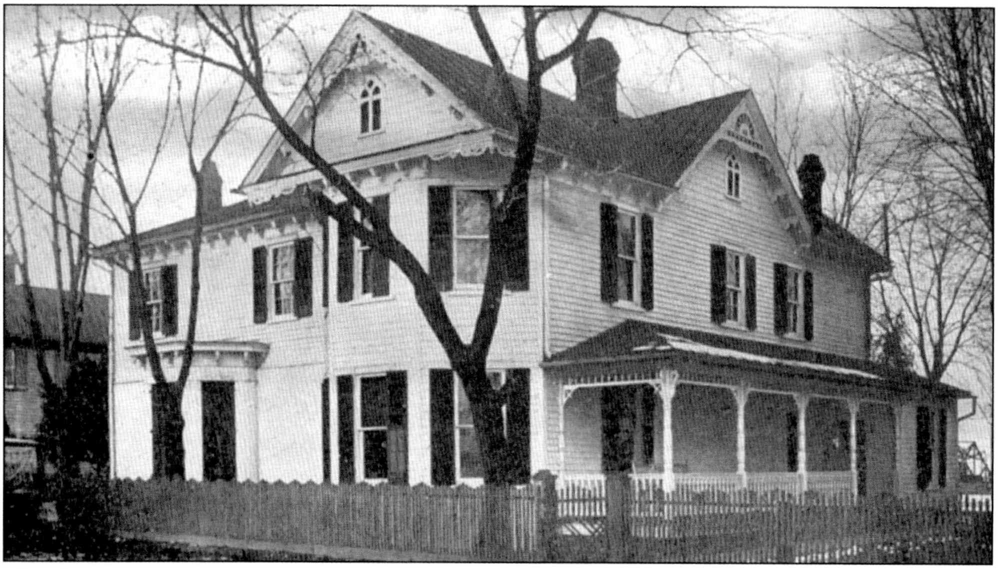

The O'Bannon House was built in the 1830s and was the first tavern in Sperryville. It was also the first brick structure in town. One previous owner, Presely Henry O'Bannon, joined the Confederate army at the age of 14. He contracted measles and came home. O'Bannon later rejoined the unit commanded by Col. John S. Mosby and surrendered at Appomattox Courthouse. (Courtesy of the Estes family.)

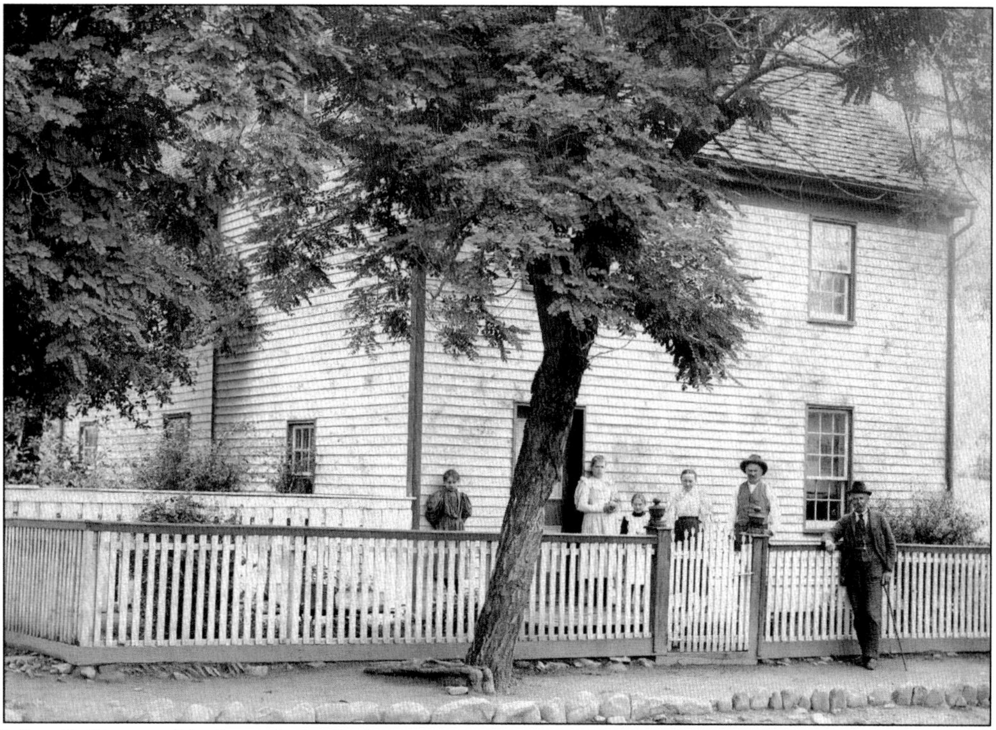

John B. Kiger, a blacksmith, built Conestoga wagons in this location in the late 1820s. It later became the home of the James Hitt family, shown standing near the house. (Courtesy of the Estes family.)

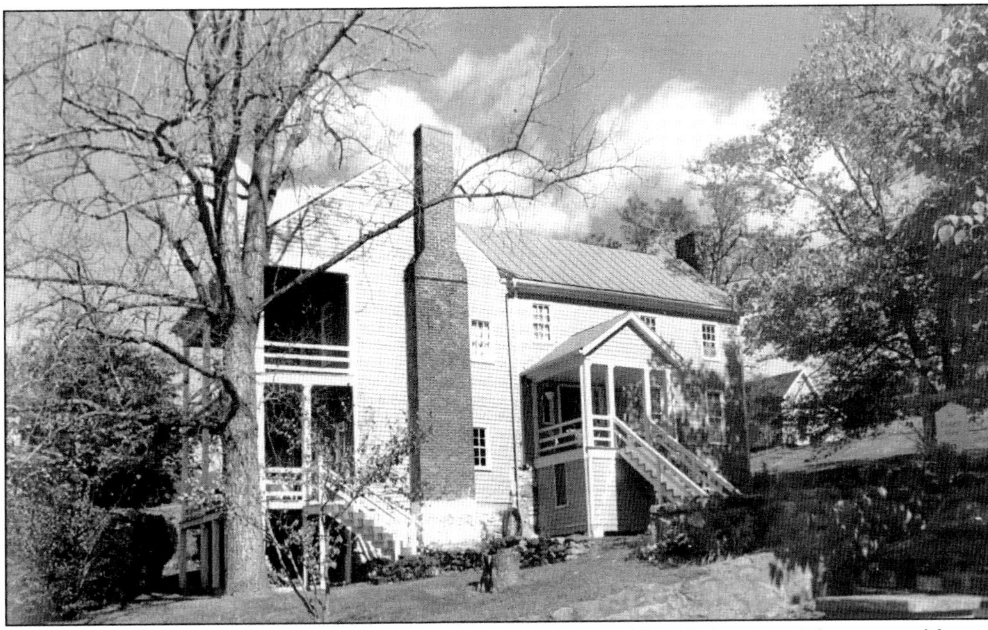

The Conyers House on Slate Mills Road is a blend of the old and the new. The original house was built around 1810. The front part, known as Conyers Store, was attached in 1815. As time went by and owners changed, additions were incorporated. In the mid-1800s and early 1900s, it was known as Finks General Store. (Courtesy of Sandra Cartwright-Brown.)

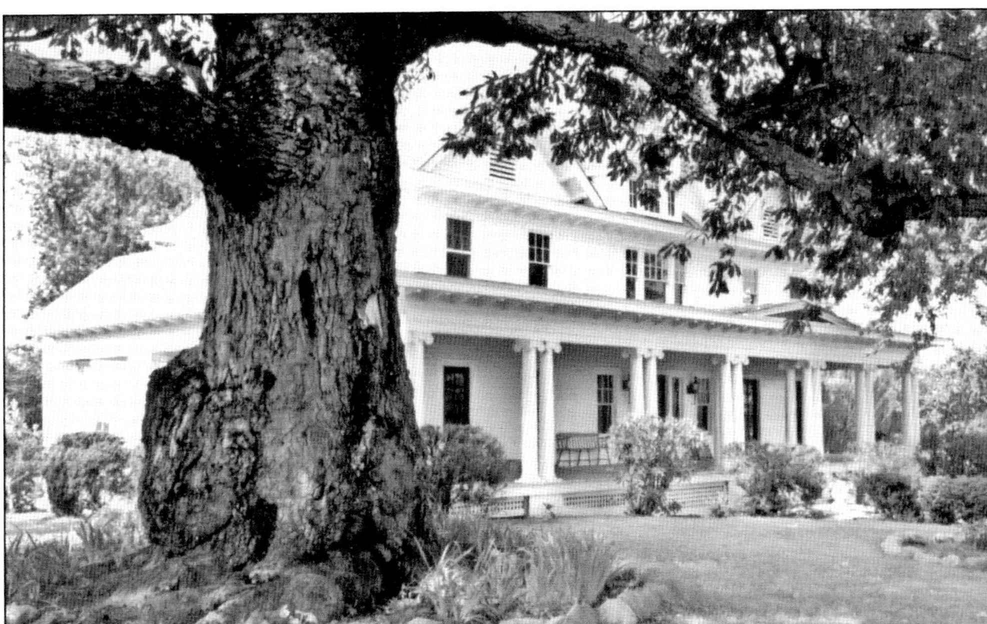

In the 1820s, John Miller built Oak Hill, a stately house situated on a hill above Sperryville surrounded by great old oaks and beautiful gardens. The house was seized by Union general Franz Sigel during the Union occupation of Sperryville of 1862 and served as Sigel's headquarters for six weeks. The house and an estimated 400-year oak tree were destroyed in a fire in 1996. (Courtesy of the Rappahannock Historical Society.)

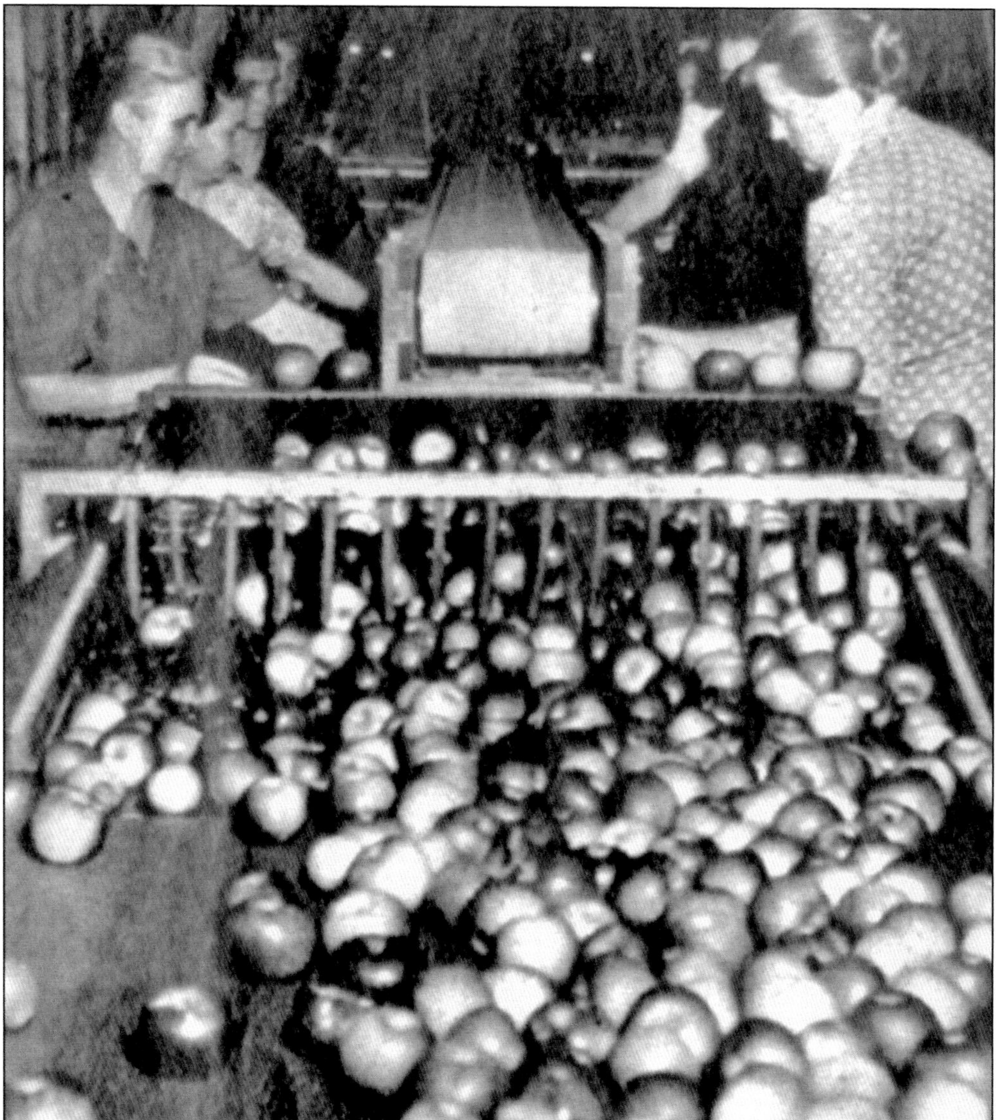

As the apples arrived at the cold storage facility, they were dumped on a conveyor belt that took them to the cleaner and on to the sorting table, where they were separated into those suitable for eating and other uses. (Courtesy of the Rappahannock Historical Society.)

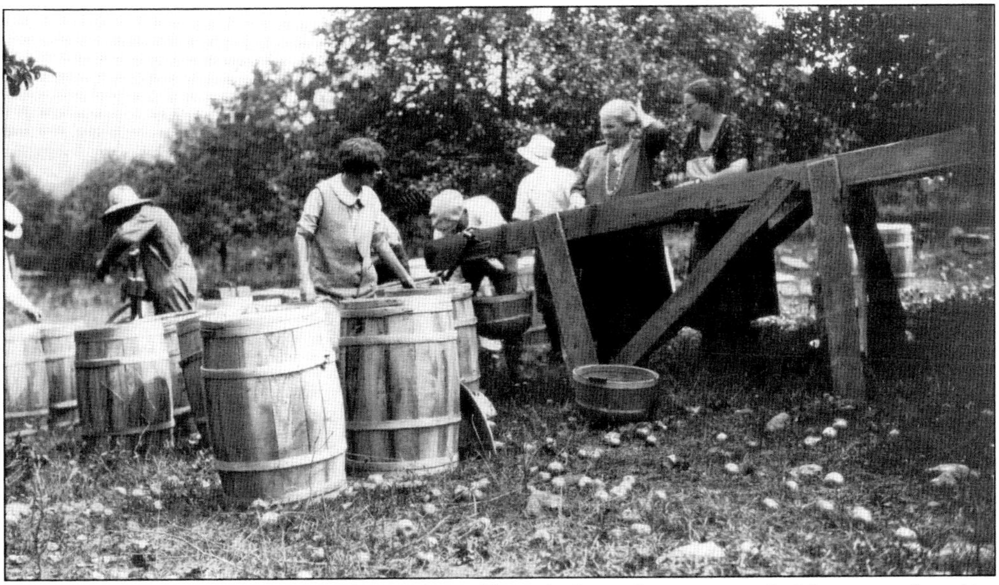

In this orchard, apples were placed on a slanted board where they were graded for size and quality before being packed into boxes. (Courtesy of Bob Johnson.)

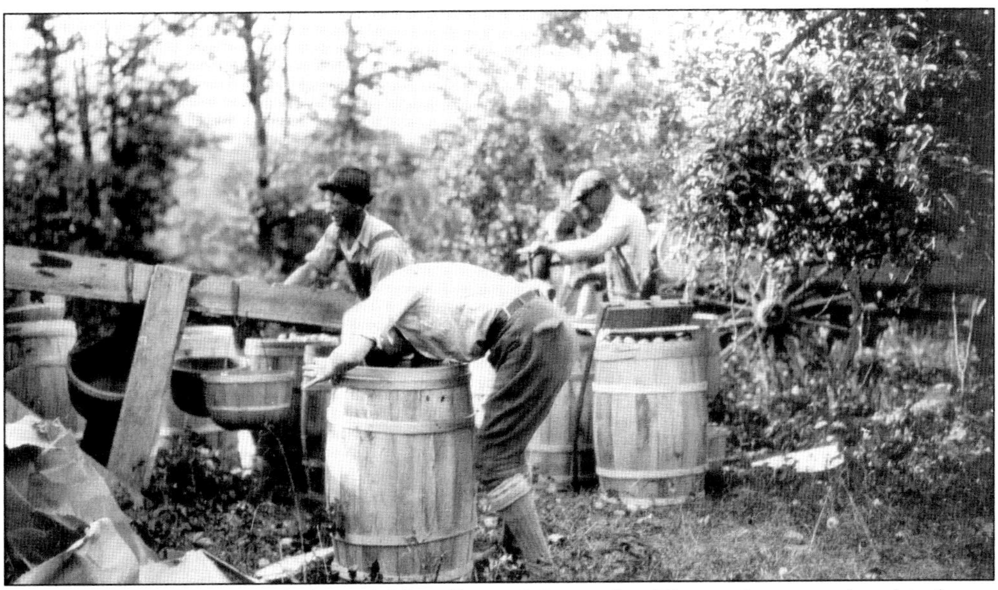

The packing process entailed careful handling of the apples. The apples were placed in boxes to prevent bruising. They were then made ready to be taken to a distribution point. (Courtesy of Bob Johnson.)

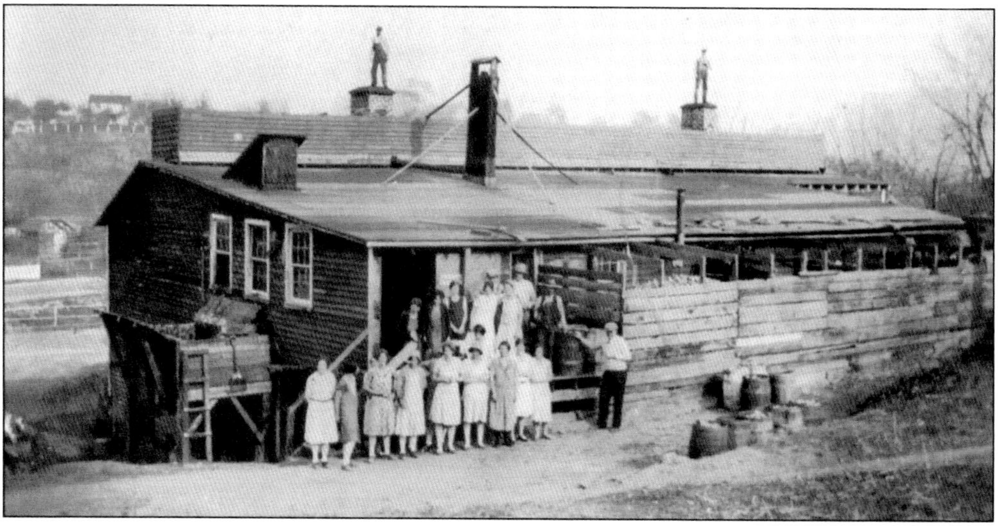

The Rappahannock Evaporating Plant opened in 1918 and operated until the end of 1937. This plant furnished employment to many local residents. It served as a major outlet for the processing of thousands of apples harvested and sold throughout the county. The plant was one of the last industries in Sperryville. (Courtesy of Aline Johnson.)

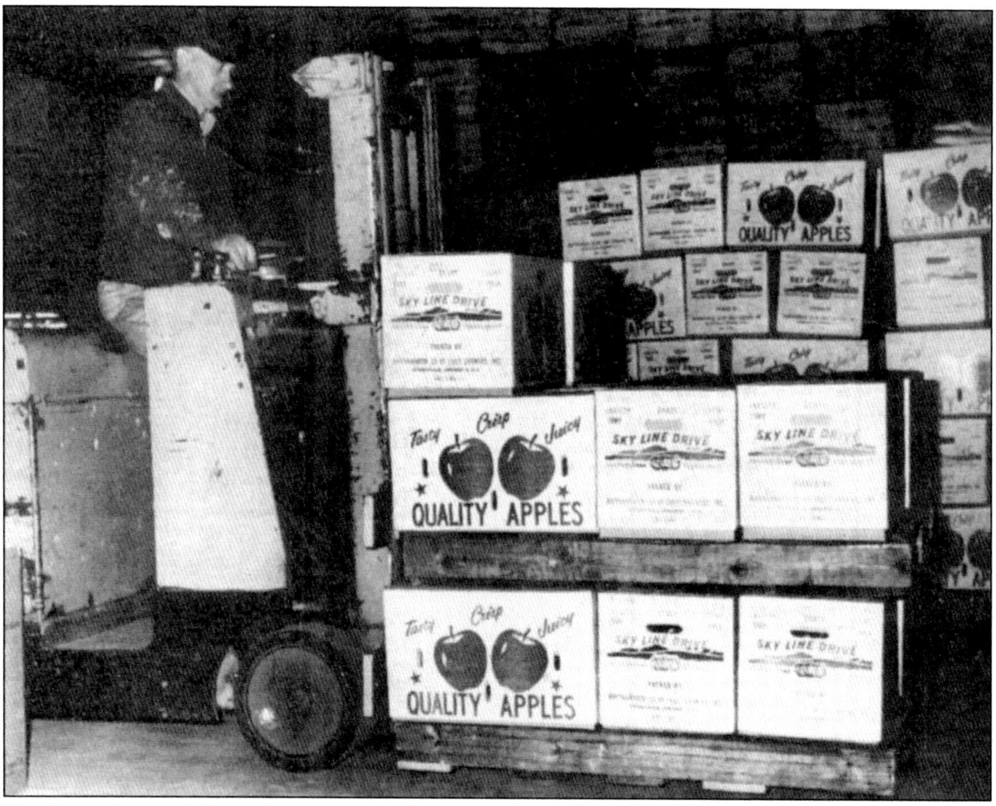

The Rappahannock Fruit Growers moved large numbers of boxed apples, some being shipped to stores and others sent to the Blue Ridge Fruit Growers Co-op next door, where juice was made and sold under the brand name "Skyline Drive." (Courtesy of the Rappahannock Historical Society.)

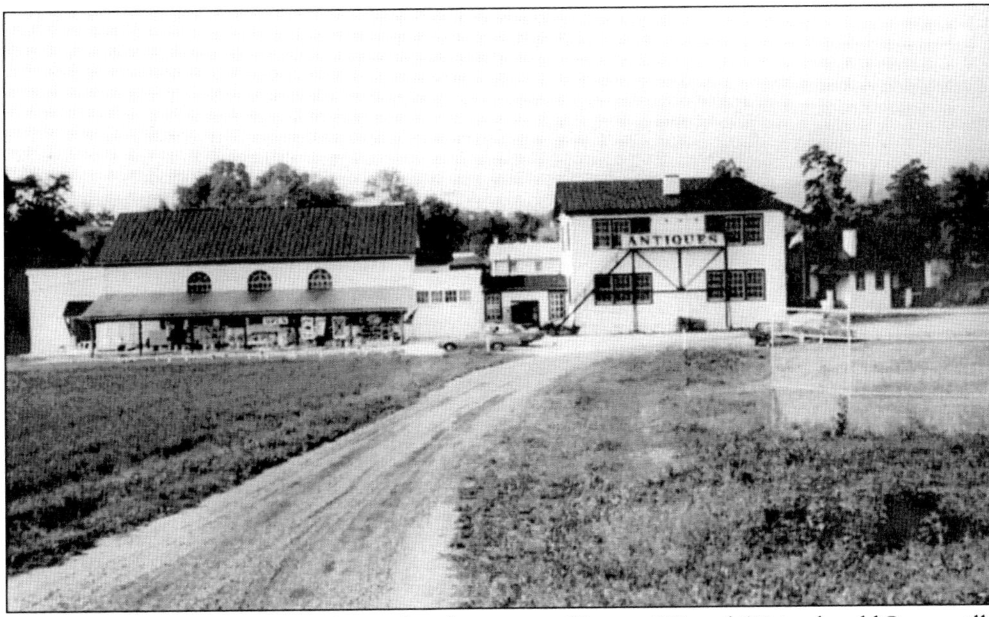

The Sperryville Emporium was located at the corner of Routes 211 and 522 in the old Sperryville School building. It was the largest business in Sperryville in the 1970s and 1980s. Antiques, new furniture, gifts, and souvenirs were sold here. (Courtesy of Martha Hitt.)

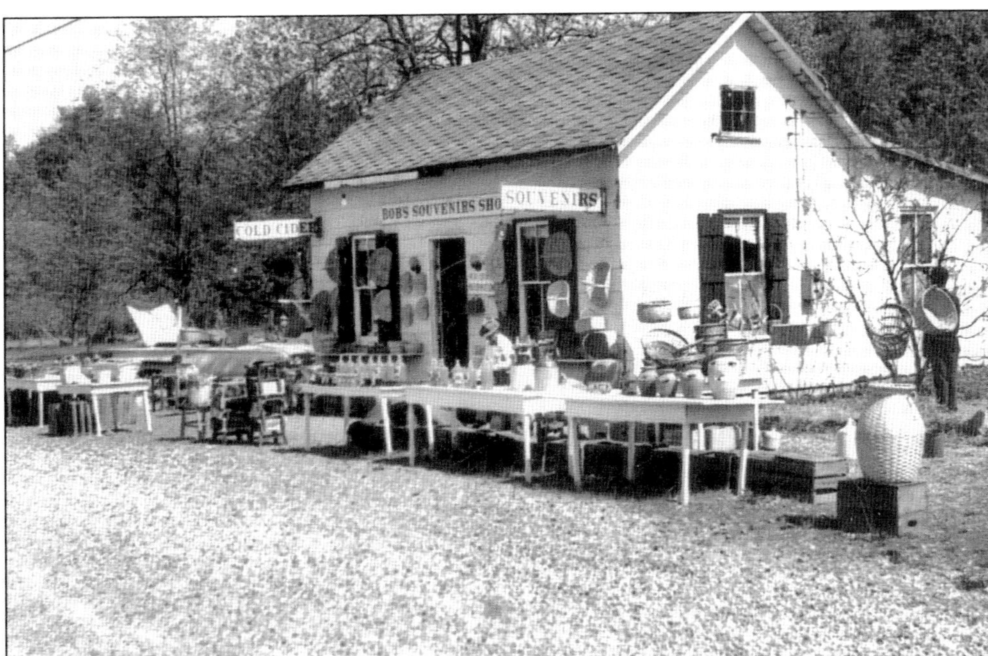

Souvenir stands dotted the highway along Route 211 in Sperryville. They sold local products such as apples, cider, jams, and jellies. (Courtesy of the Rappahannock Historical Society.)

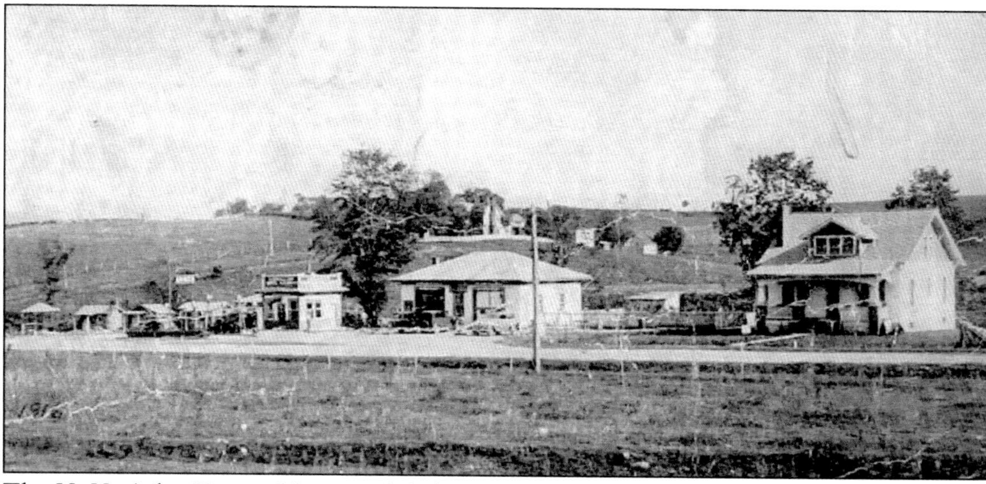

The H. H. Aylor Tourist Home and Cabins are shown on Route 211 in 1936. (Courtesy of Ranny Aylor.)

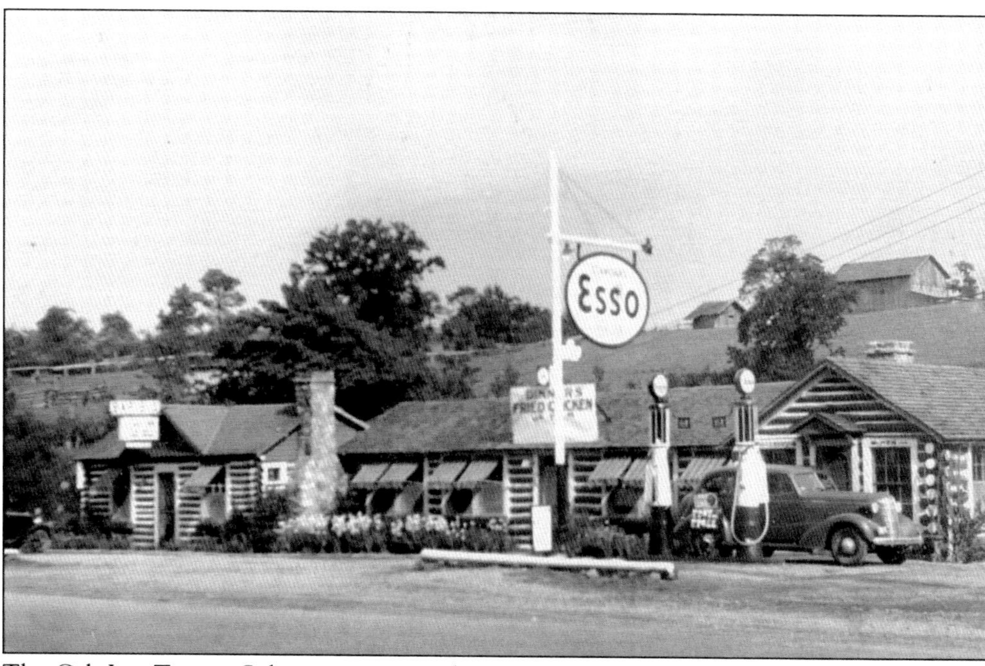

The Cab Inn Tourist Cabins were erected around 1940 to service the many visitors to the Shenandoah National Park. The dining room served meals and an Esso gas station provided full service to its patrons. (Courtesy of the Estes family.)

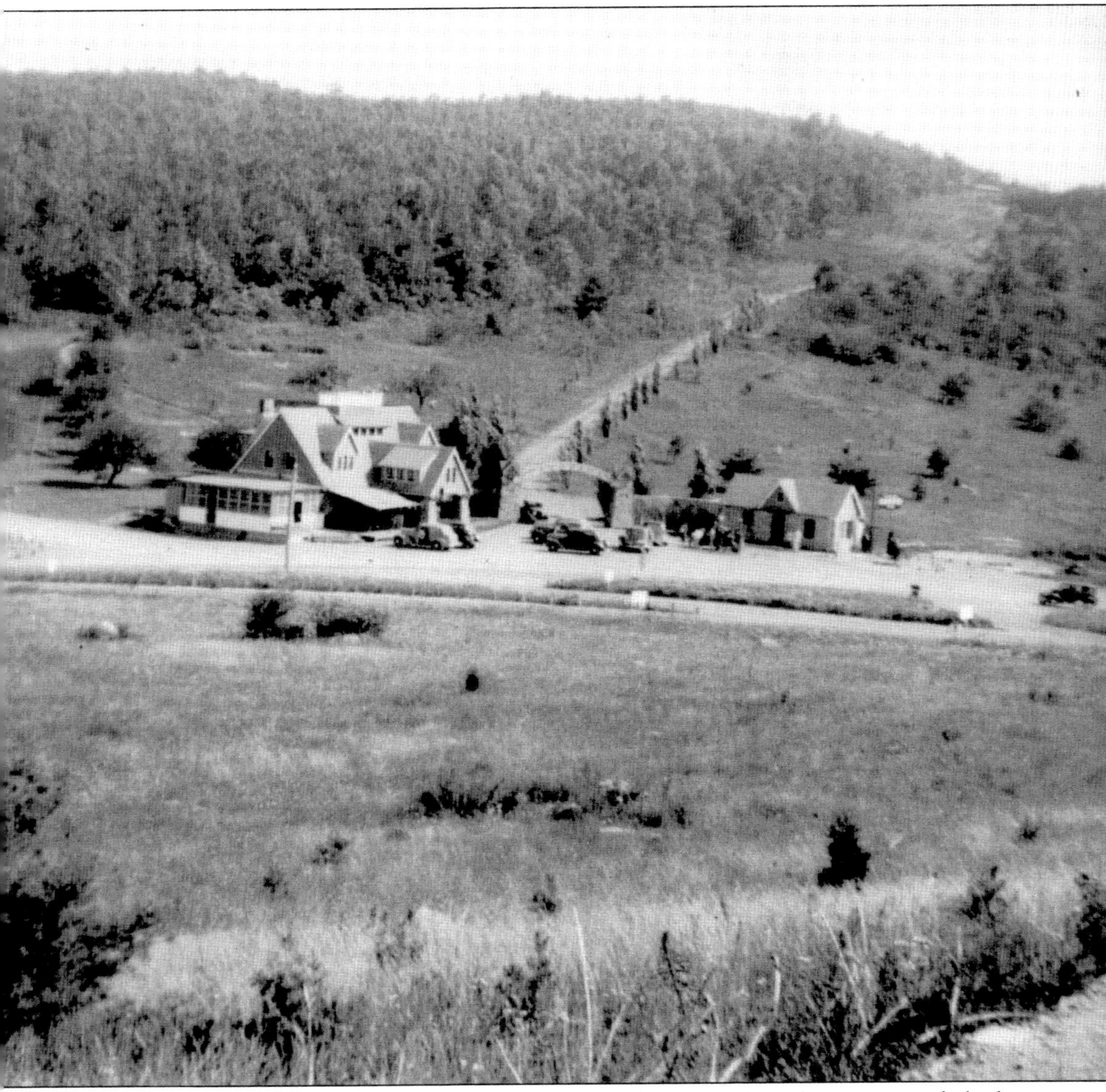

Located on Lee Highway, the Panorama Tea Room was built in the 1920s of stone, most of which was hauled from quarries at the foot of the mountain. It consisted of a lobby, three guest rooms, three rooms for servants, a small dining room, a kitchen, and a small cellar. Behind the tea room was a garage and shower with hot and cold running water. (Courtesy of Peter Luke.)

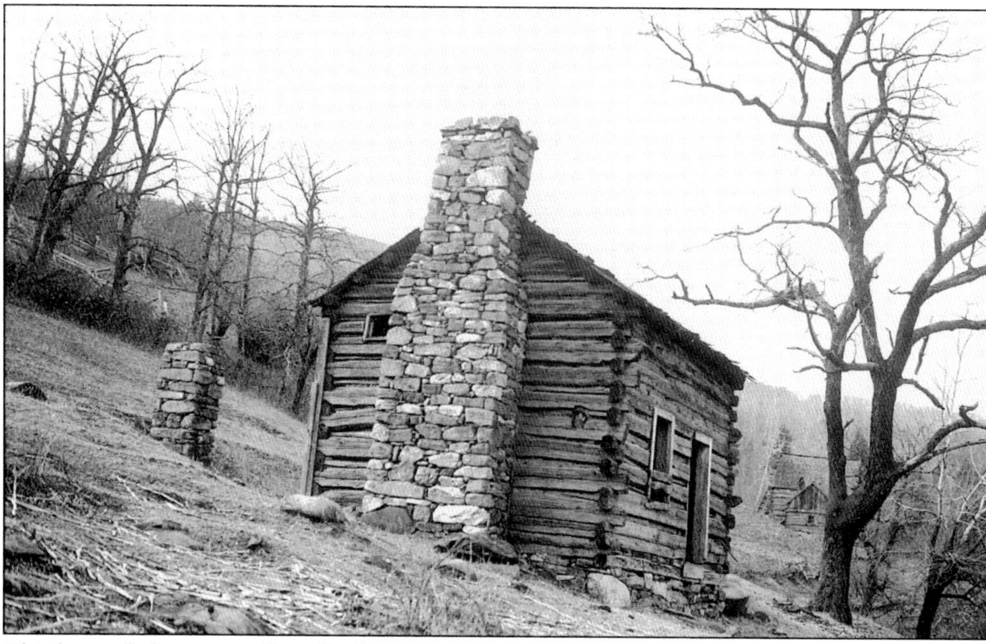

This home, belonging to Boot Dodson, was a one-room log cabin in the Blue Ridge Mountains. The builder was very skilled and proud of his work, judging from the precise placement of the logs and the stones in the chimney. (Courtesy of the Shenandoah National Park Archives, Reed Engle.)

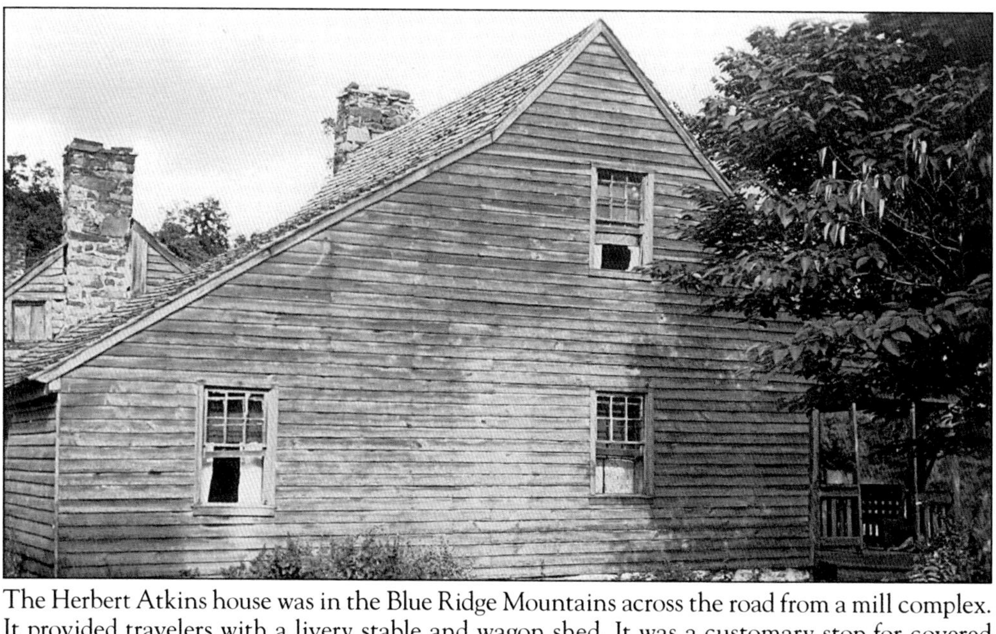

The Herbert Atkins house was in the Blue Ridge Mountains across the road from a mill complex. It provided travelers with a livery stable and wagon shed. It was a customary stop for covered wagons carrying produce from the Shenandoah Valley to eastern Virginia. The wagon often brought manufactured goods on the return trip. (Courtesy of the Shenandoah National Park Archives, Reed Engle.)

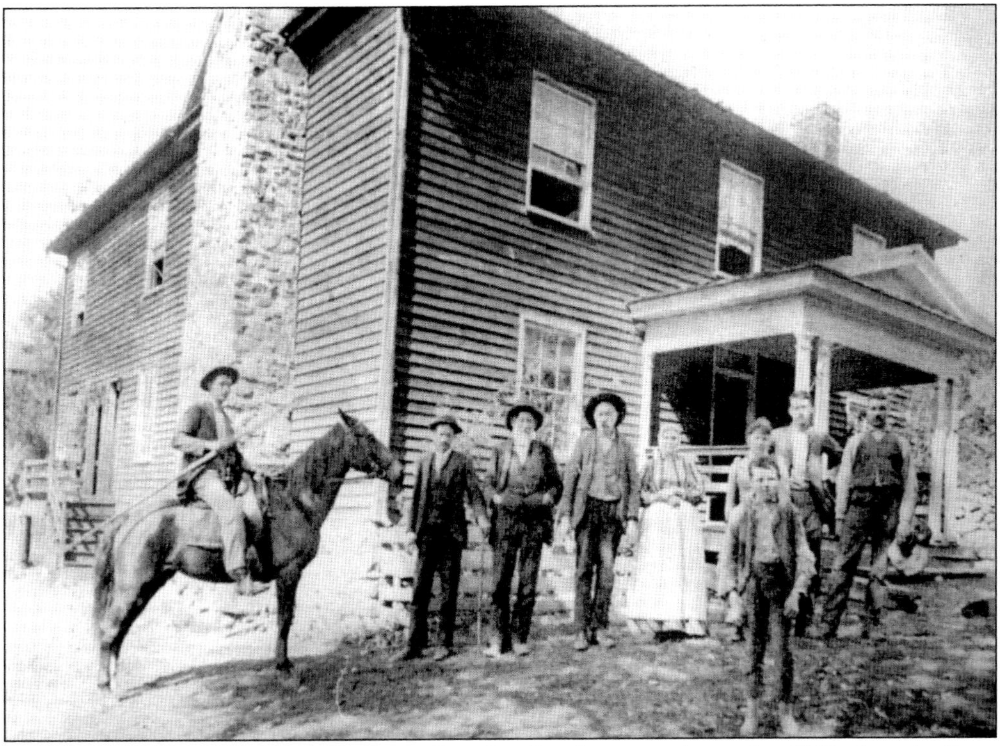

The Bolen homestead, located near Piney Run Fire Road, was condemned in 1930 when the State of Virginia was buying land in the Blue Ridge Mountains to establish the Shenandoah National Park. (Courtesy of the Shenandoah National Park Archives, Reed Engle.)

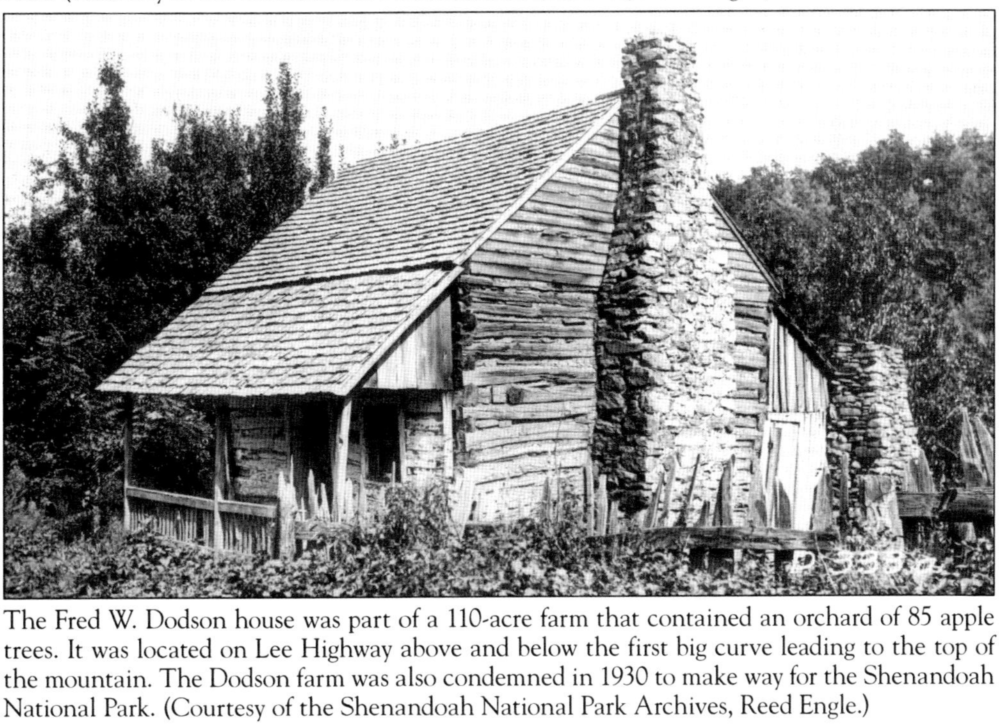

The Fred W. Dodson house was part of a 110-acre farm that contained an orchard of 85 apple trees. It was located on Lee Highway above and below the first big curve leading to the top of the mountain. The Dodson farm was also condemned in 1930 to make way for the Shenandoah National Park. (Courtesy of the Shenandoah National Park Archives, Reed Engle.)

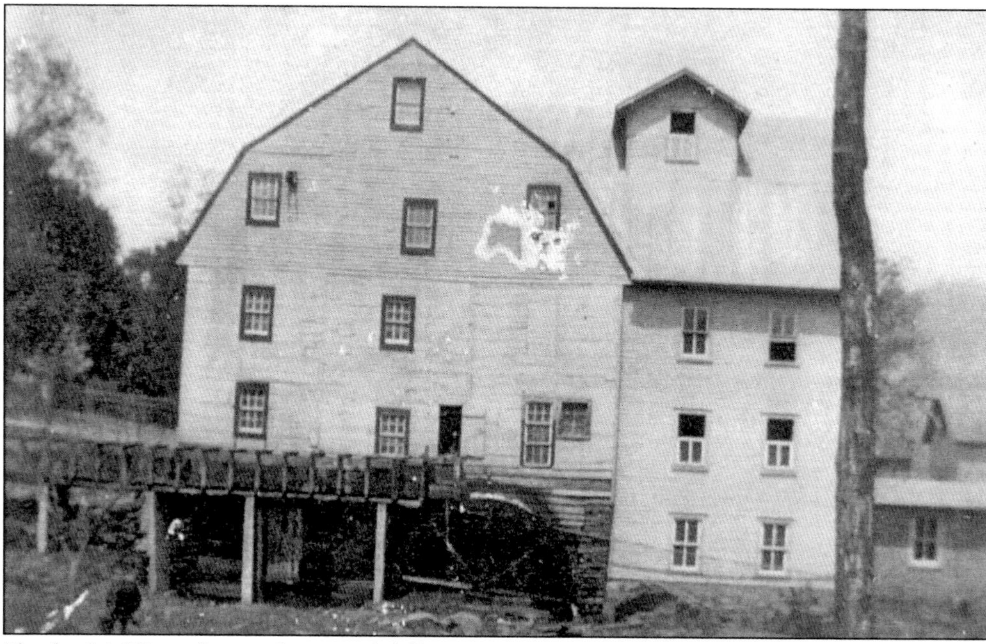

Fletcher's Mill was known by several different names over the years. The mill was mentioned in a deed dated April 1, 1819. It was one of the largest and busiest of the mills and was the last one to close. The mill produced meal and two different grades of flour. It closed in 1956. (Courtesy of the Estes family.)

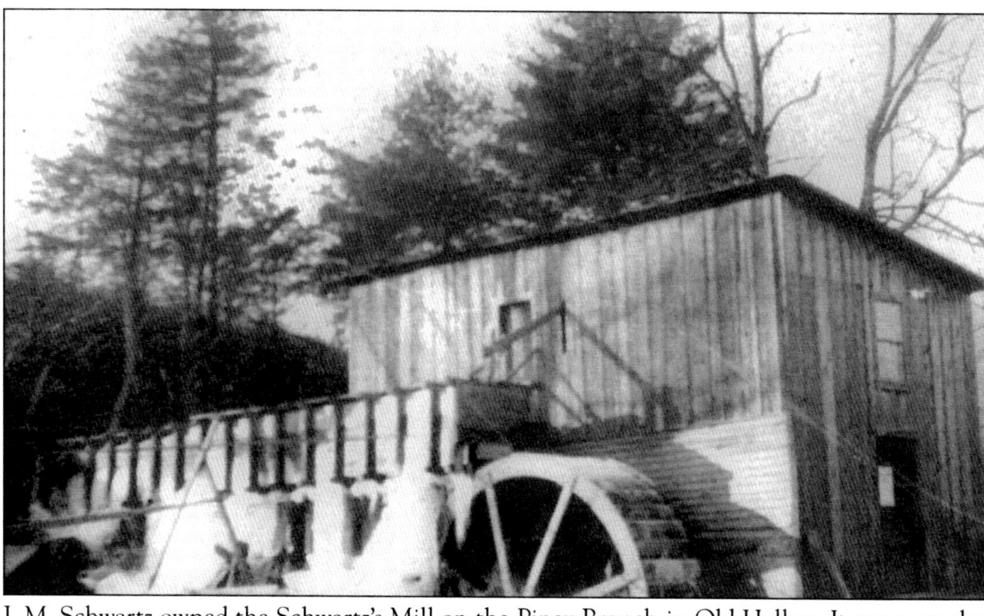

J. M. Schwartz owned the Schwartz's Mill on the Piney Branch in Old Hollow. It was a woolen mill. The South Fork Woolen Factory wove heavy products such as blankets and rugs. (Courtesy of the Estes family.)

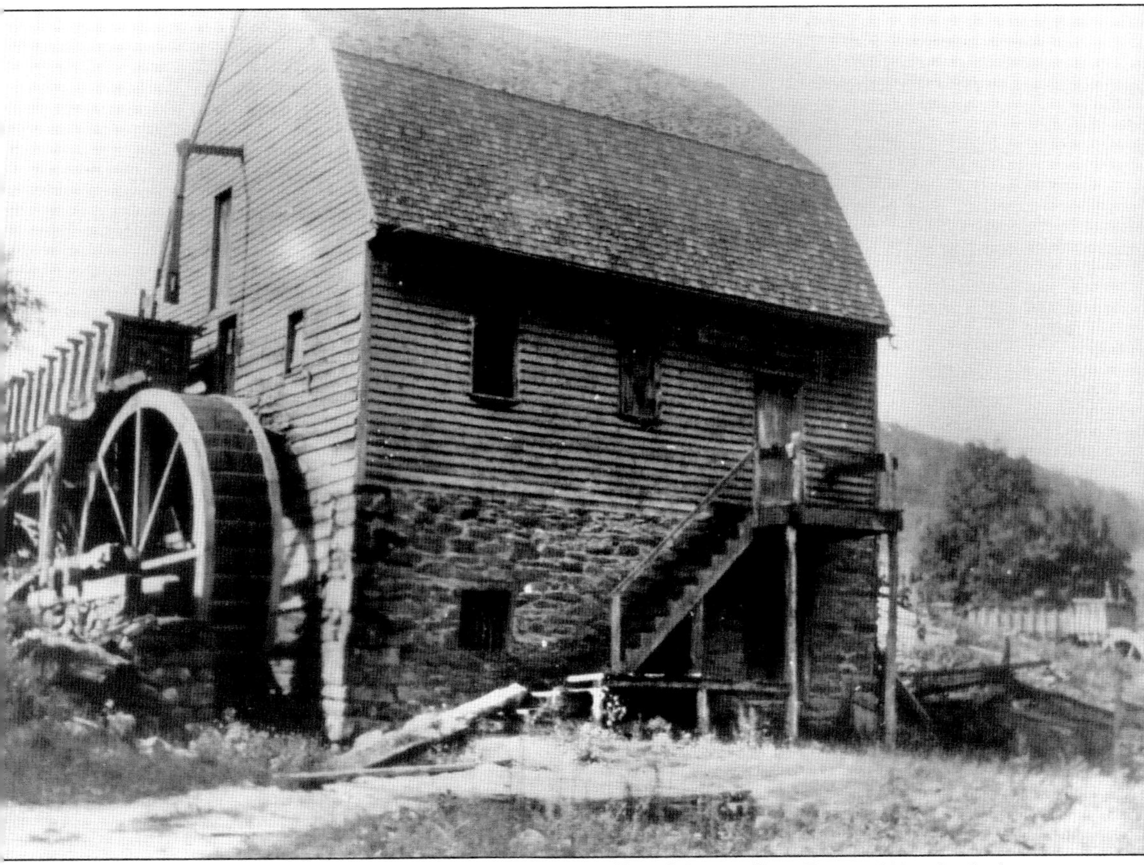

James Woodward originally owned the Estes Grist Mill and Sawmill on Route 211, which dates to around 1836. James A. Estes owned the mill in 1900 and ground cornmeal and buckwheat there. The gear wheels are now in possession of the Smithsonian's National Museum of American History. (Courtesy of the Estes family.)

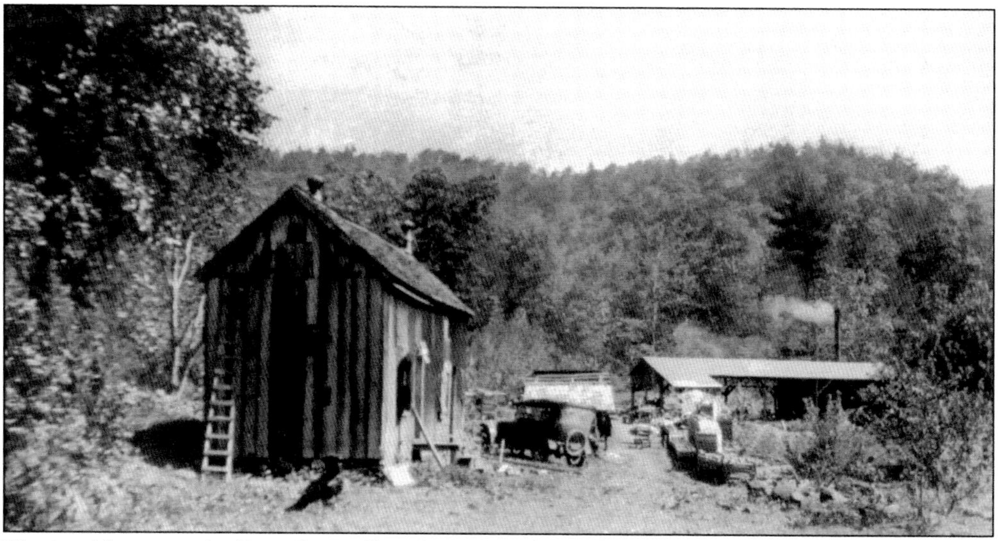

The bunkhouse at the Estes Sawmill on Piney Run housed workers before 1933. This area is now part of the Shenandoah National Park. (Courtesy of the Estes family.)

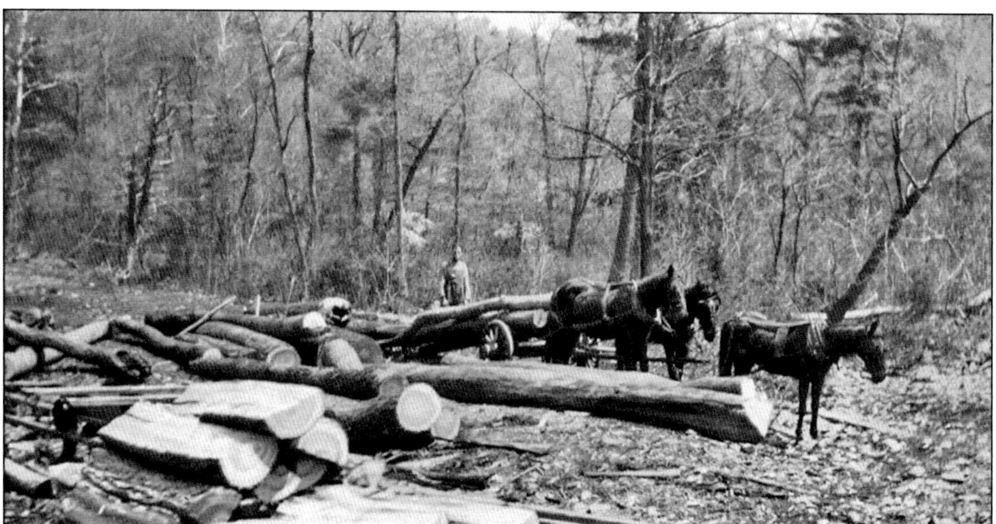

Horses are shown pulling logs near a steam-powered sawmill. The logs were cut into locust posts for fencing. Poplar was used to make staves that were made into barrels for the apple industry. (Courtesy of the Estes family.)

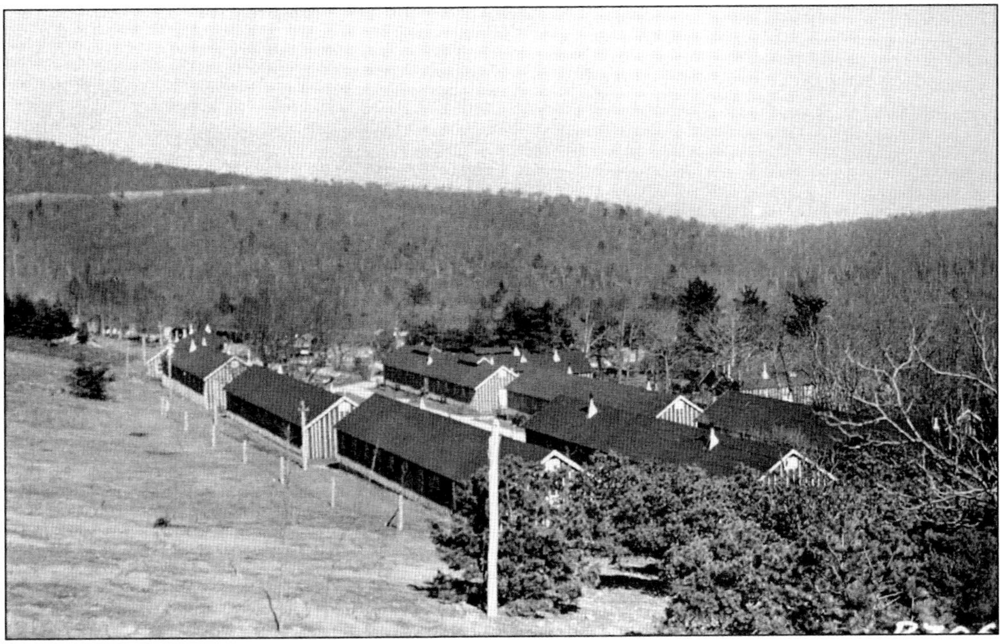

Civilian Conservation Corps (CCC) camps were established to provide employment for men out of work during the Depression. This is the Pinnacles Camp, a large camp near Sperryville. (Courtesy of the Shenandoah National Park Archives, Reed Engle.)

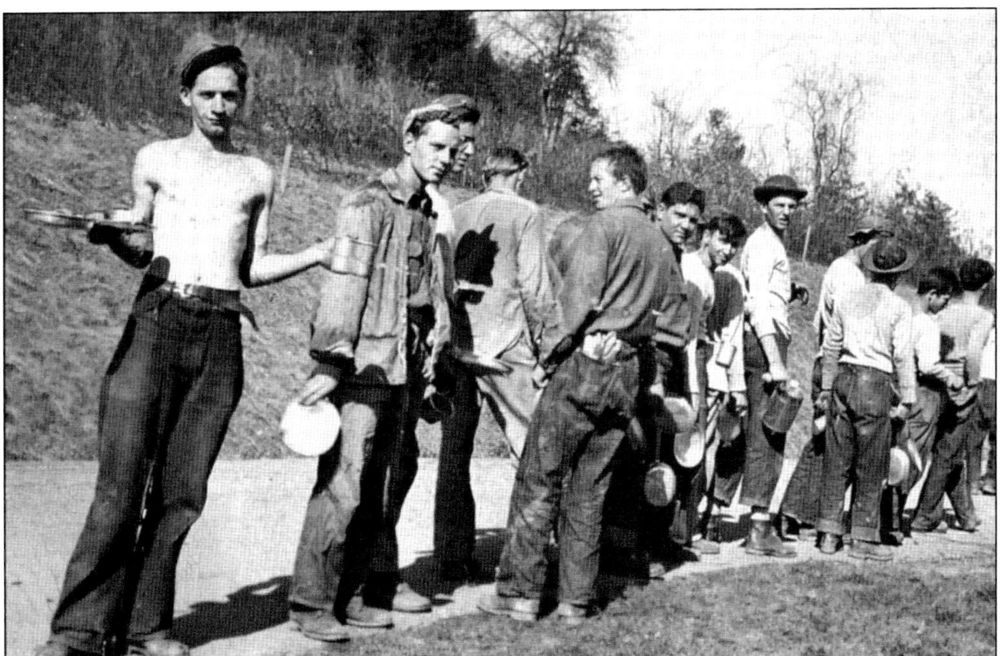

A group of CCC workers are shown standing in line waiting to fill their water containers. These men were fed, clothed, housed, and paid $30 per month in exchange for labor building roads and trails. (Courtesy of the Shenandoah National Park Archives, Reed Engle.)

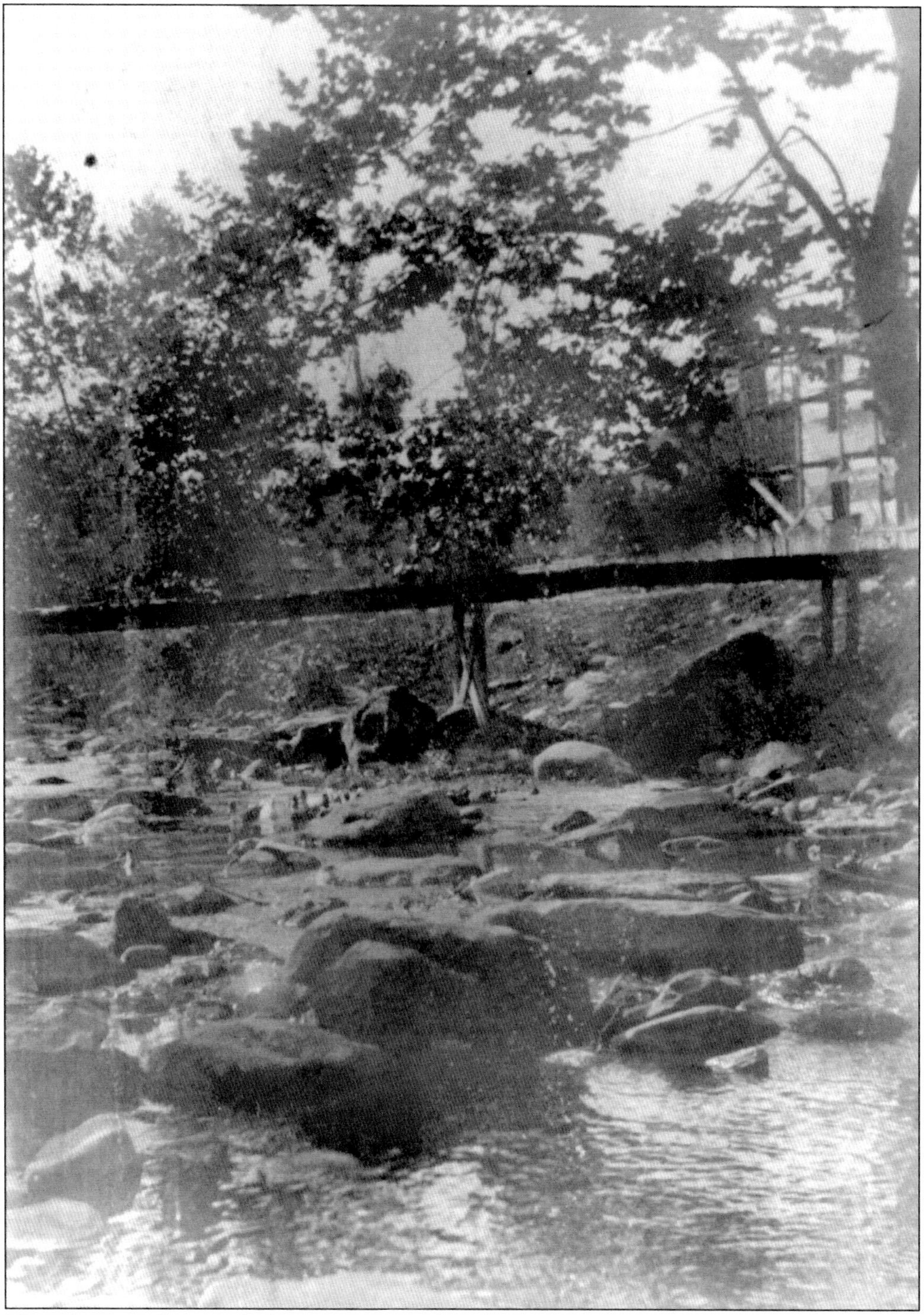

The Thornton River, which originates in the Blue Ridge Mountains, runs along Route 211 through Sperryville. A footbridge was constructed near Main Street to allow people to cross the river. (Courtesy of the Estes family.)

Five

WASHINGTON

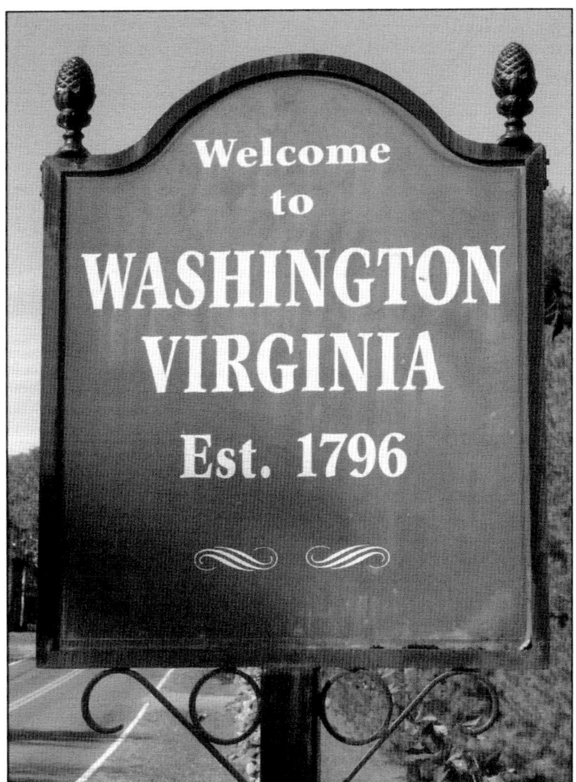

Washington was established in 1794 and incorporated in 1796. When Rappahannock County was established, the village was chosen as the county seat in 1833 because of its central location within the county. The Washington Historic District is listed on the National Register of Historic Places and the Virginia Landmarks Registry. (Courtesy of John Tole.)

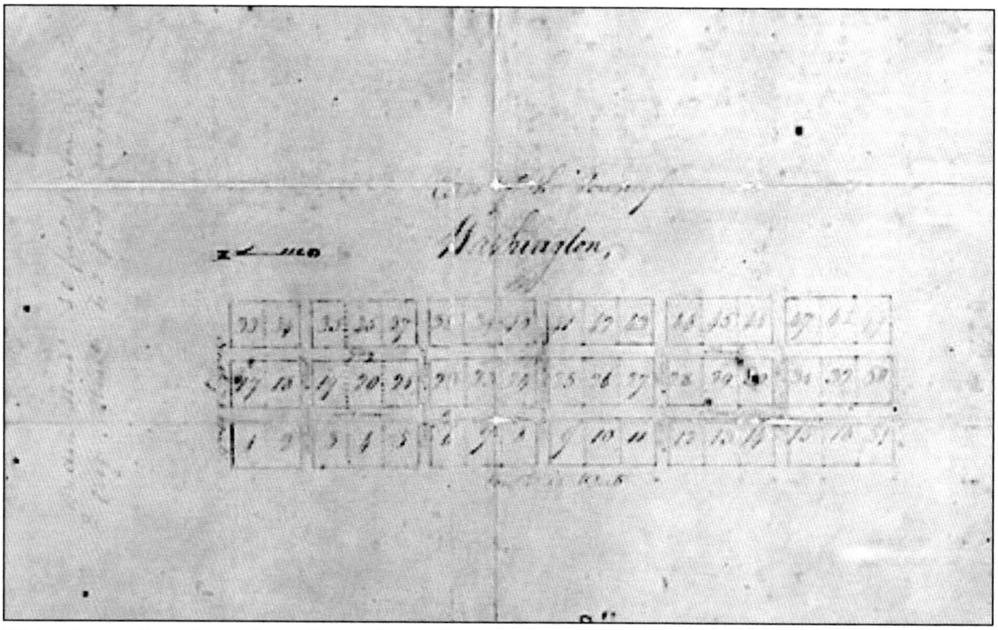

This plat is thought to have been drawn by a young George Washington in 1749. The town was laid out in half-acre lots and has remained virtually unchanged. The streets are named for old families, including Porter, Jett, Calvert, and Wheeler. (Courtesy of the Rappahannock Historical Society.)

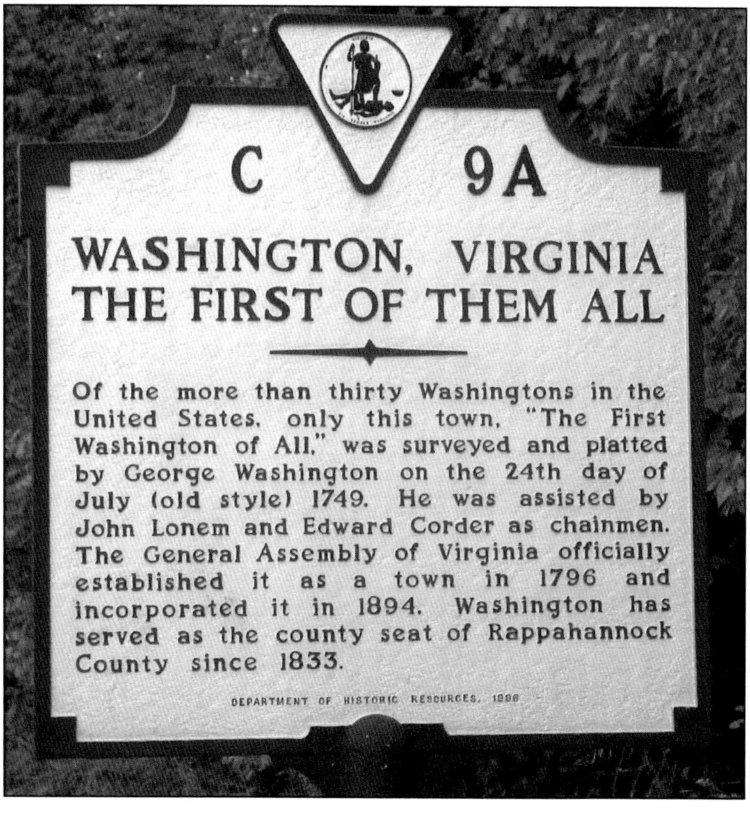

A Virginia Department of Historic Resources sign identifies the village of Washington as one of more than 30 such named towns in the United States. Washington, Virginia, is known as "The First Washington of Them All." (Courtesy of John Tole.)

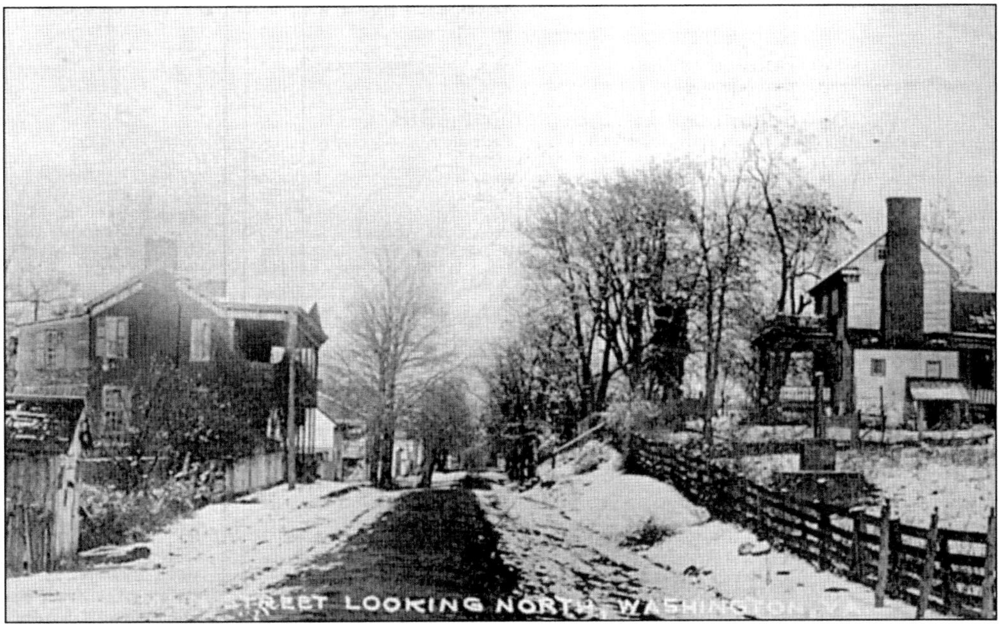

This is Main Street looking north around 1917. Notice the unpaved street, the old Menefee home, and the former Episcopal parsonage, also known as the Massie home. (Courtesy of the Rappahannock Historical Society.)

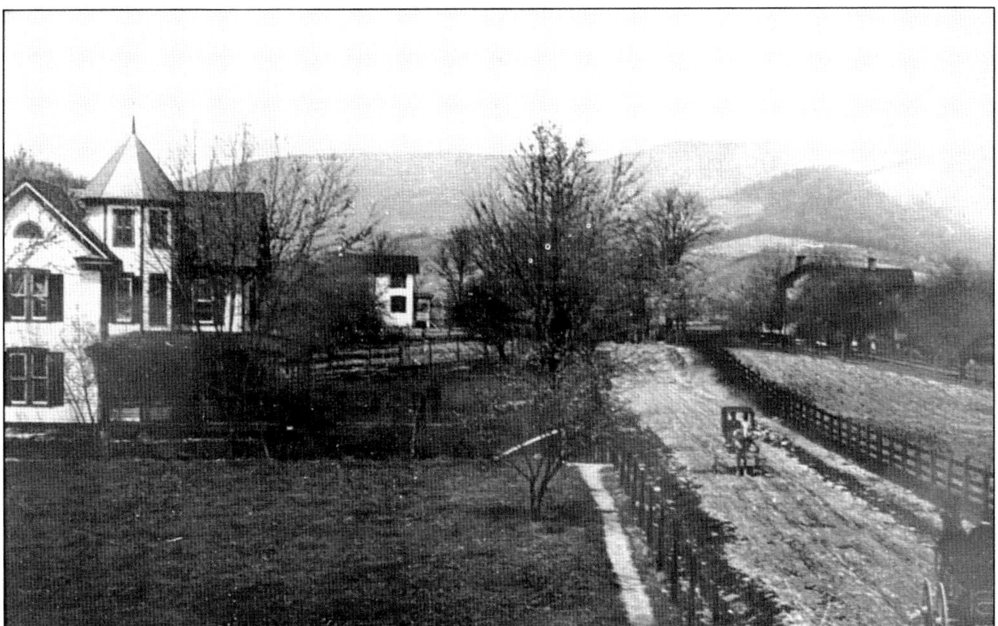

This is Blue Ridge Avenue looking west as you proceed into Harris Hollow. Notice the horse and buggy making their way along the road. (Courtesy of the Rappahannock Historical Society.)

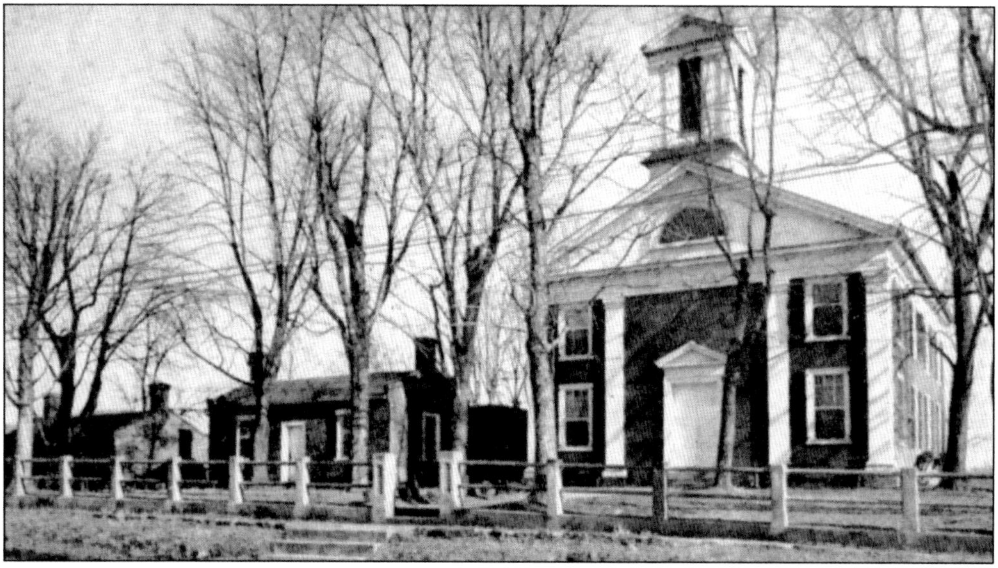

The courthouse, clerk's office, and treasurer's office were built in 1835. There have been a series of additions and renovations to the building over the years. (Courtesy of Diane Bruce.)

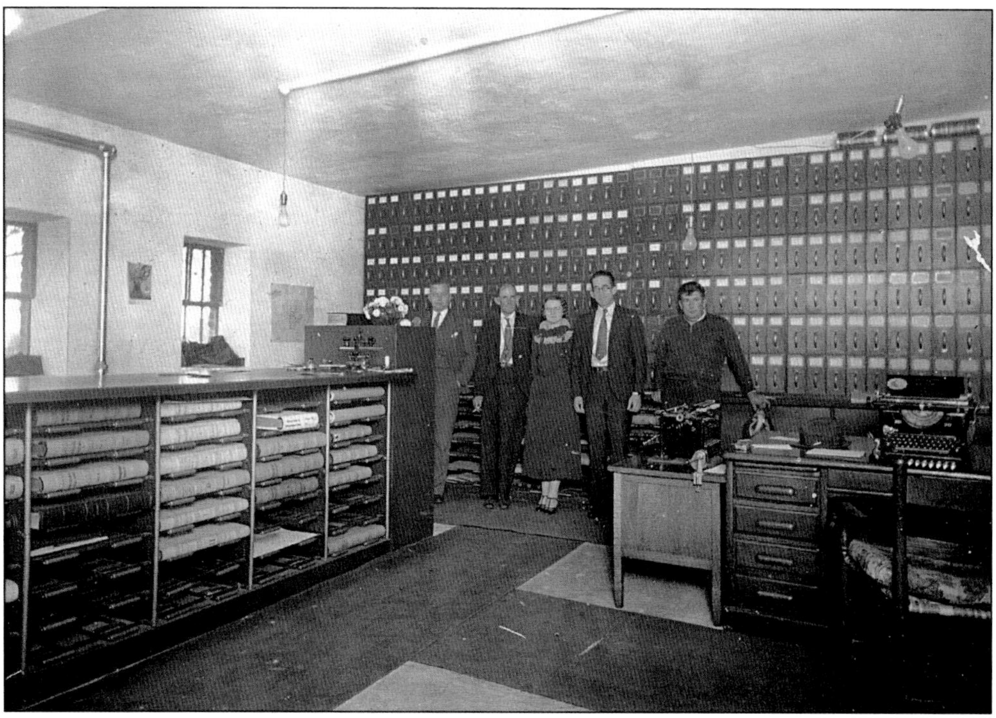

A view of the inside the clerk's office in the 1940s shows an array of deed books and drawers that served as filing cabinets. A new clerk's office was built to the right of the courthouse in 1978 and contains all the official records of the county dating back to 1833. (Courtesy of Diane Bruce.)

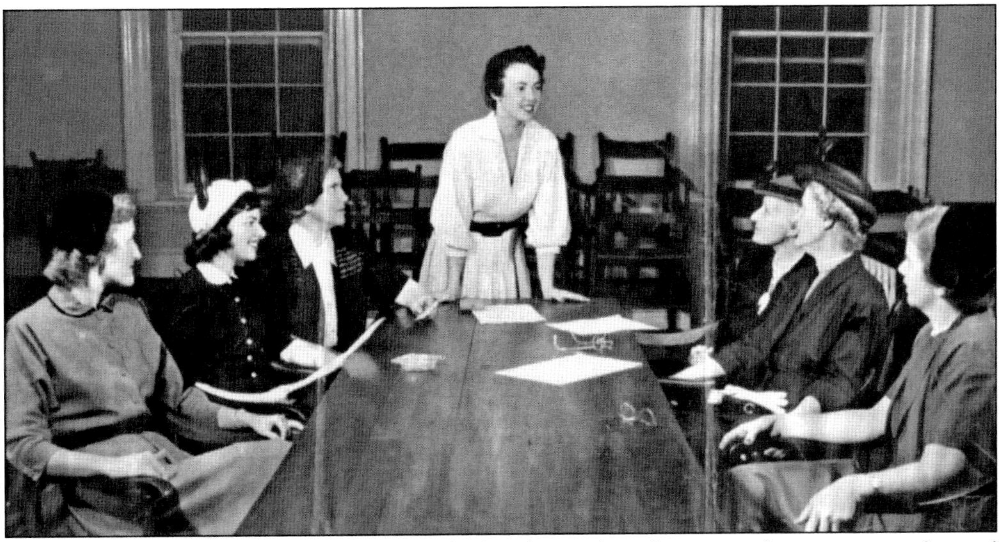

Begun as a practical joke after the mayor declined to seek reelection and no one came forward to run, a judge thought it a novel idea to run an all-woman slate. Dorothy Cox Davis was elected mayor in 1950 along with an all-woman council. The town of Washington made history. The women were featured in an article in *Collier's* magazine entitled "Washington 'She-Town.' "

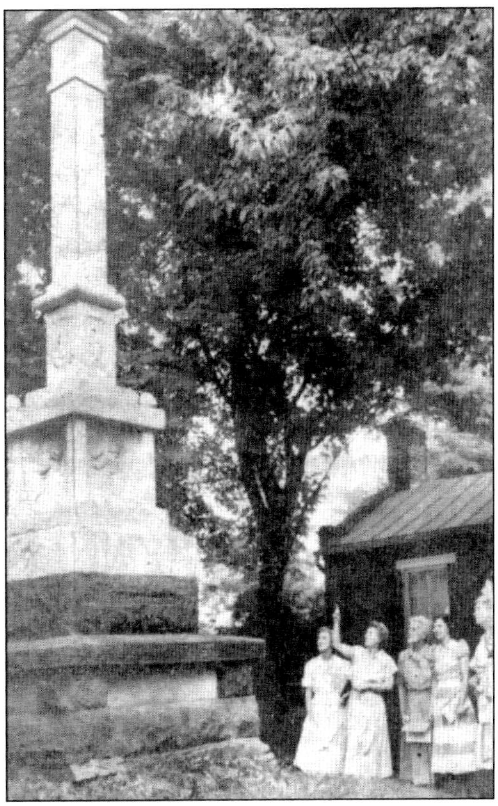

The six women on the town council visit the courthouse complex to inspect the loss of the top ornament on the Confederate monument in Washington. The six women council members were, in alphabetical order, Robbie Critzer, Dorothy Hawkins, Ruby Jenkins, Achsah Dudley Miller, Louise Miller Price, and Nellie Elizabeth Racer. (Courtesy of the Rappahannock Historical Society.)

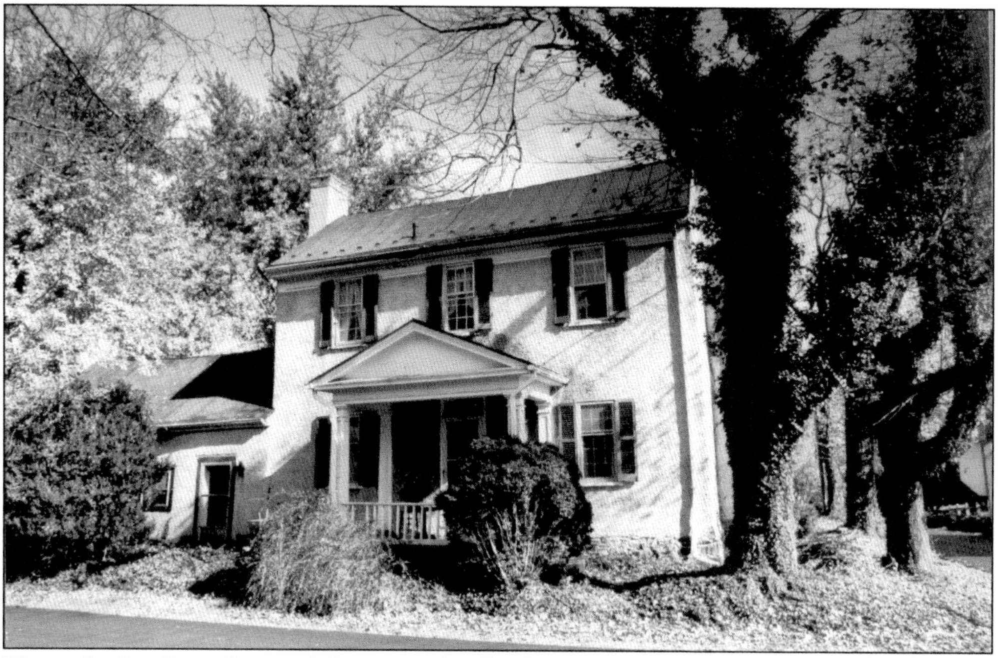

This is the first Rappahannock County Jail and Jailer's House, located at the corner of Main and Calvert Streets. (Courtesy of the Rappahannock Historical Society.)

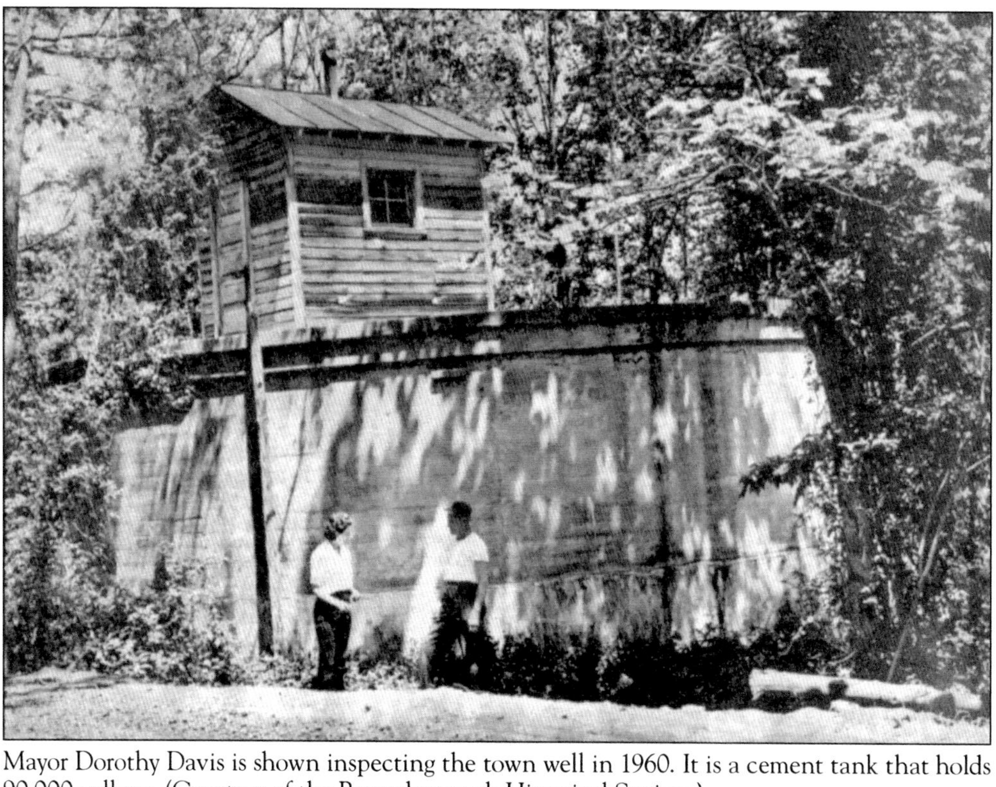

Mayor Dorothy Davis is shown inspecting the town well in 1960. It is a cement tank that holds 90,000 gallons. (Courtesy of the Rappahannock Historical Society.)

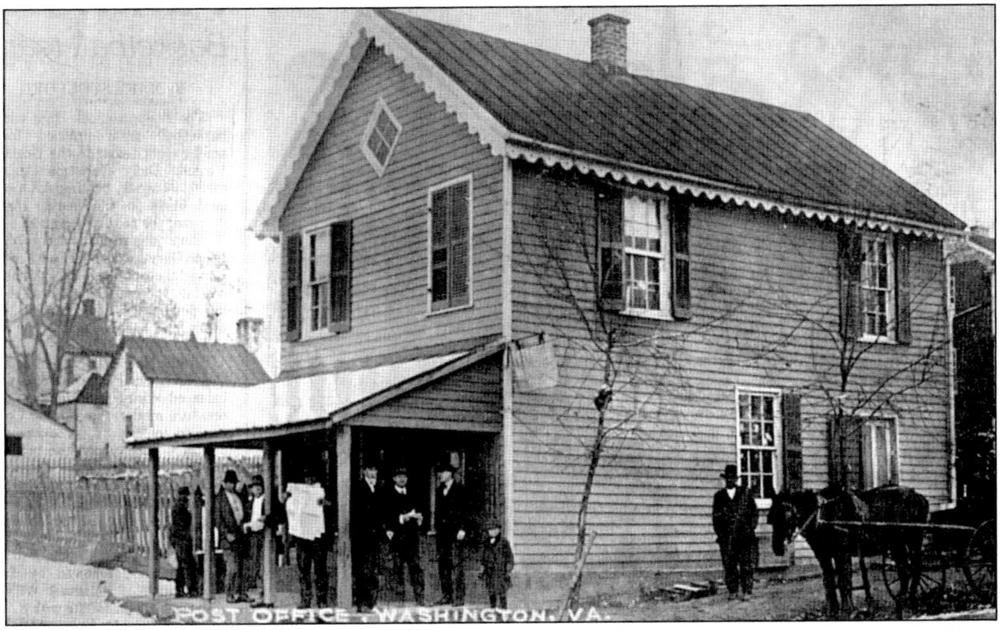

Local people are shown gathered at the Washington Post Office on the corner of Main and Jett Streets in 1917. (Courtesy of the Rappahannock Historical Society.)

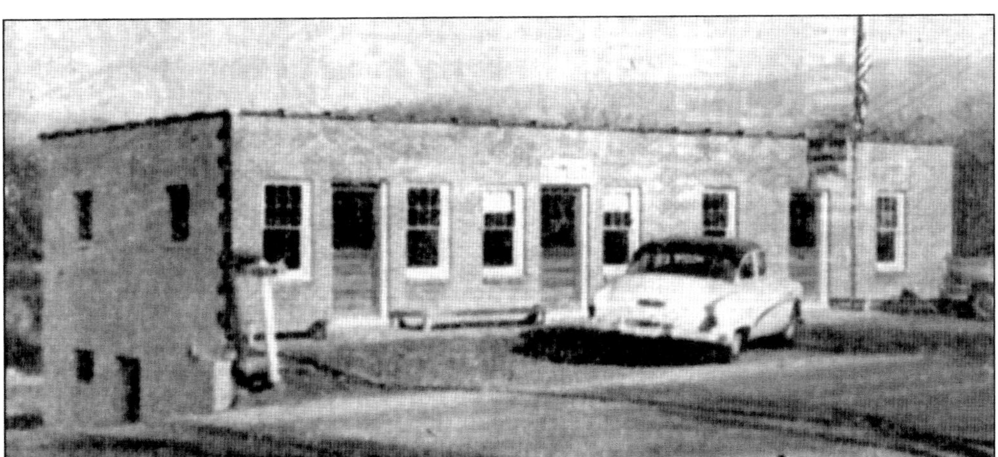
The Washington Post Office was located in this building on Main Street in 1956. (Courtesy of the Rappahannock Historical Society.)

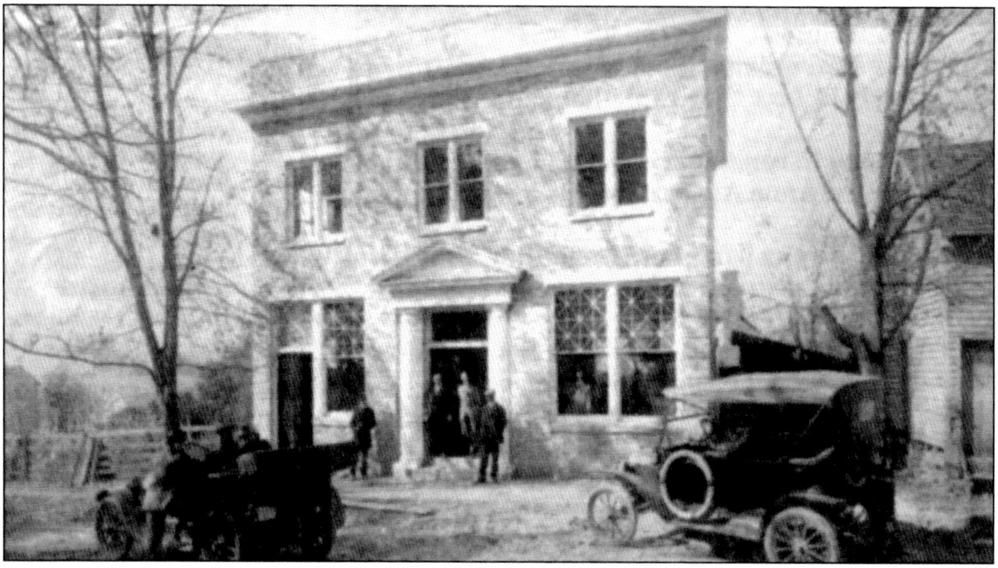

The Rappahannock National Bank opened for business in September 1902. The bank operated at this location until 2003, when a new bank was erected on Route 211. (Courtesy of the Rappahannock Historical Society.)

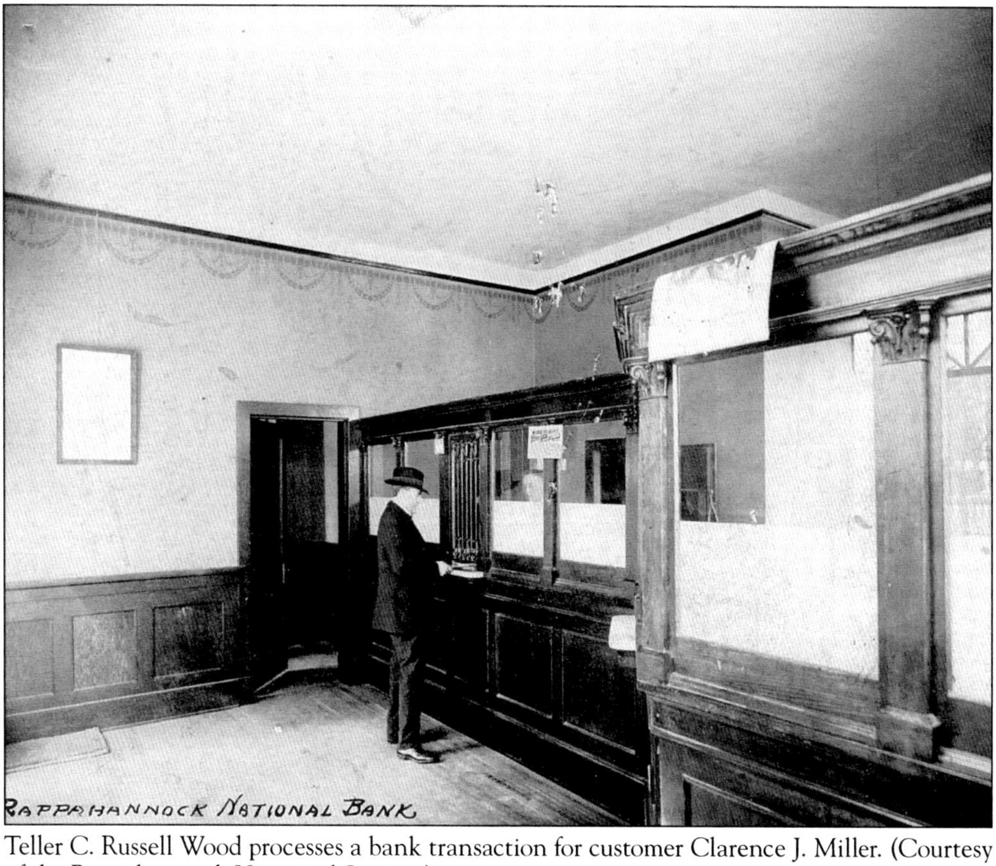

Teller C. Russell Wood processes a bank transaction for customer Clarence J. Miller. (Courtesy of the Rappahannock Historical Society.)

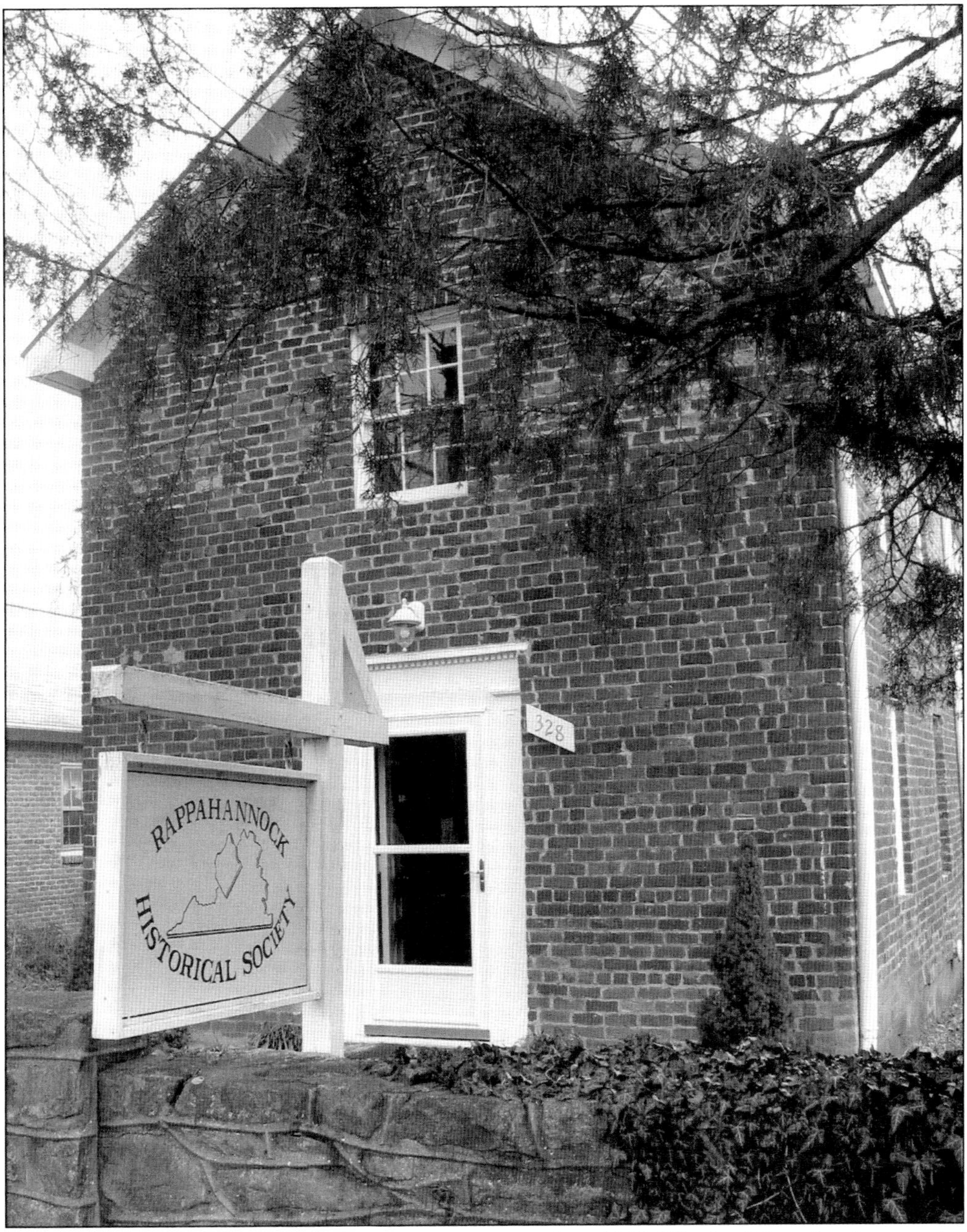

The Rappahannock Historical Society was organized in 1965. The building that houses the historical society was built in 1820. It once served as an outbuilding for a manor house called Avon Hall. (Courtesy of the Rappahannock Historical Society.)

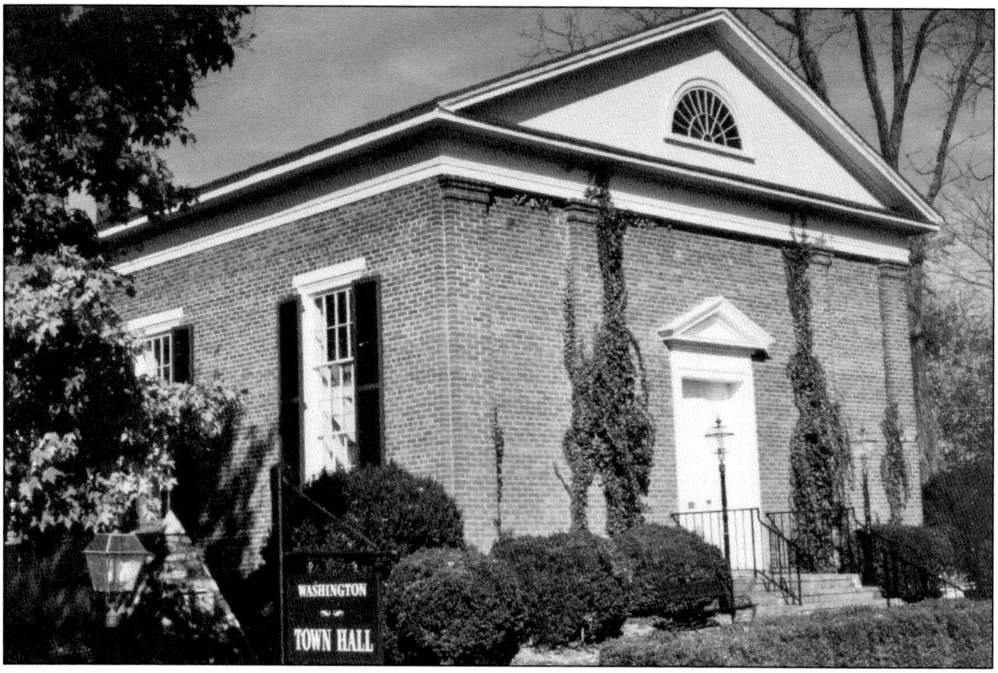

The Washington Presbyterian Church was built by James Leake Powers in 1856 of brick in the Doric architectural style. It served its congregation until 1939, when the building was sold. It was used from 1963 to 1990 as the Rappahannock County Library. It now serves as the Washington Town Hall. (Courtesy of the Rappahannock Historical Society.)

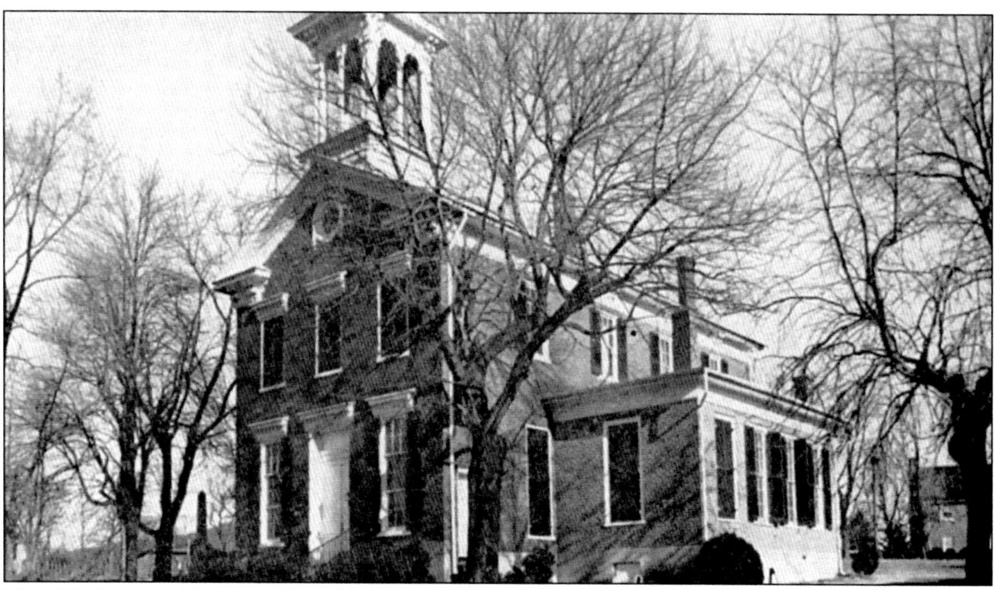

The Washington Baptist Church was constructed in 1882. The Washington Lodge No. 78 of the Ancient Free and Accepted Masons used the upstairs of the building. (Courtesy of the Rappahannock Historical Society.)

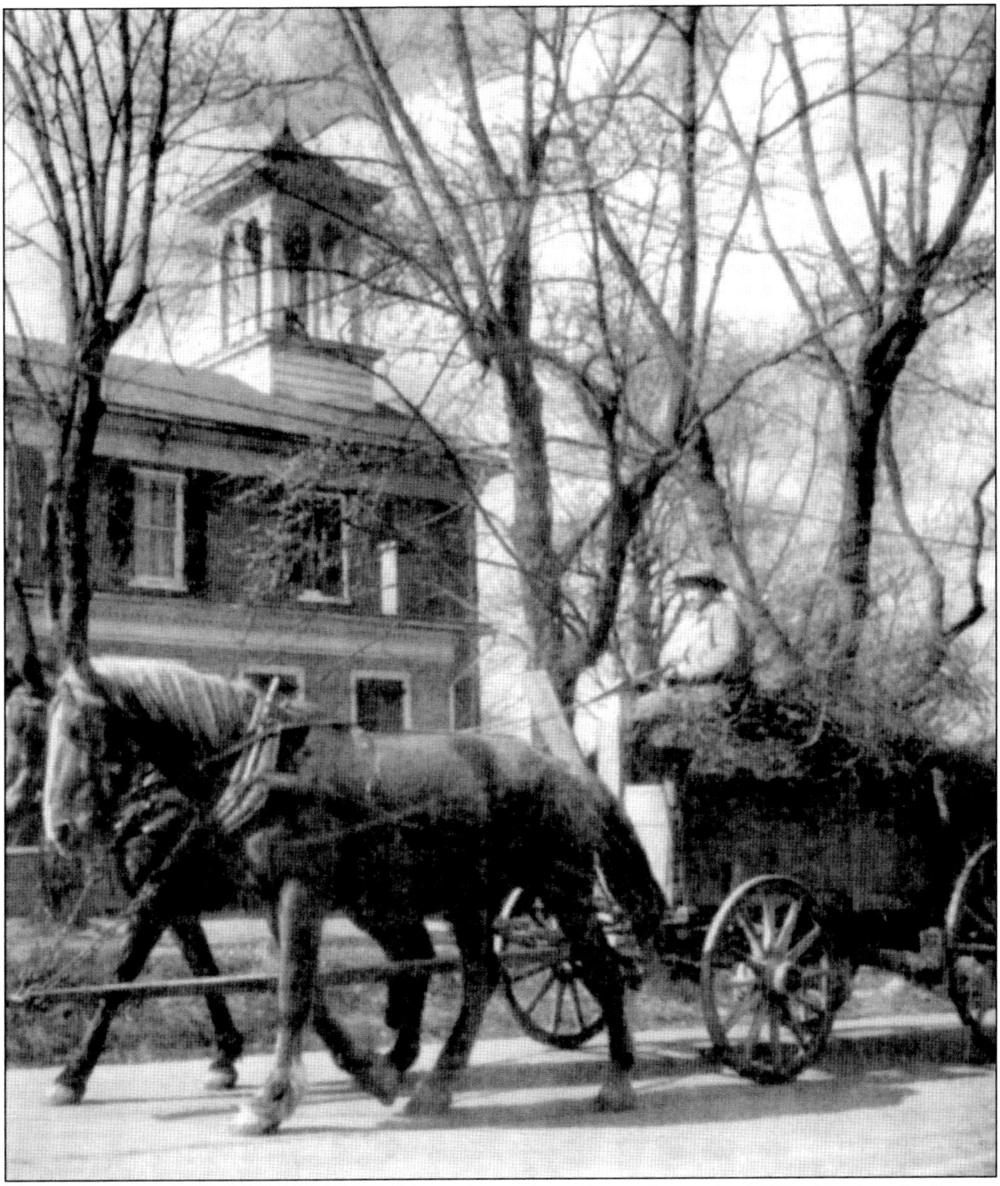

The Washington Baptist Church is shown from the side in the early 1950s. Notice the horse-drawn wagon carrying tree branches that were removed from a nearby property. (Courtesy of the Rappahannock Historical Society.)

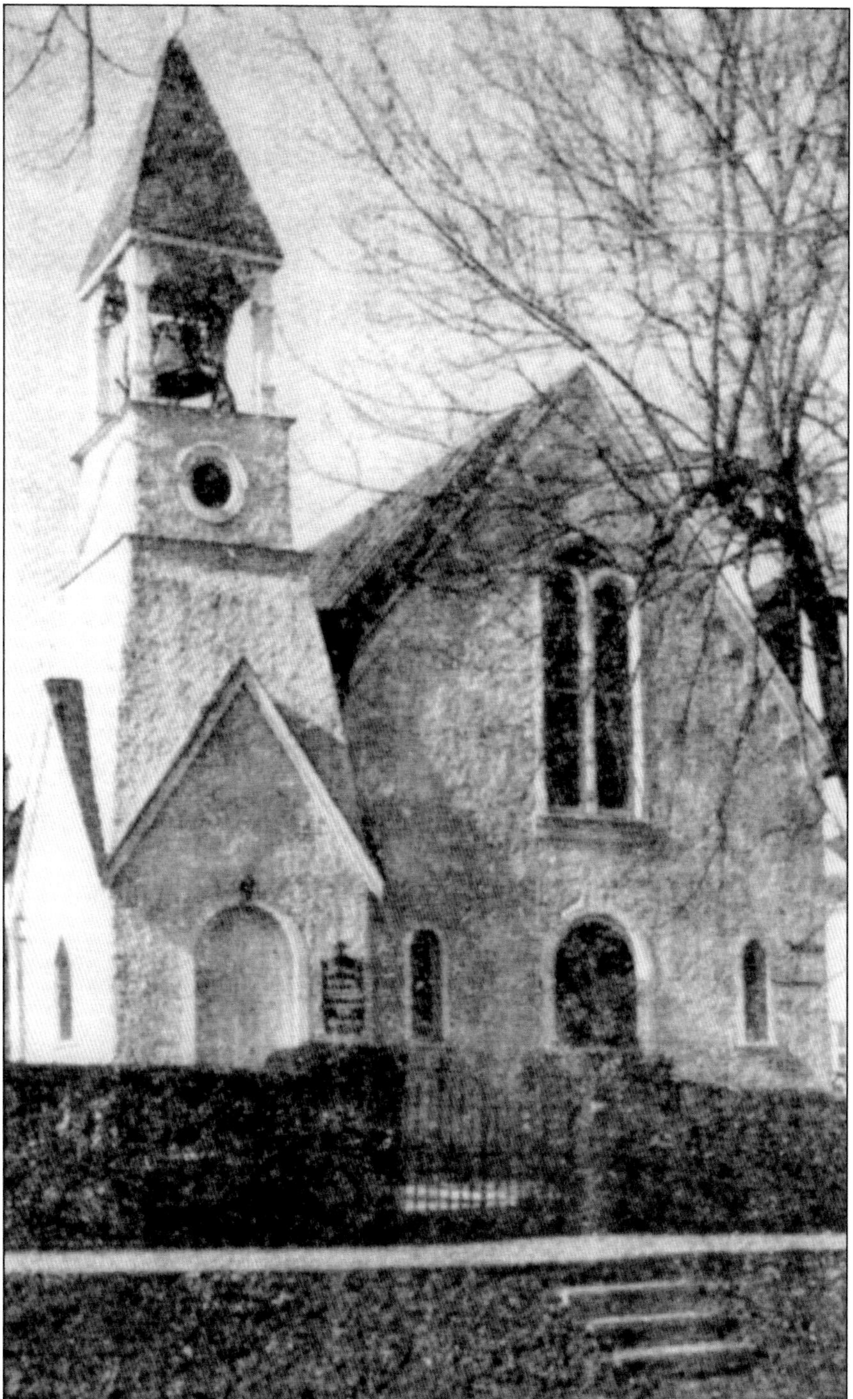

Trinity Episcopal Church was built in 1857 with the cornerstone laid by the Masonic Lodge of Washington. Several items are contained in the cornerstone: a Book of Common Prayer, the journal of the 61st annual convention of the Protestant Episcopal Church of Virginia, and other printed material, along with several coins in use at the time. (Courtesy of Diane Bruce.)

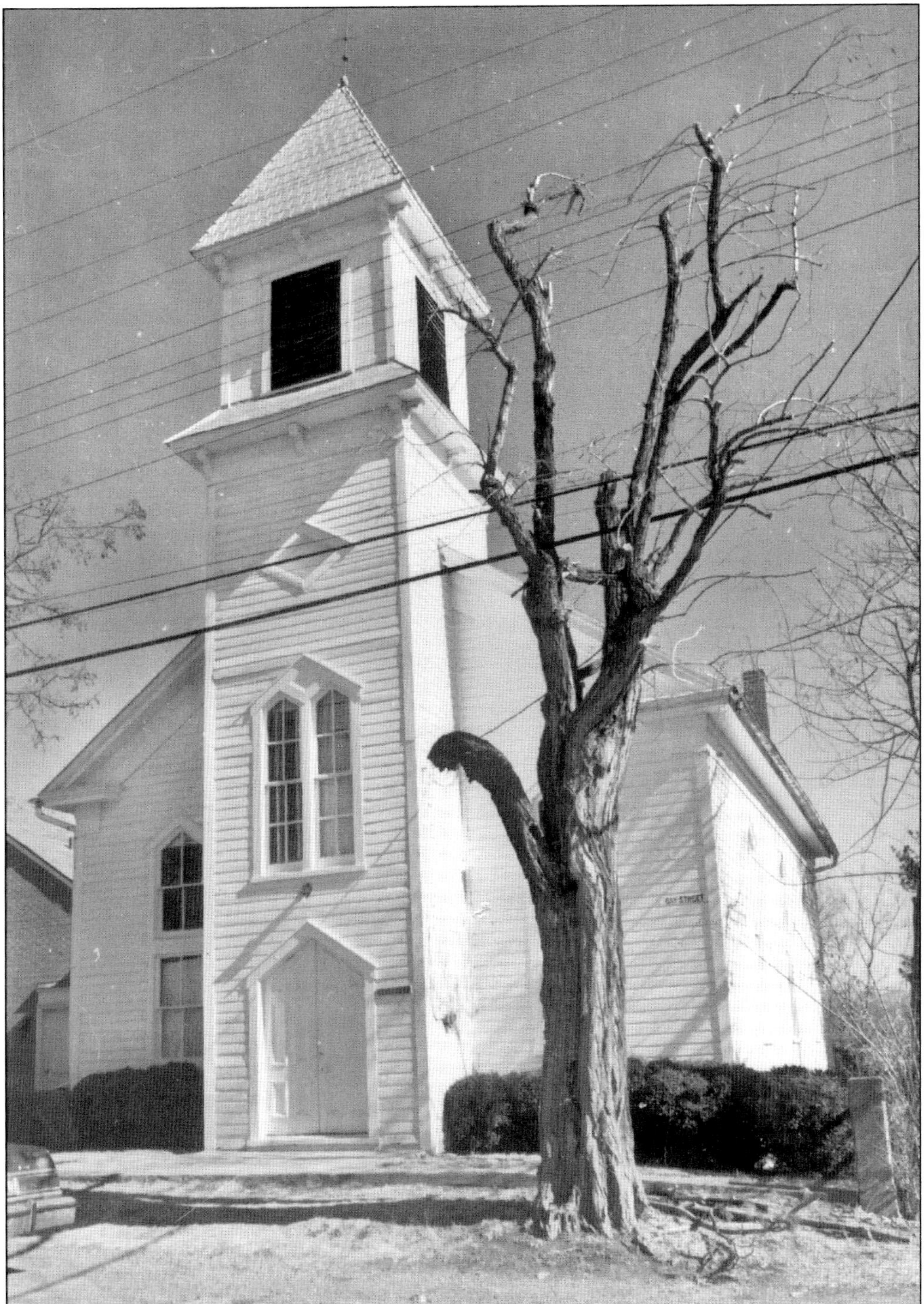

The Washington United Methodist Church was built in 1889. Washington Lodge No. 78 of the Ancient Free and Accepted Masons laid the cornerstone. The church closed in 1979. (Courtesy of the Rappahannock Historical Society.)

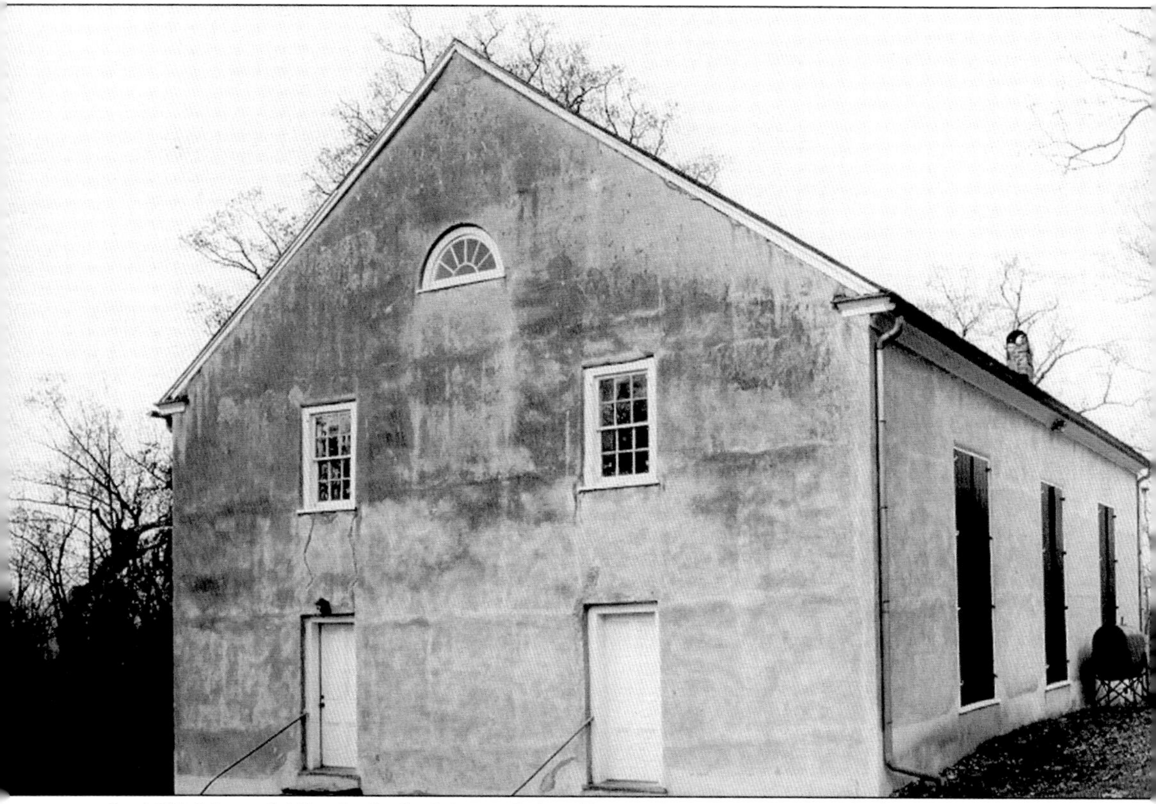

In 1855, Henry Miller built the Mount Salem Baptist Meeting House, also known as the Mount Salem Baptist Church. The building was constructed in the Federal style with Greek Revival influences on the interior. The church closed in 1942. The building is on the National Register of Historic Places and the Virginia Landmarks Registry. (Courtesy of John Tole.)

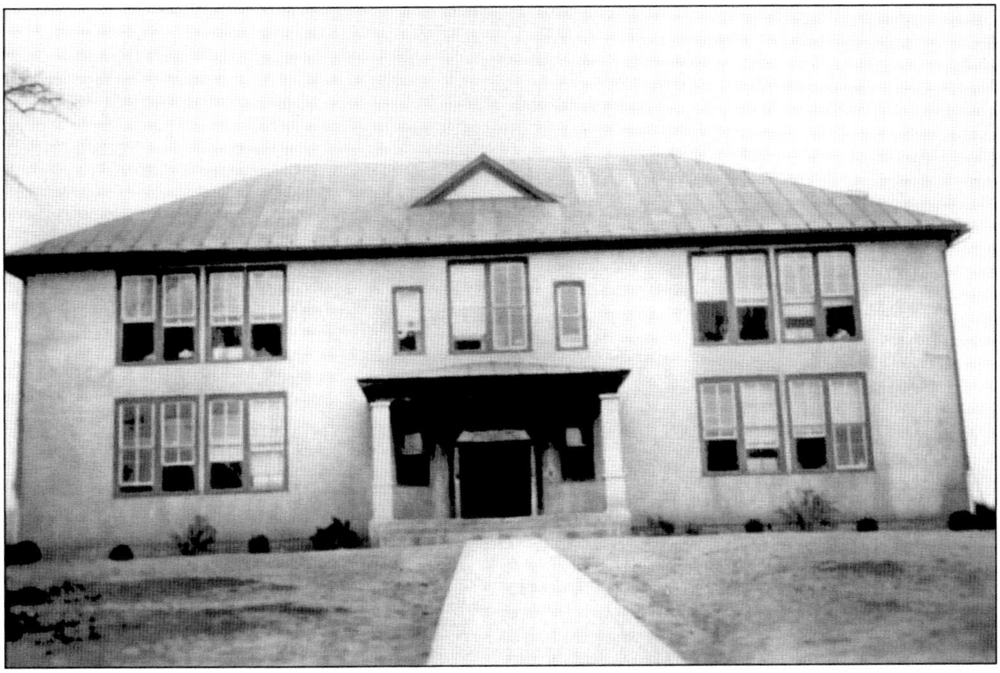

Washington High School was built in 1908. It is shown in the 1940s. The school ceased to be a high school in 1960 and served as an elementary school until 1969. (Courtesy of the Rappahannock Historical Society.)

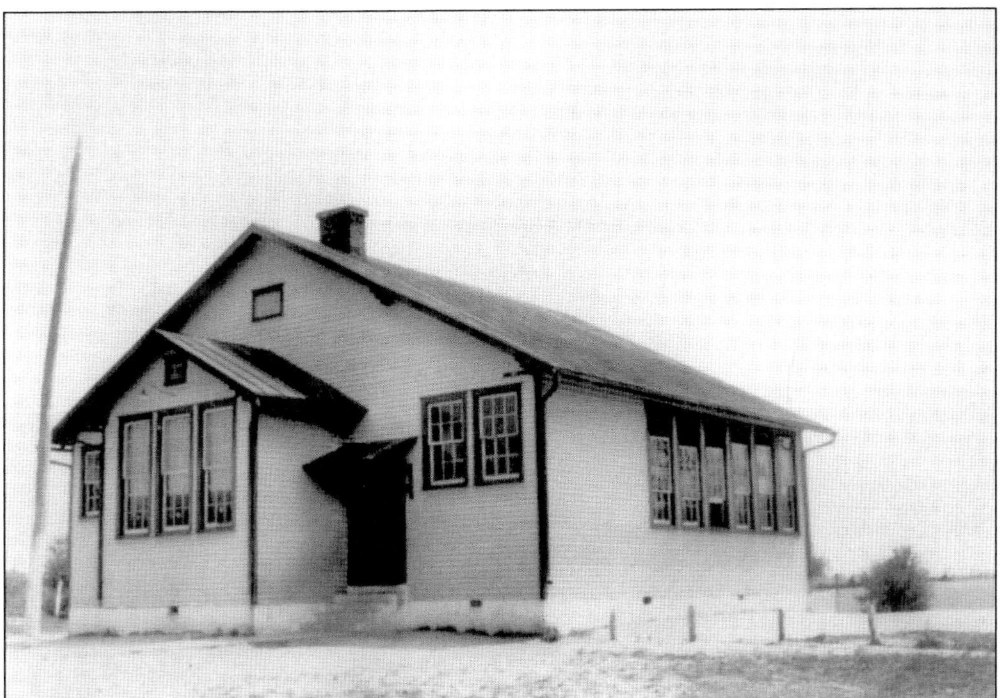

The Washington Graded School was constructed in 1924 on Piedmont Avenue. It was one of four Rosenwald Funds schools in the county. (Courtesy of the Rappahannock Historical Society.)

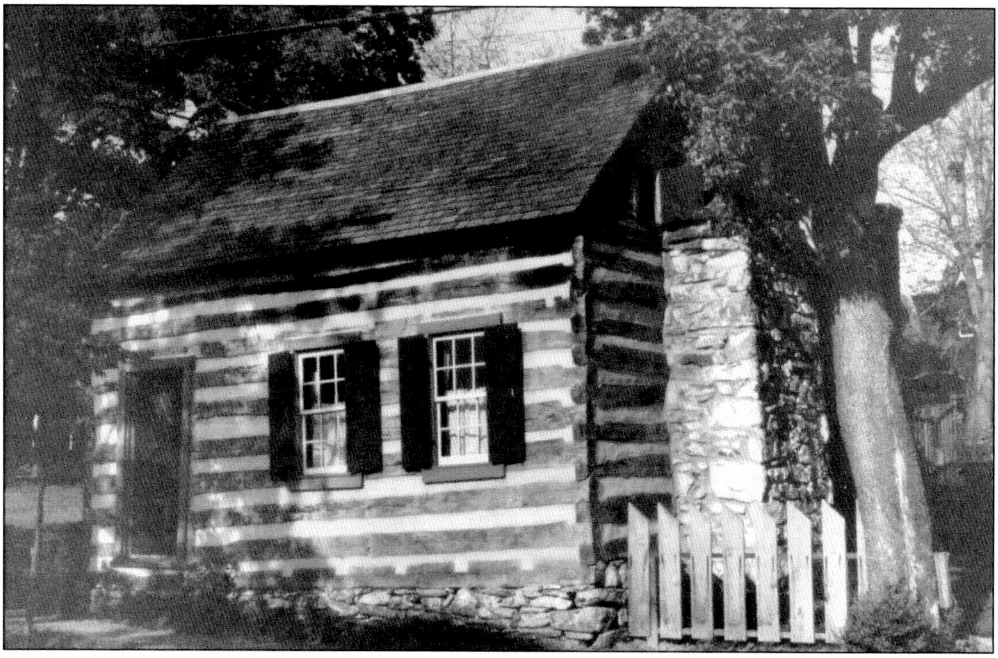

This log cabin on Main Street is one of six log cabins thought to have been here before 1749. (Courtesy of the Rappahannock Historical Society.)

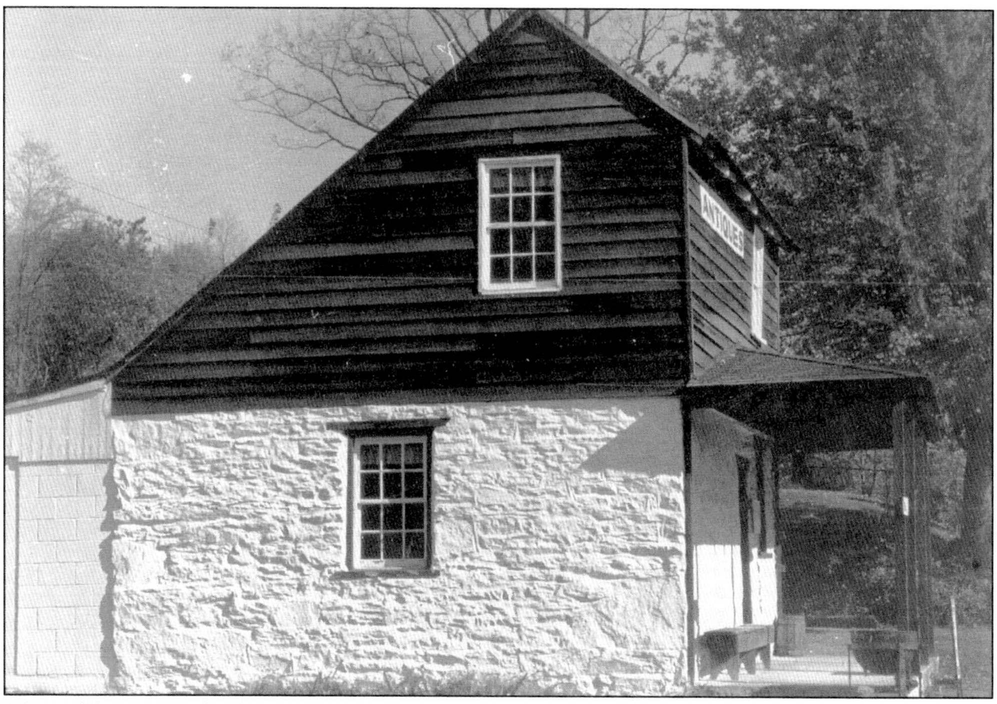

This tollhouse was built in 1853 when the Sperryville-Rappahannock Turnpike Company came into existence. Tolls were collected here until at least 1916. There were several buildings at intervals of approximately every 12 miles along Route 211 used as tollhouses. This is the only one still in existence. (Courtesy of the Rappahannock Historical Society.)

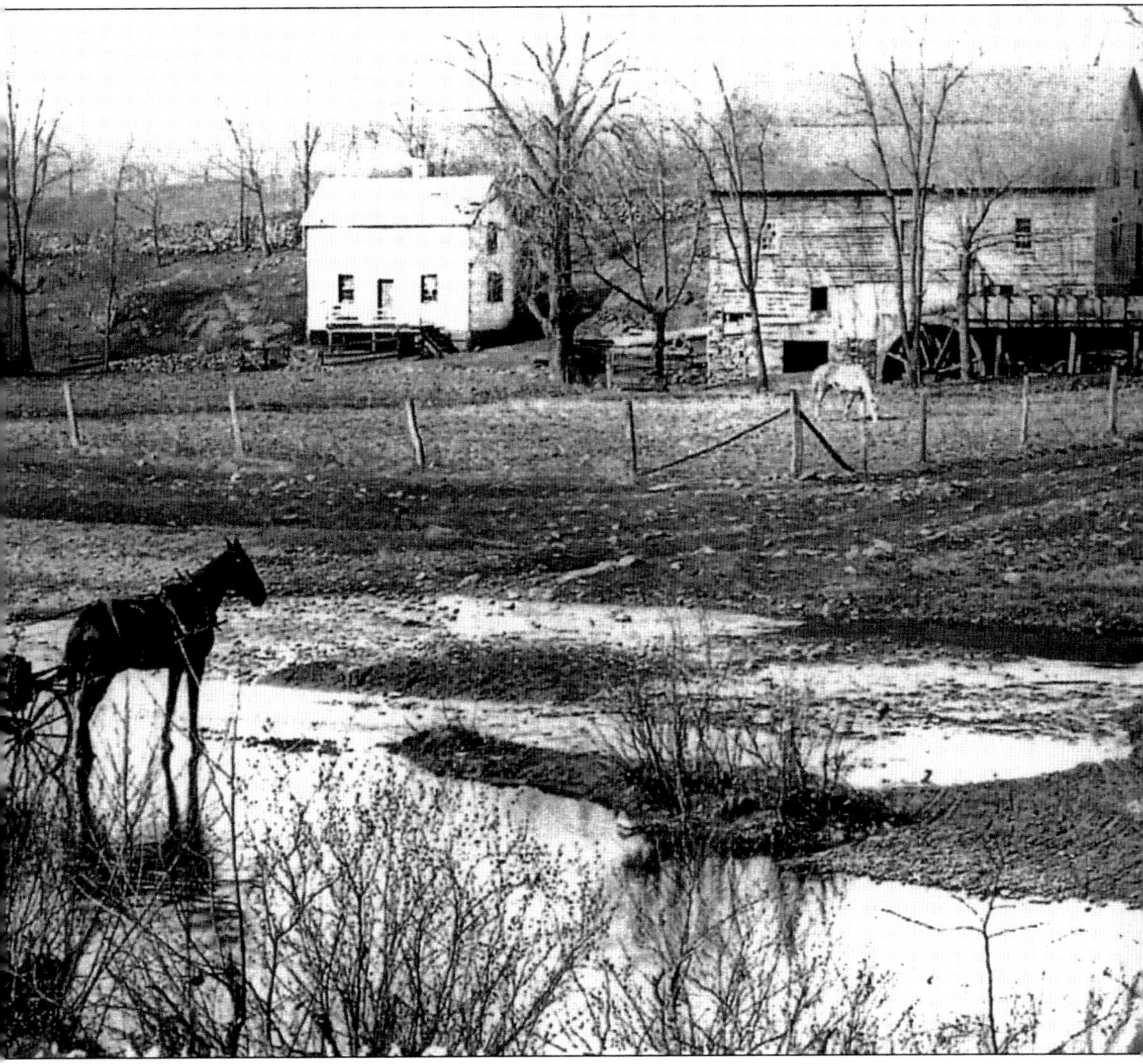

Baggarly's Mill, also known as Calvert Mill and Washington Mill, is a gristmill dating from 1777 to 1779. It sits on a site above the Rush River just outside of Washington. It is thought to have served as a neutral trading spot during the Civil War. The mill is listed on the National Register of Historic Places and the Virginia Landmarks Registry. (Courtesy of the Rappahannock Historical Society.)

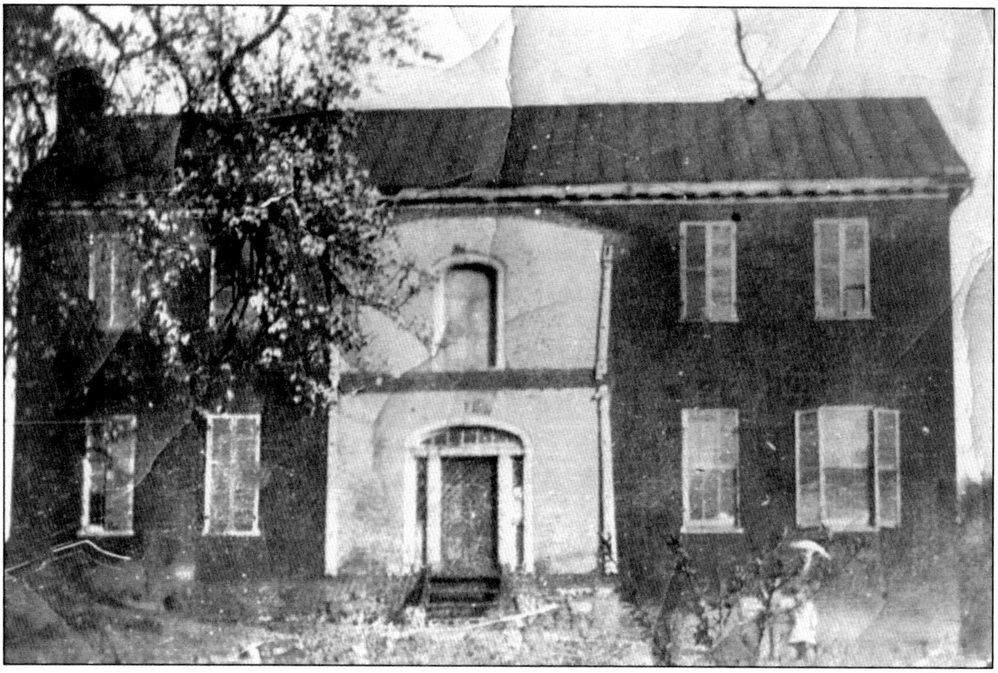

James Jett built Ellerslie in 1814. The manor house originally had a fancy portico with brick columns. The gardens contained beautiful old English boxwoods that were taken as slips from a neighboring estate called Rose Hill and planted in 1815. The house is shown in the 1920s. It was destroyed by fire in 1933. (Courtesy of the Rappahannock Historical Society.)

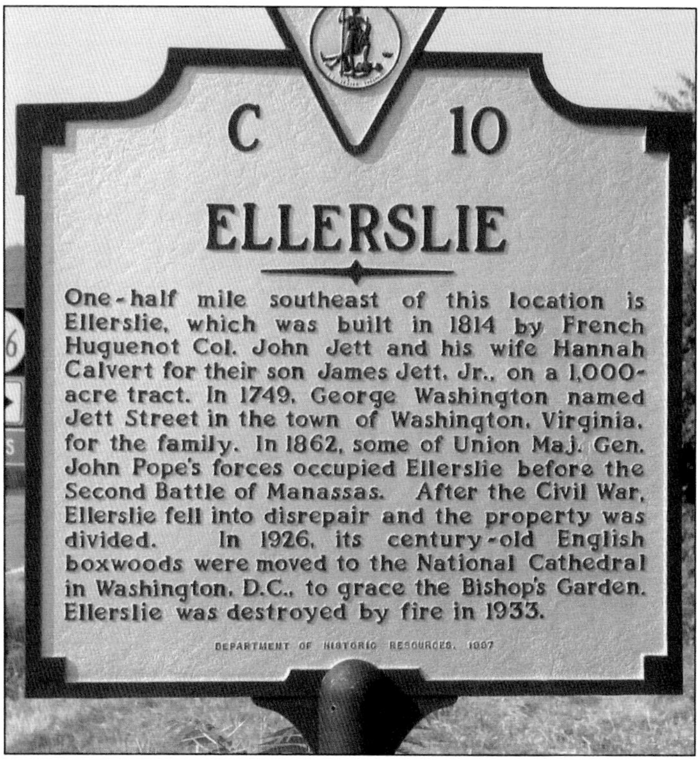

A Virginia Department of Historic Resources sign states that in 1926, the boxwoods from Ellerslie were moved to the Bishop's Garden at the National Cathedral in Washington, D.C. (Courtesy of John Tole.)

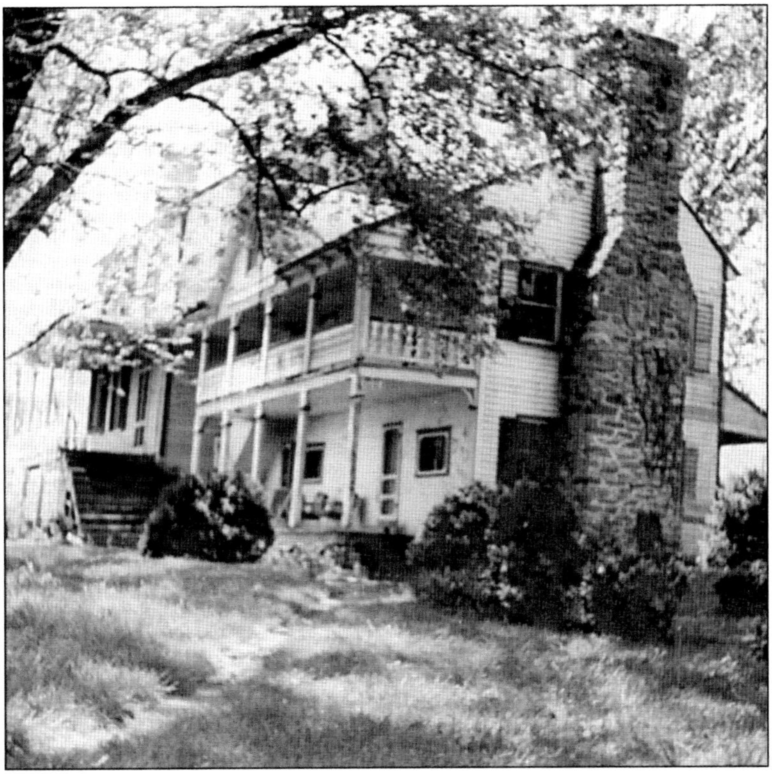

The Meadows began as a log cabin built in the early 1740s. It has been expanded several times over the years. During the Civil War, it served as a hospital for Union soldiers. After the Civil War, owner Judge Strother couldn't keep servants because they thought the house was haunted. (Courtesy of the Rappahannock Historical Society.)

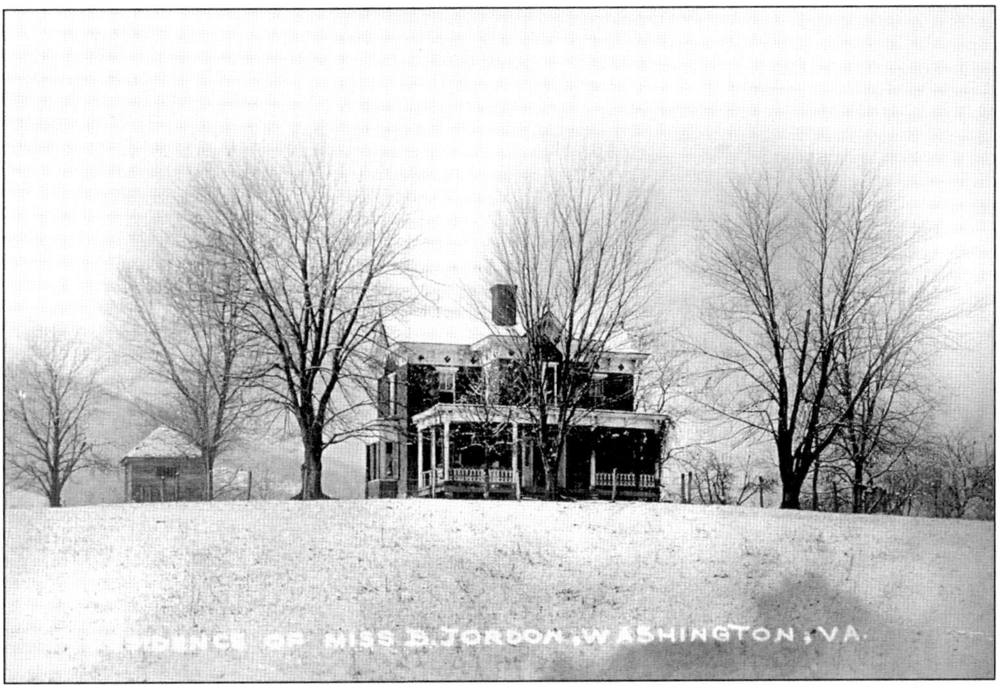

In 1850, the Jordan family built Mount Prospect about a quarter-mile from the center of Washington on Main Street. Constructed of red brick produced on the property, the Victorian-Italianate–style home was typical of the period with high ceilings and large rooms. (Courtesy of Eve Willis.)

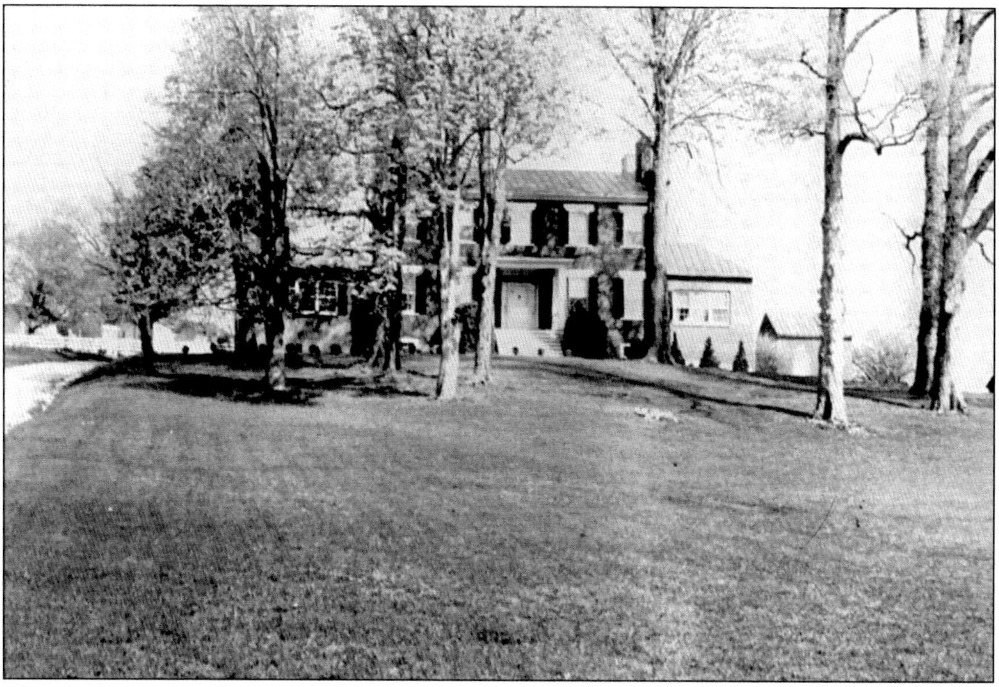

The Maples is located on Main Street. Middleton Miller built the large, Federal-style house in the 1840s with bricks hand kilned on the property. He owned a woolen mill just outside the county that produced the wool fabric known as "Confederate Gray." (Courtesy of the Rappahannock Historical Society.)

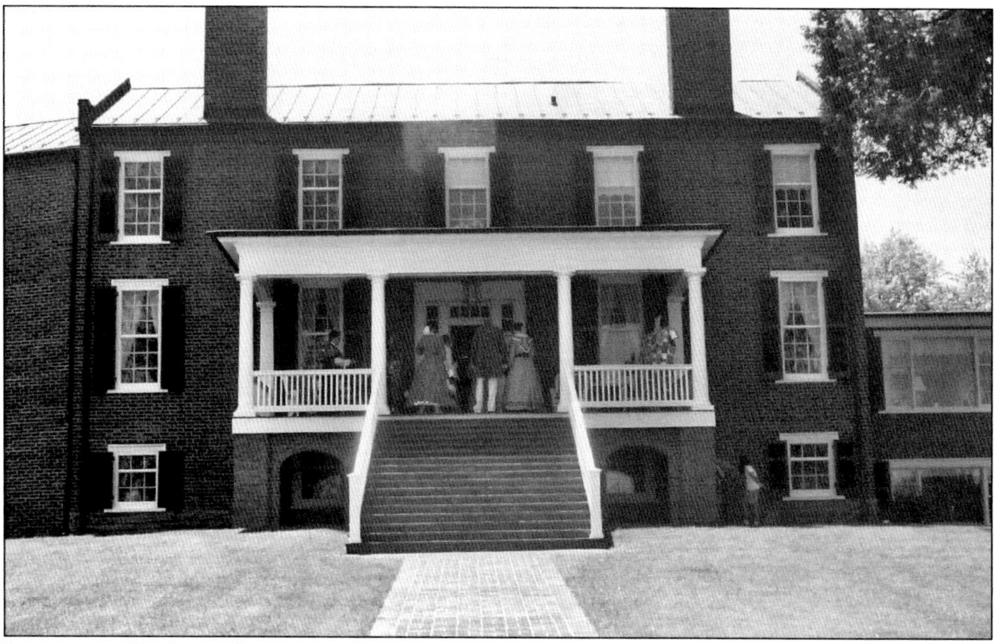

Jessamine Hill is located in Tiger Valley and is one of the area's most historic homes. In 1830, Thomas Clark Fletcher built the three-story main house with both Federal and Jeffersonian influences, reminiscent of an antebellum estate. (Courtesy of the Rappahannock Historical Society.)

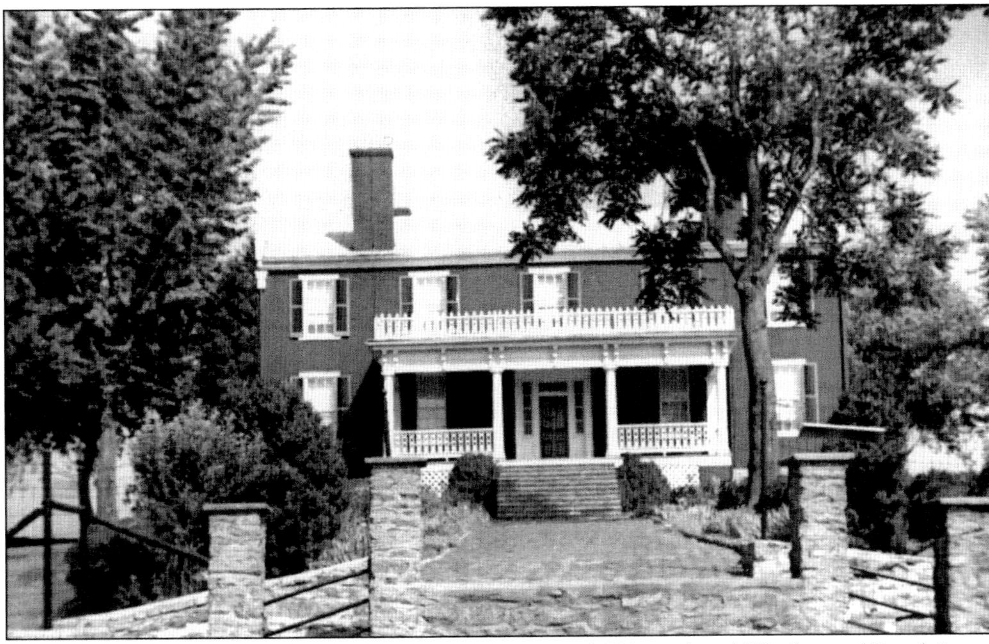

Ben Venue Farms sits at the crossroads of Routes 211 and 729 on the old Richmond Road. James Leake Powers built the manor house between 1844 and 1846. A formal boxwood garden provides a dramatic contrast to the expansive fields surrounding the property. Ben Venue or Gaines Crossroads, as it was known in the 1860s, saw most of the Union and Confederate forces pass by during the marches and retreats to and from Antietam and Gettysburg. Ben Venue Farms is on the National Register of Historic Places and the Virginia Landmarks Registry. (Courtesy of the Rappahannock Historical Society.)

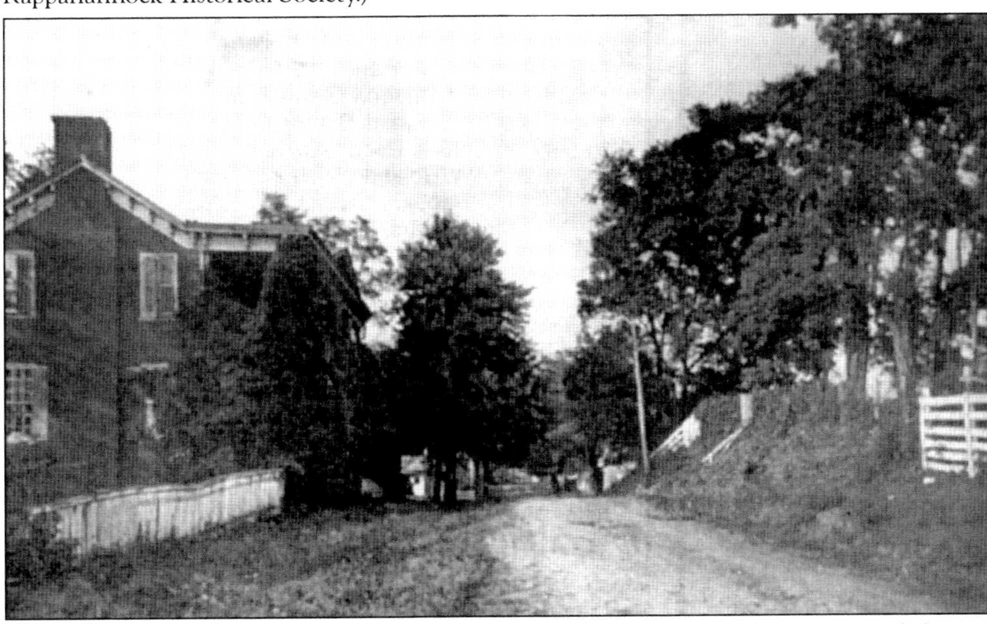

The J. Y. Menefee House was located where the Rappahannock News building is currently located on Main Street. This two-story brick home had two front porches. The Menefee family bought the first automobile in town. (Courtesy of the Rappahannock Historical Society.)

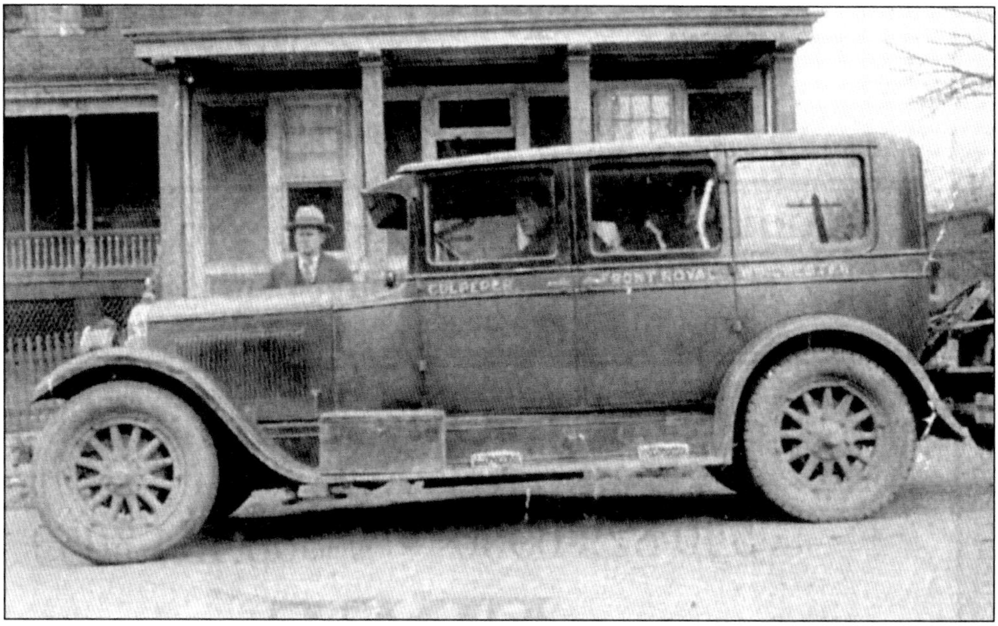

In the late 1920s and early 1930s, Walker Jenkins operated a bus route between Culpeper, Front Royal, and Winchester. The bus made frequent stops in Washington. (Courtesy of Mary Jenkins.)

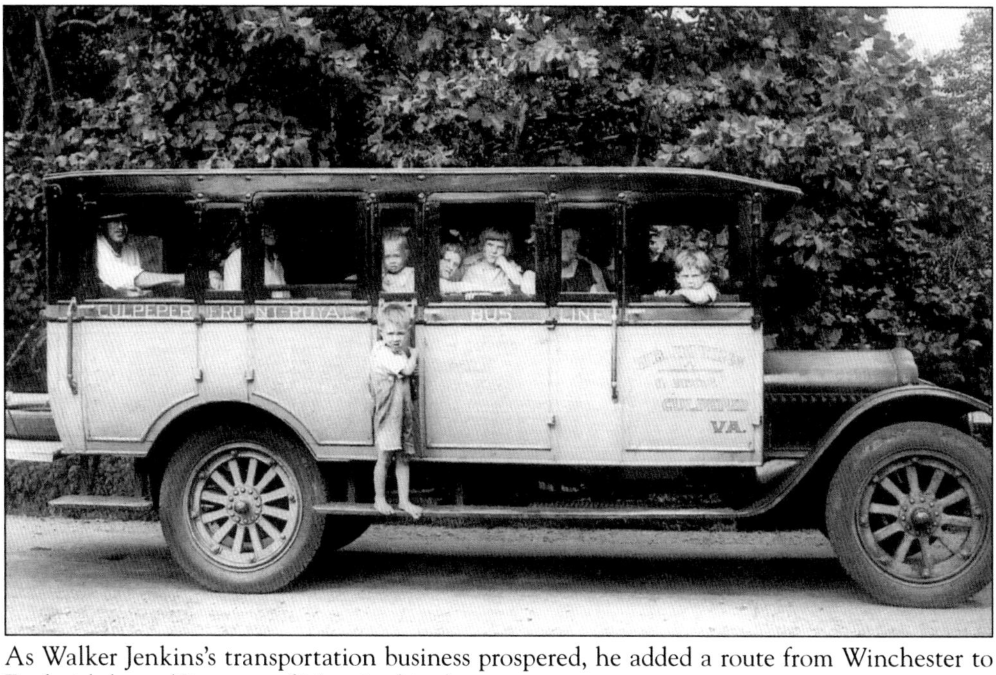

As Walker Jenkins's transportation business prospered, he added a route from Winchester to Fredericksburg. (Courtesy of Mary Jenkins.)

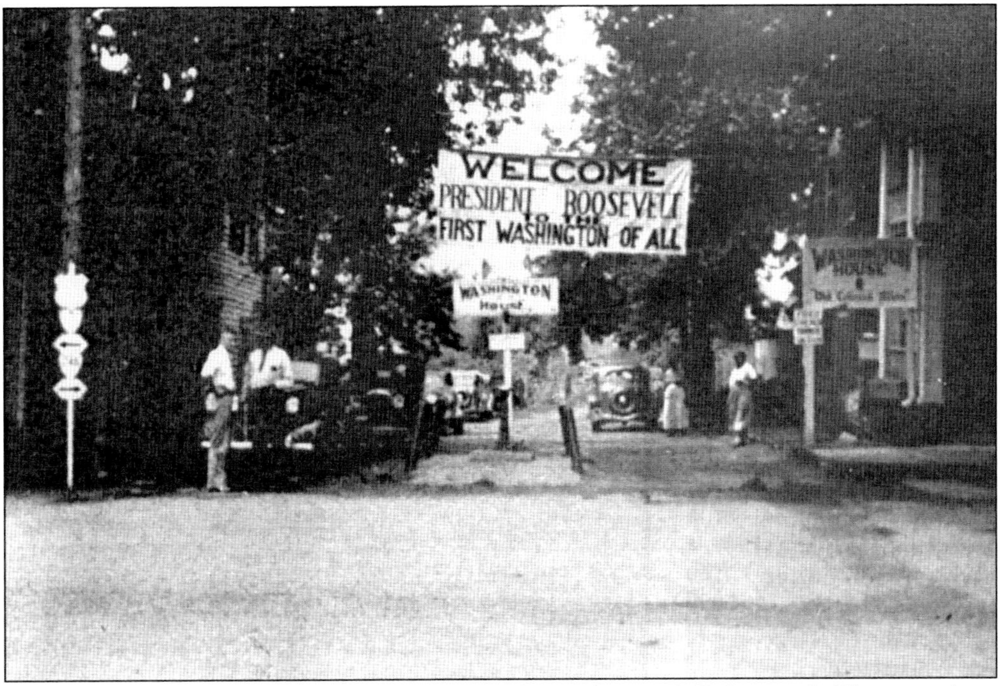

Residents were full of anticipation at the prospect of a visit by Pres. F. D. Roosevelt. The party chose to take another route to the camp in the Blue Ridge Mountains instead of coming through town, much to the disappointment of everyone. (Courtesy of the Rappahannock Historical Society.)

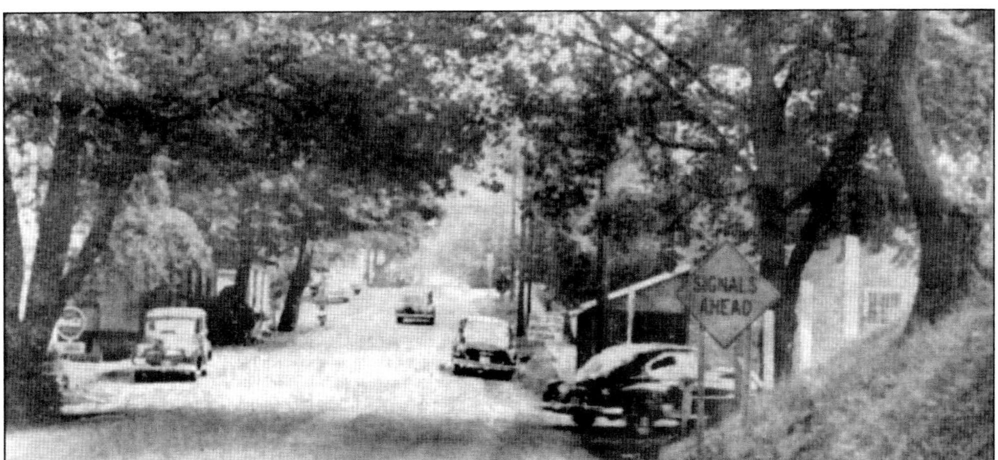

Main Street, near the corner of Jett Street, is pictured as it appeared in the 1950s when some of the large, old trees were still standing. Before the Route 211 bypass was built, travelers came through Washington on Main Street. (Courtesy of the Rappahannock Historical Society.)

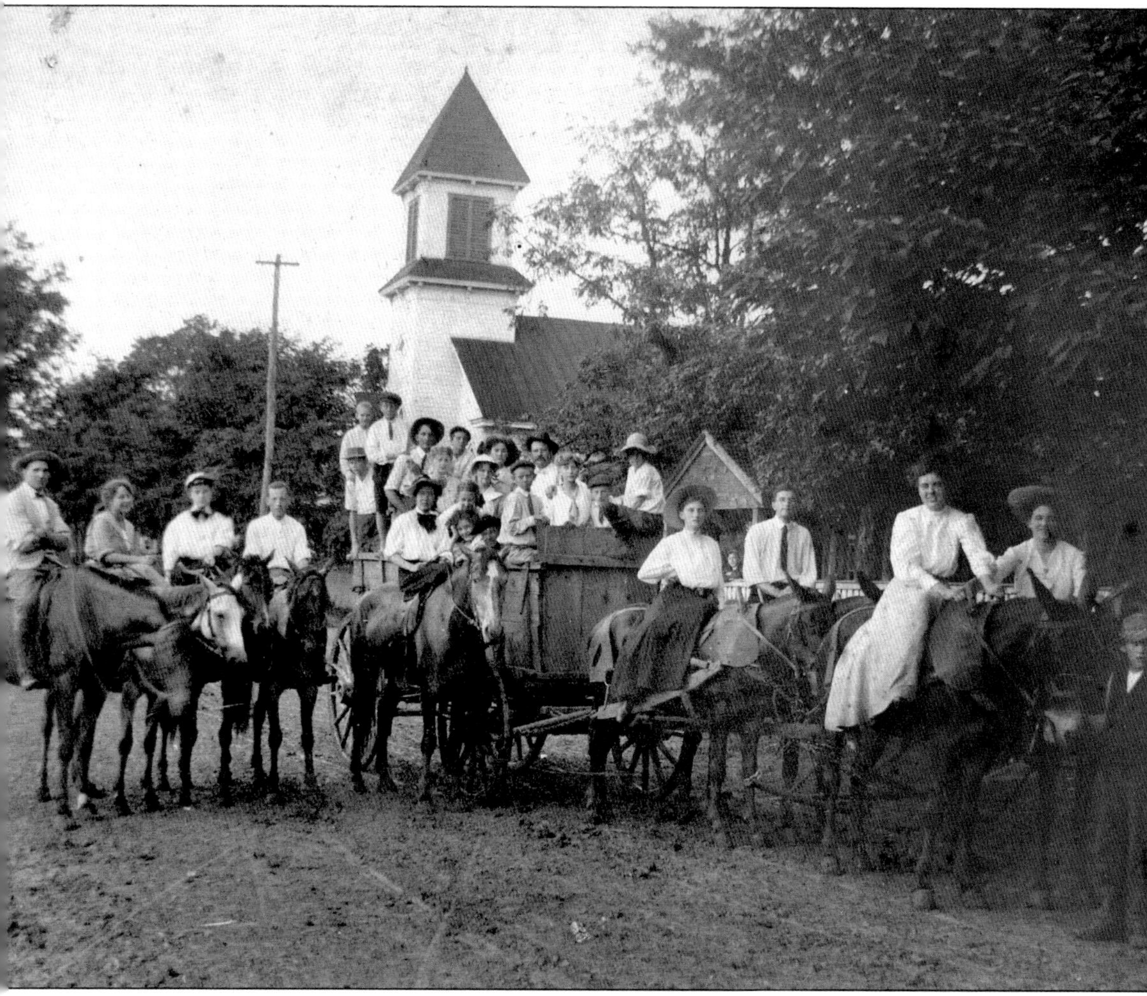

A group of people line up in front of the Washington United Methodist Church before leaving for an outing to Big Devil's Staircase in Harris Hollow in 1900. (Courtesy of the Rappahannock Historical Society.)

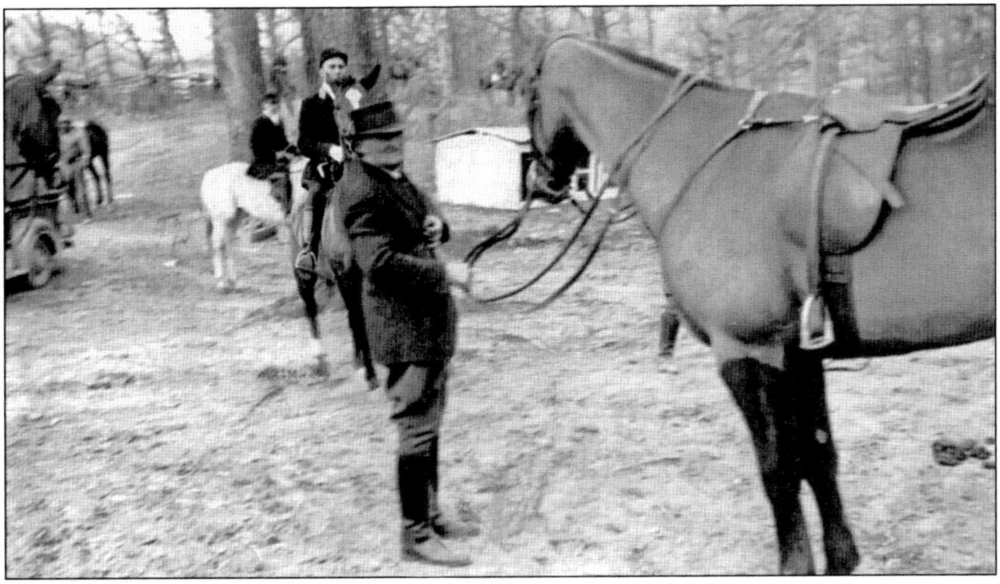

"Jelly" Payne holds onto his horse while Jack Bruce sits astride his mount at the fairgrounds in 1940. Records were set by some of the riders during the fair and horse show. (Courtesy of Diane Bruce.)

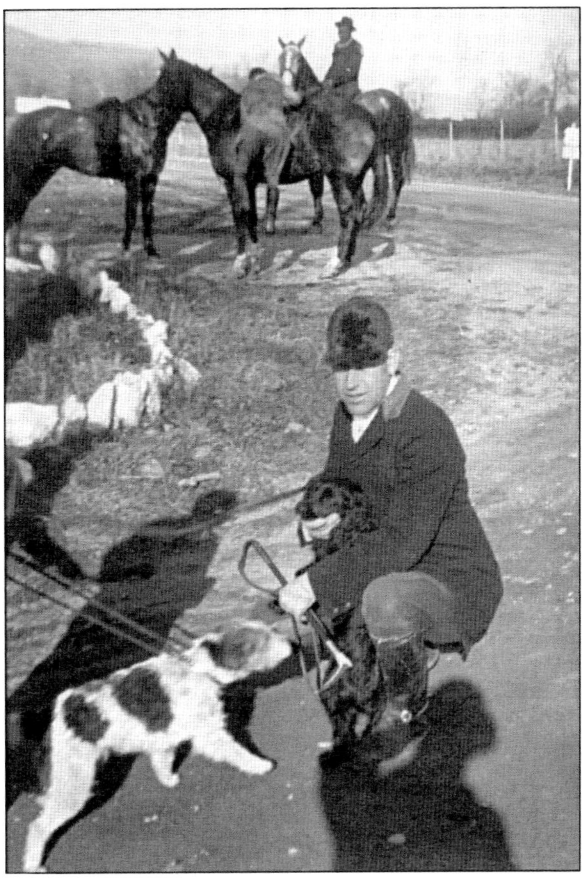

W. Arthur Miller, a master of hounds, prepares to judge a horse show at the fairgrounds. (Courtesy of Eve Willis.)

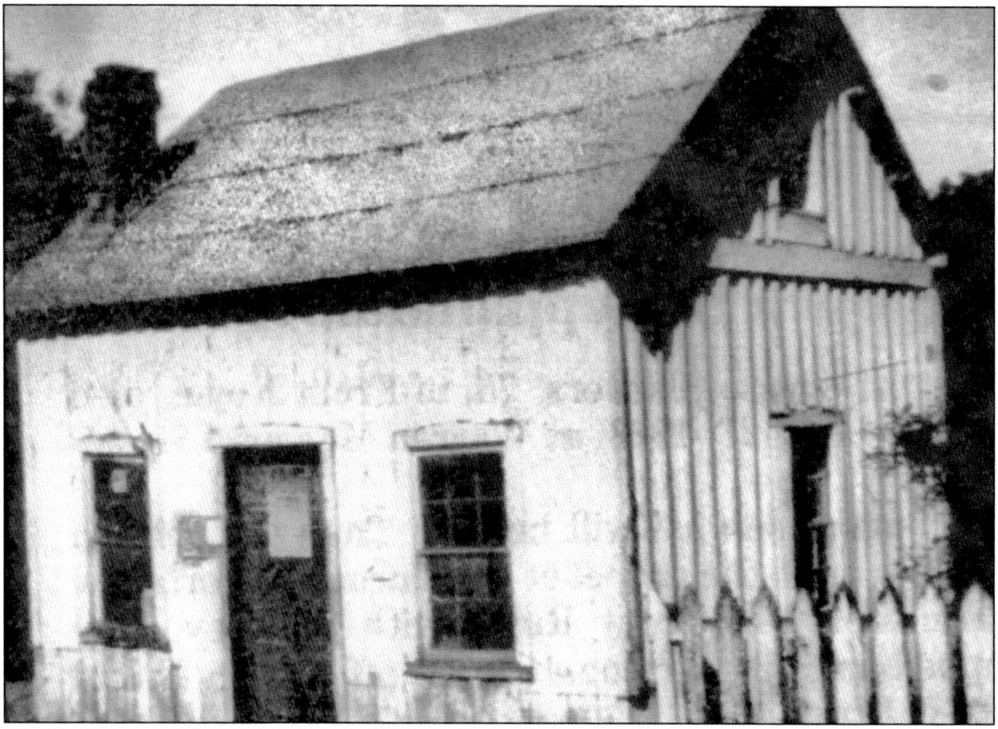

This building once housed the *Blue Ridge Guide*, one of a succession of newspapers in Rappahannock County. Started in 1888, the *Blue Ridge Guide* was managed by George E. Cary for 47 years and folded in 1936. (Courtesy of the Rappahannock Historical Society.)

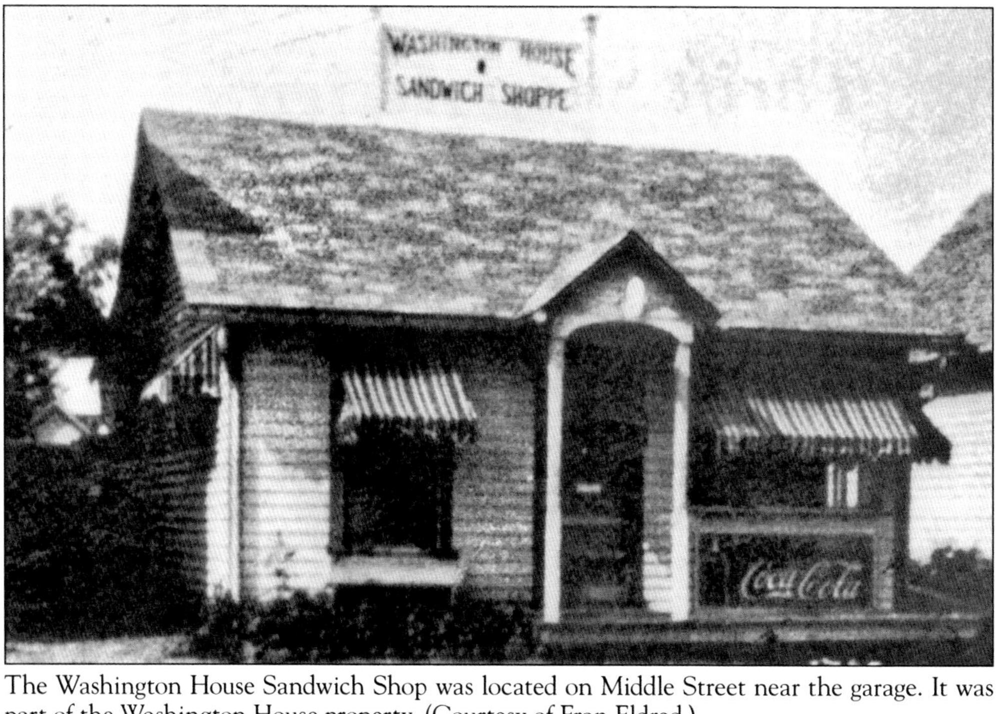

The Washington House Sandwich Shop was located on Middle Street near the garage. It was part of the Washington House property. (Courtesy of Fran Eldred.)

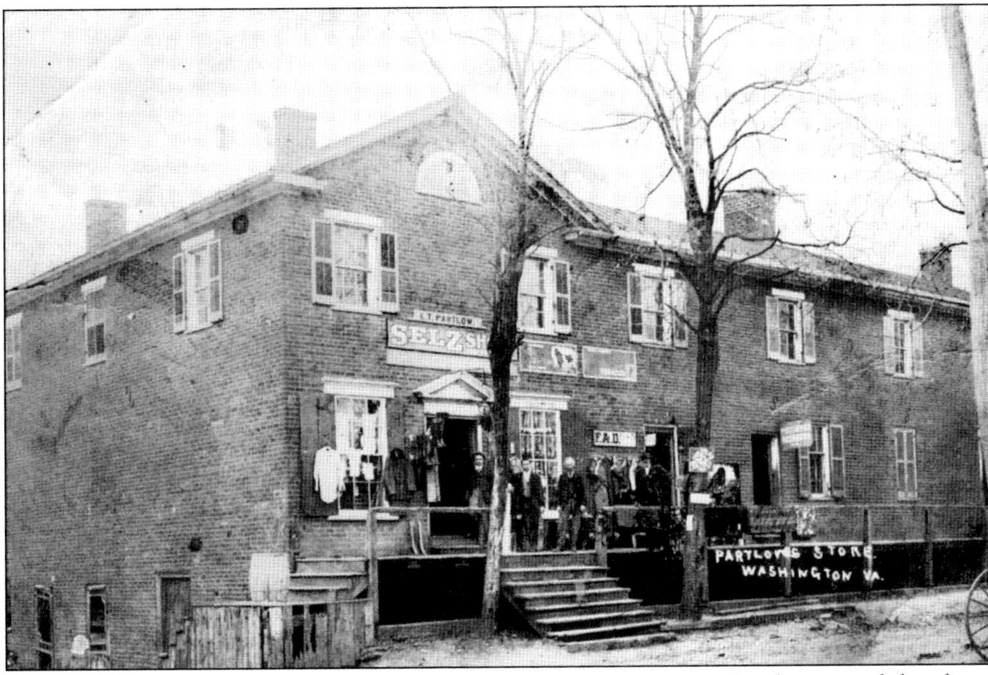

Partlow's Store was located at the corner of Gay and Jett Streets. L. T. Partlow owned this three-story brick building. Notice the sign above the door that reads "Selz Shoes." The building was destroyed and was replaced by a new building in the 1930s. (Courtesy of the Rappahannock Historical Society.)

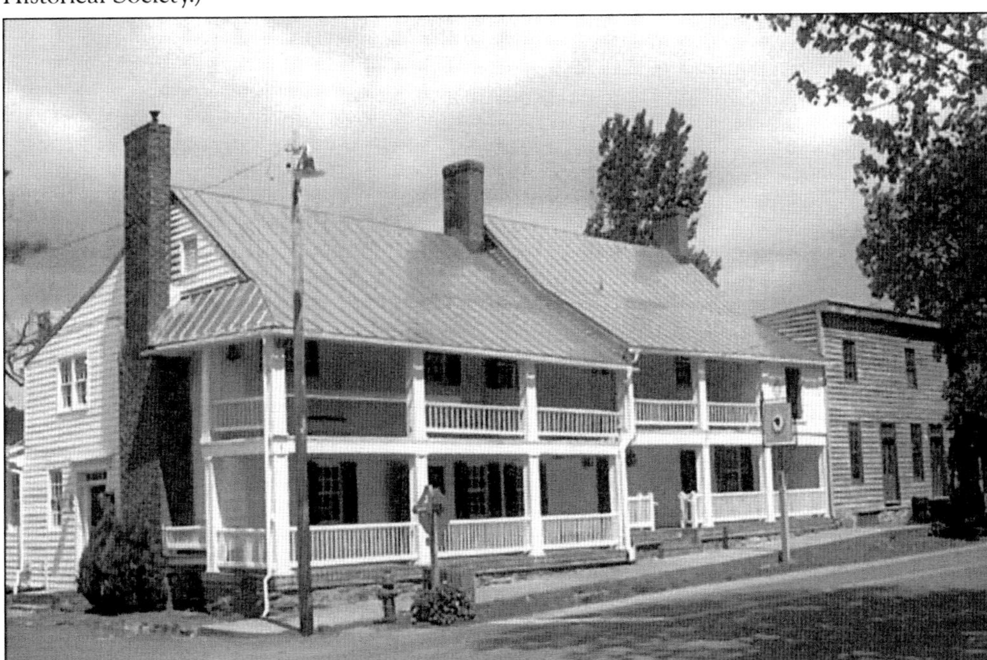

The Washington House was built in 1740. It was owned and operated as a tavern by Anne Calvert Coxe in 1833. In 1900, it was renamed the Washington House. It was known as Mrs. Coxe's Tavern in the 1990s. (Courtesy of the Rappahannock Historical Society.)

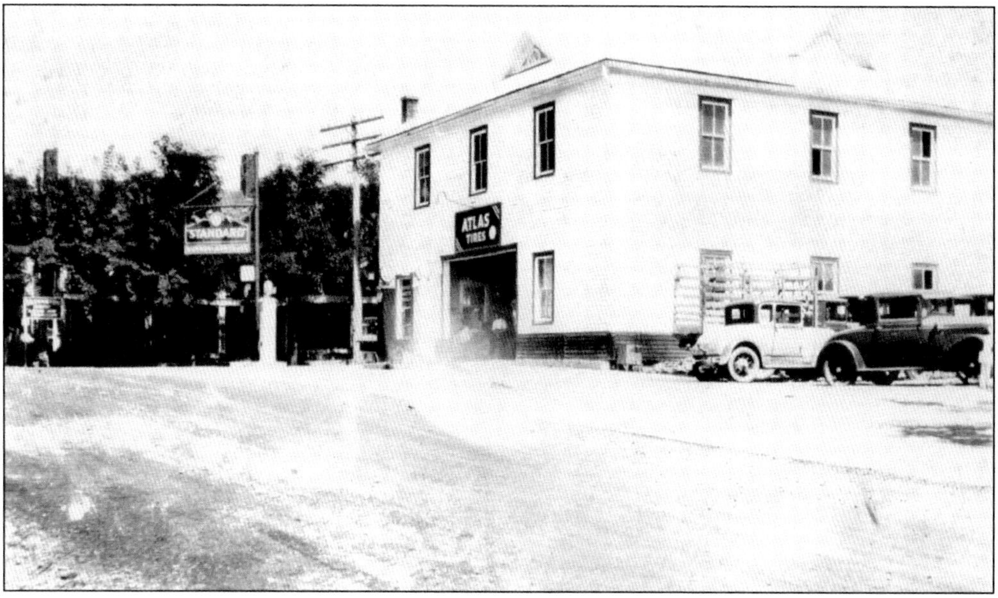

The garage at the corner of Middle and Main Streets was previously Thornton's and later Merrill's Garage. The upstairs was used as a theater to show silent movies. In 1978, the property was transformed into the Inn at Little Washington. (Courtesy of the Rappahannock Historical Society.)

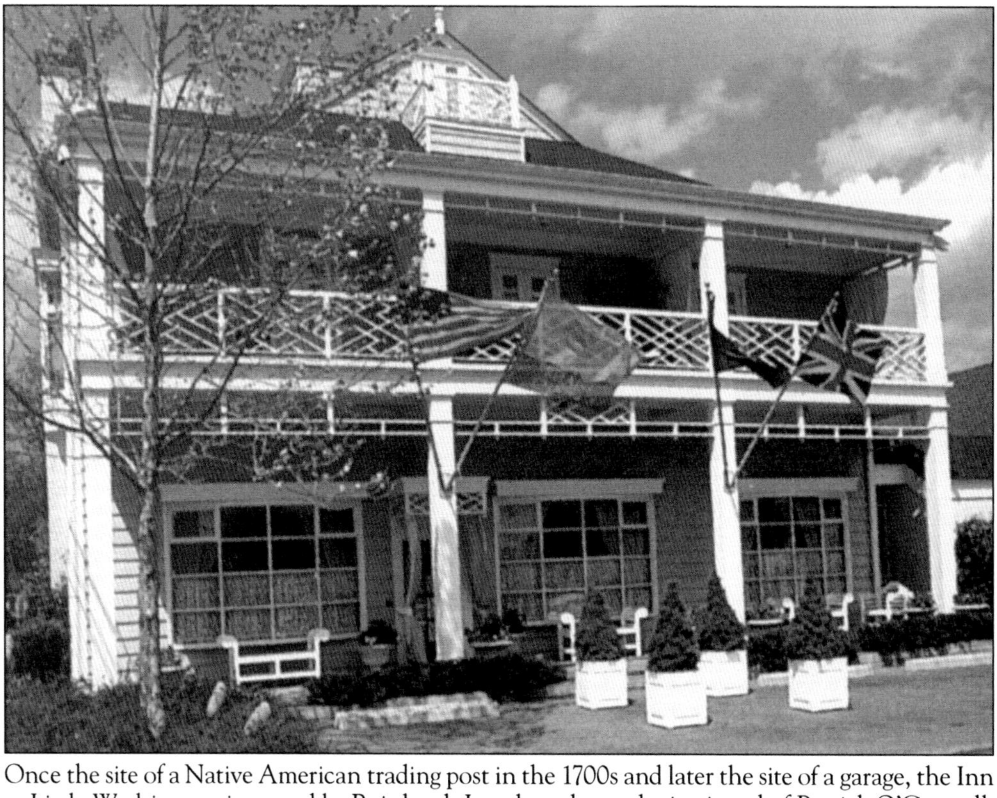

Once the site of a Native American trading post in the 1700s and later the site of a garage, the Inn at Little Washington is owned by Reinhardt Lynch and award-winning chef Patrick O'Connell. (Courtesy of the Rappahannock Historical Society.)

Six

WOODVILLE

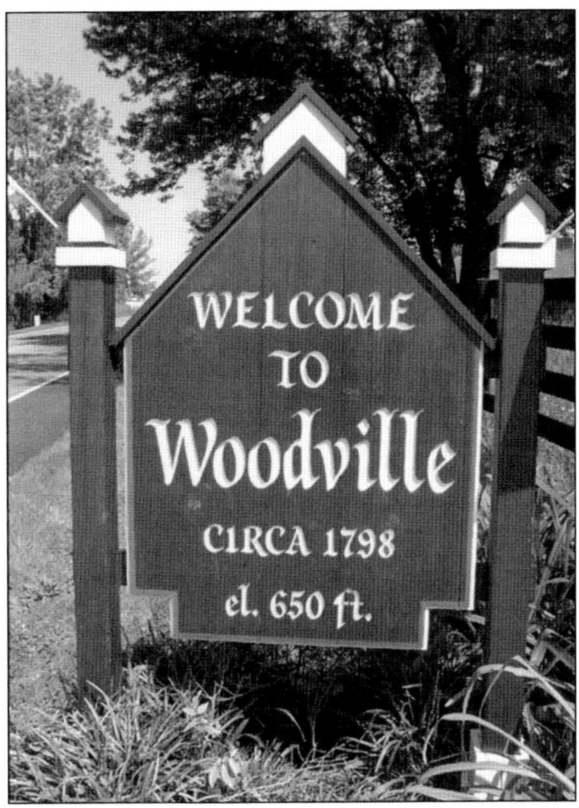

Woodville was established in 1798. The village was laid out in half-acre lots. Some believe the town was named for a Rev. John Woodville who served St. Mark's Parish in 1794. Another theory is that it was named for trees because the streets were named Cherry, Maple, Walnut, Locust, Poplar, Willow, Apple, White Oak, and Chestnut. A post office was established in 1803 with Joseph Reid as the first postmaster. A temperance hall thrived for a time until the building became a town hall. Union forces camped for a time in the area and even used the top of Red Oak Mountain as a vantage point. A tornado ripped through the village in 1929, destroying many homes and businesses. (Courtesy of John Tole.)

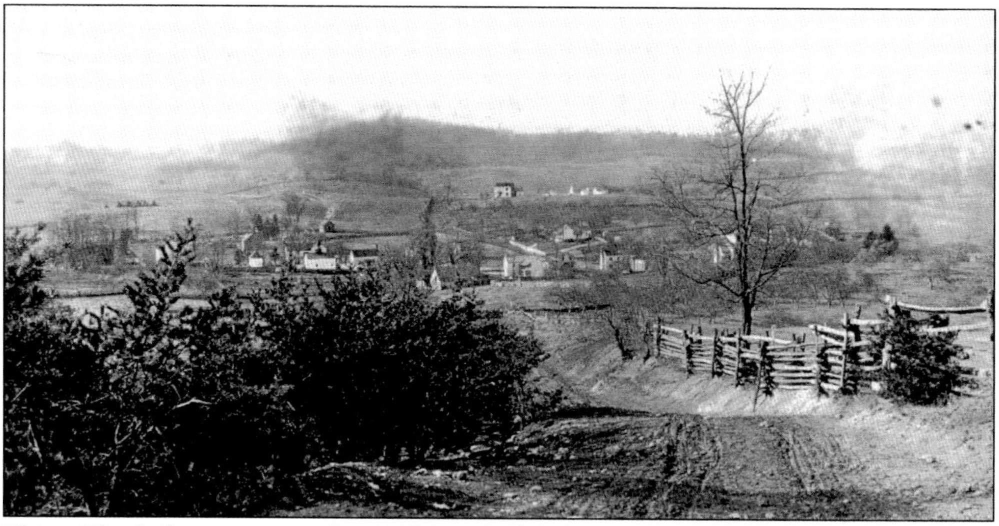

This is Woodville as it appeared in 1905 from Red Oak Mountain Road. Homes and businesses are visible along Cherry Street. (Courtesy of the Rappahannock Historical Society.)

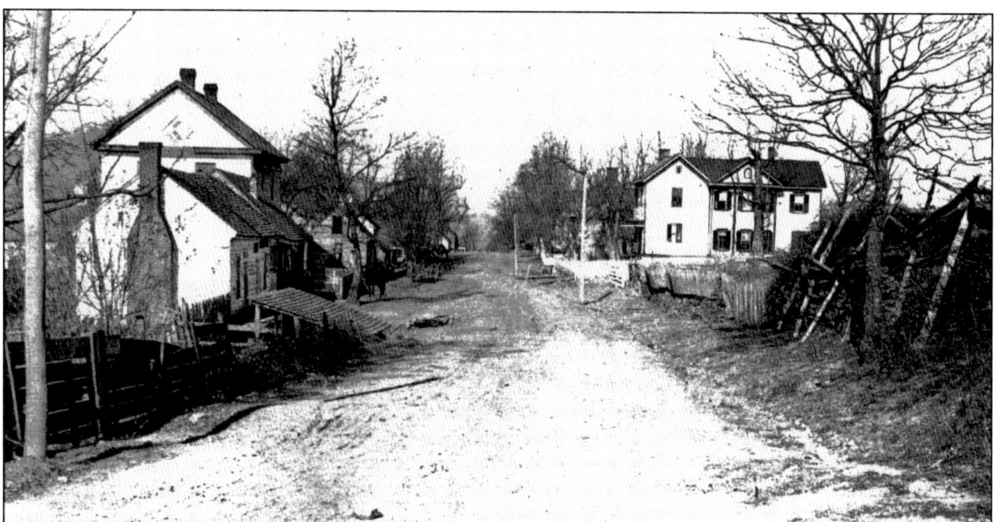

The town of Woodville is built on either side of Route 522 in a valley at the foot of Red Oak Mountain. (Courtesy of the Rappahannock Historical Society.)

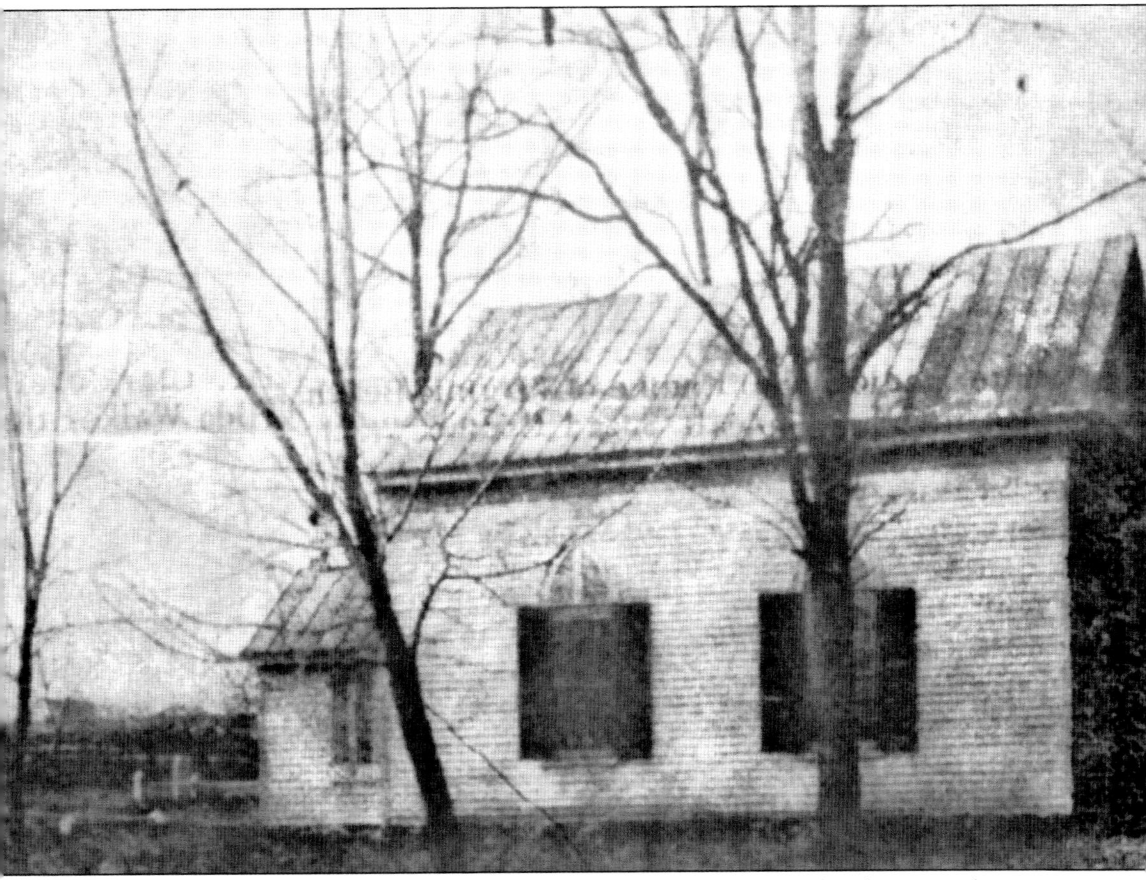

St. Paul's Episcopal Church was erected around 1840 on Hawlin Road. The church remained active until the tornado of 1929 destroyed the building, and it was never rebuilt. St. Paul's Episcopal Cemetery remains in use. (Courtesy of the Rappahannock Historical Society.)

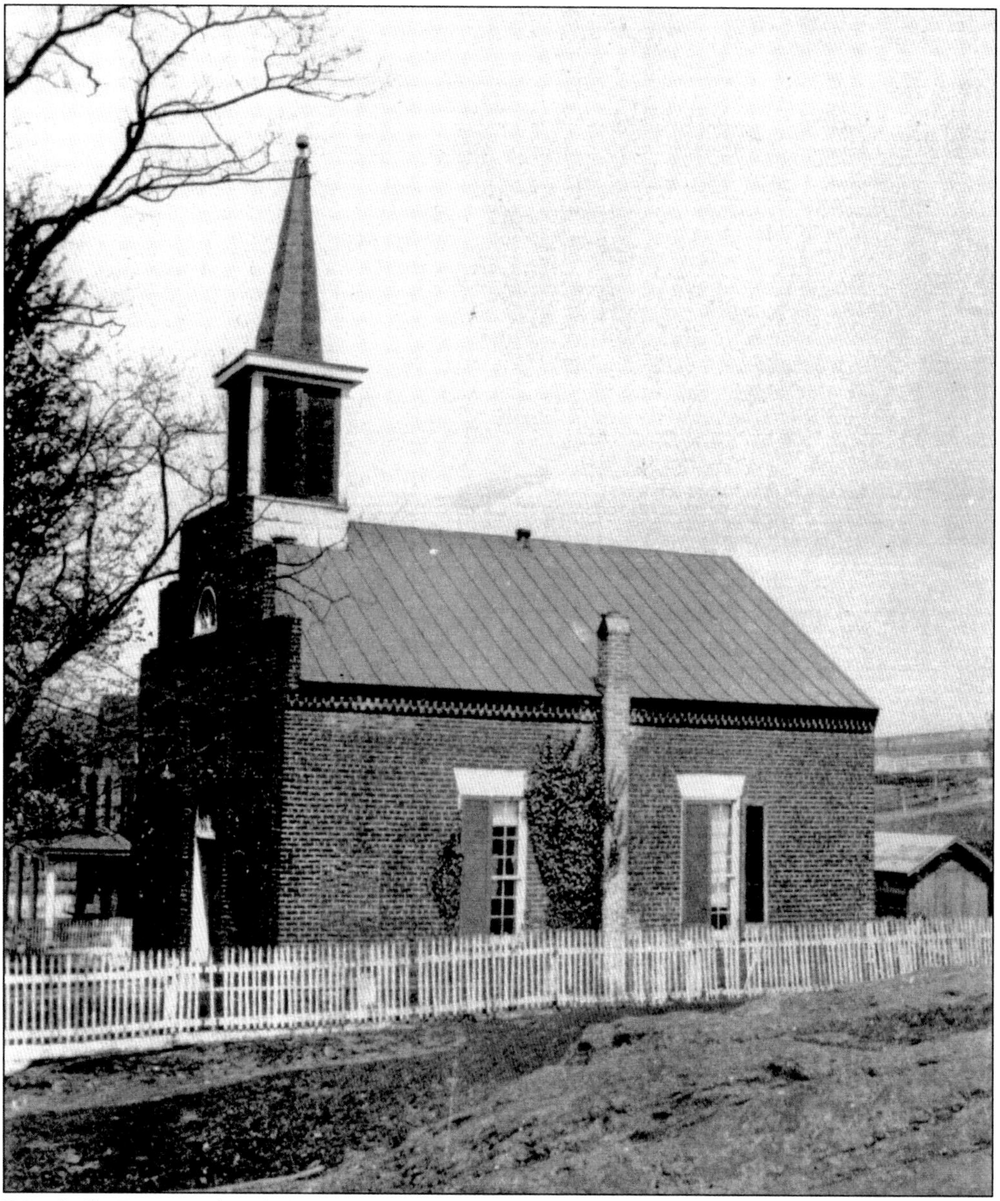

Woodville Baptist Church, located on Route 522, was organized in 1852. The church had to be rebuilt after it was destroyed in 1929 by a tornado. The new church building was dedicated in 1930. (Courtesy of the Rappahannock Historical Society.)

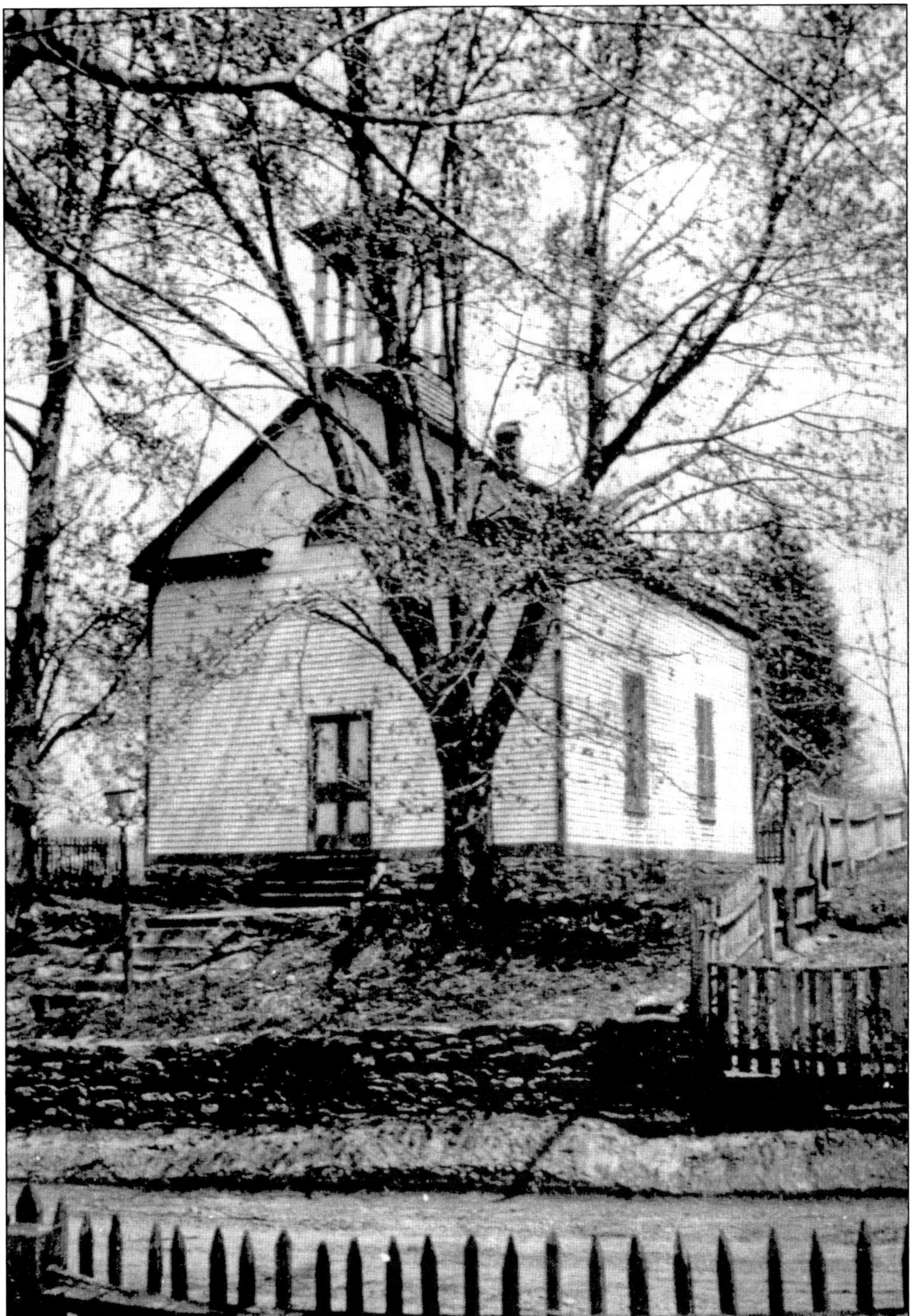

Woodville Methodist Church was a casualty of the 1929 tornado. The church building was not rebuilt. (Courtesy of the Rappahannock Historical Society.)

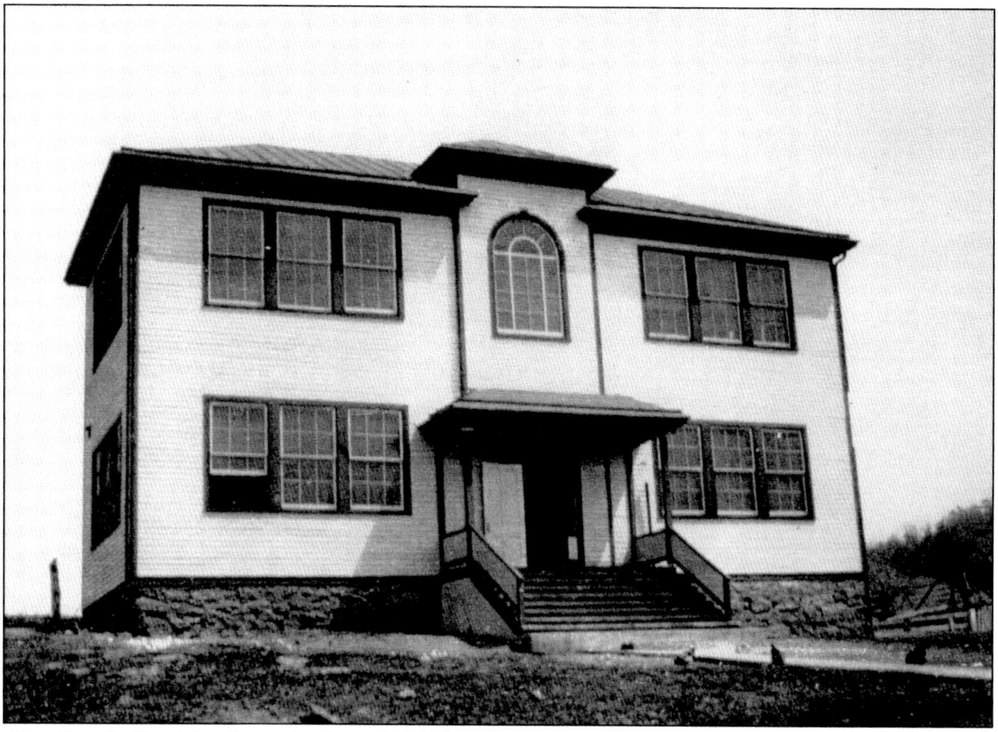

The Woodville School was built in 1909. It was a four-room school that housed students from elementary to high school. The school was completely destroyed by the tornado in 1929. (Courtesy of the Rappahannock Historical Society.)

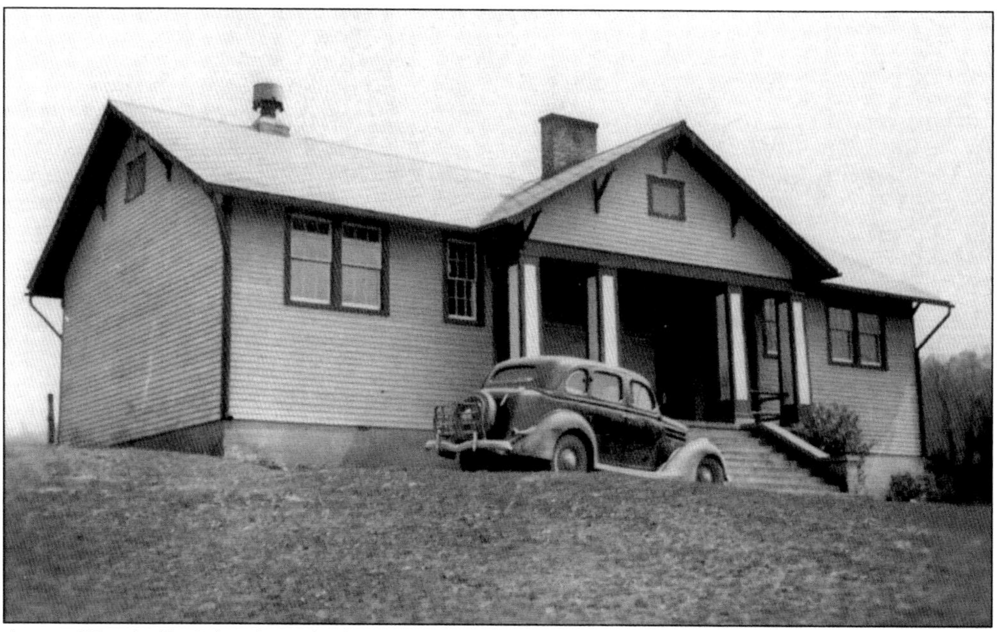

A new Woodville School was built in 1929 as a two-room elementary school to replace the four-room school. After the tornado, the high school students attended Sperryville High School. The school closed in 1954. (Courtesy of the Rappahannock Historical Society.)

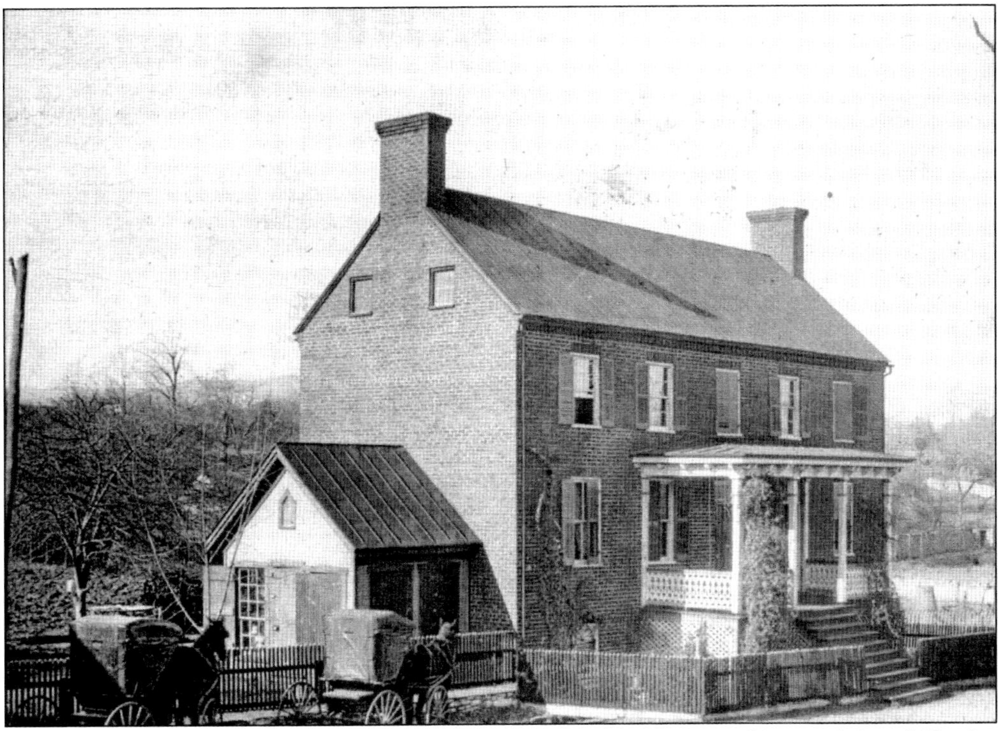

Liberty Hall, the home of Silas Johnson, was located on the corner of Route 522 and Hawlin Road. The two-story brick structure was built in 1836 but did not survive the tornado of 1929. (Courtesy of the Rappahannock Historical Society.)

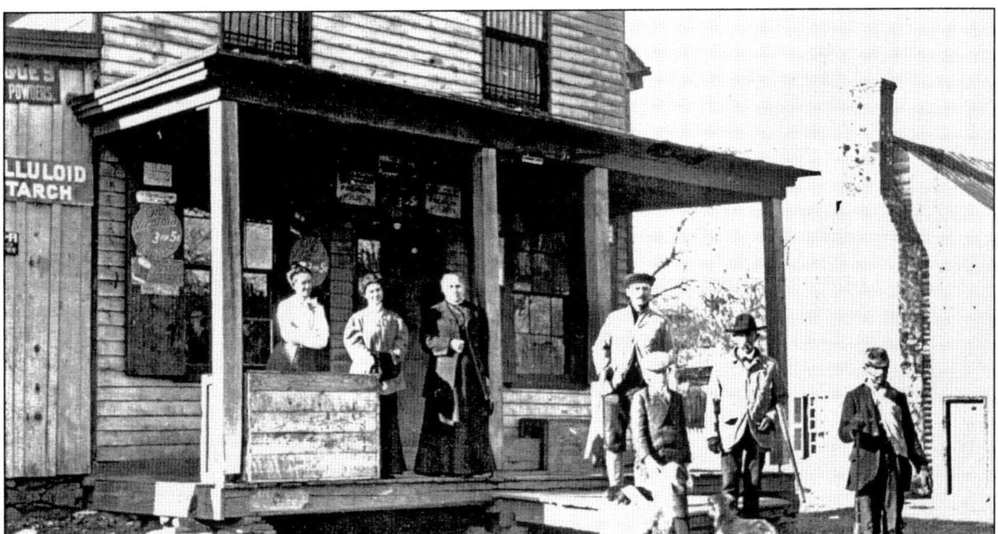

The Silas Johnson Store was located on Route 522 just to the left of Liberty Hall. One of four merchants in Woodville, Silas Johnson ran a general store in the 1880s. A small portion of the store survived the tornado of 1929. (Courtesy of the Rappahannock Historical Society.)

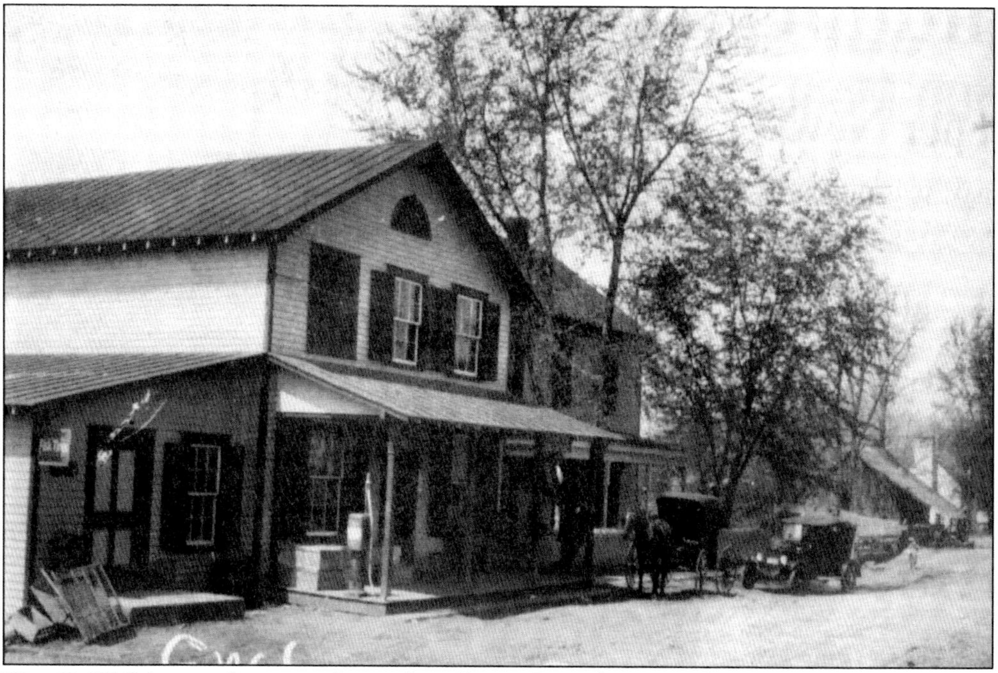

The G. W. Johnson Store was located on Route 522. The general merchandise store was in operation from the 1890s to the 1900s. (Courtesy of the Rappahannock Historical Society.)

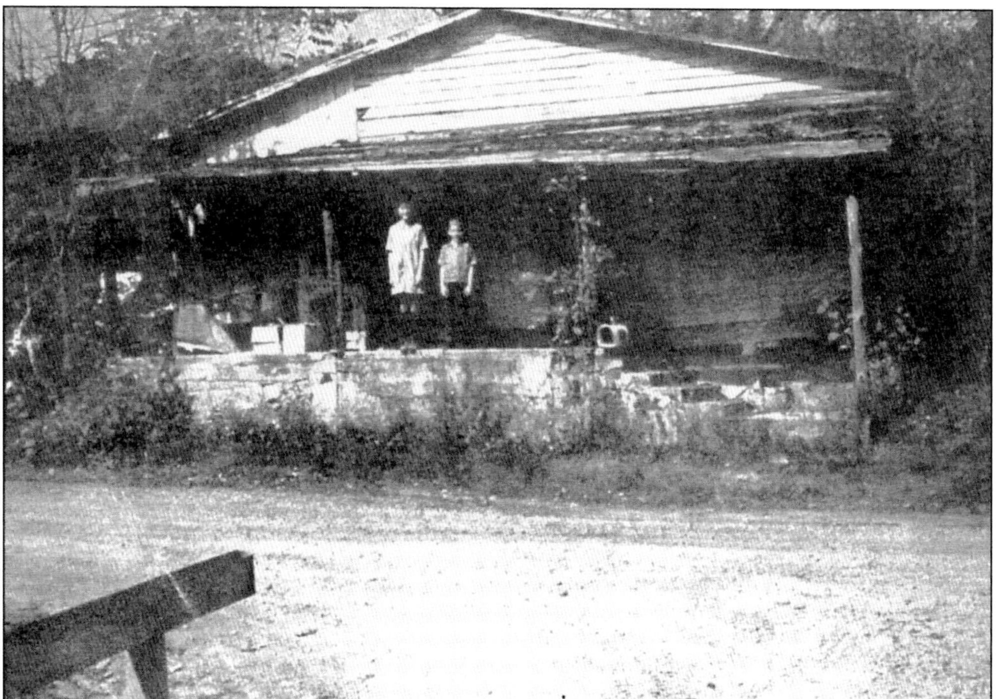

The Rock Mills Store was a gathering place for local residents to socialize, buy necessities, and gather their mail. The building is no longer standing. (Courtesy of Dan Hitt.)

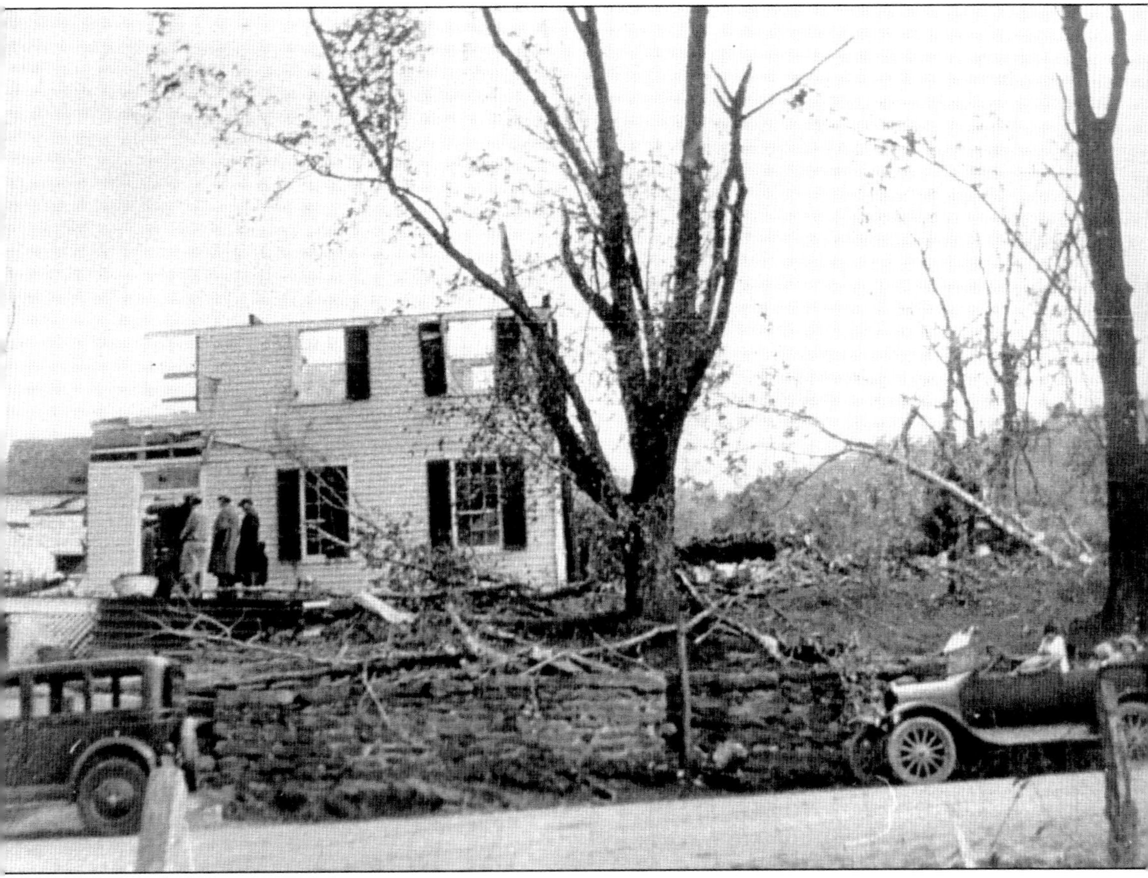

The tornado touched down on May 2, 1929, on the south side of Hawlin Road near St. Paul's Episcopal Cemetery. It tore through the center of Woodville destroying everything in its path. One child was killed and numerous others were injured. Parts of Woodville never recovered from the destruction. The tornado struck Rye Cove, Virginia, just prior to Woodville, and a song was written and performed by the Carter Family about the event. (Courtesy of the Rappahannock Historical Society.)

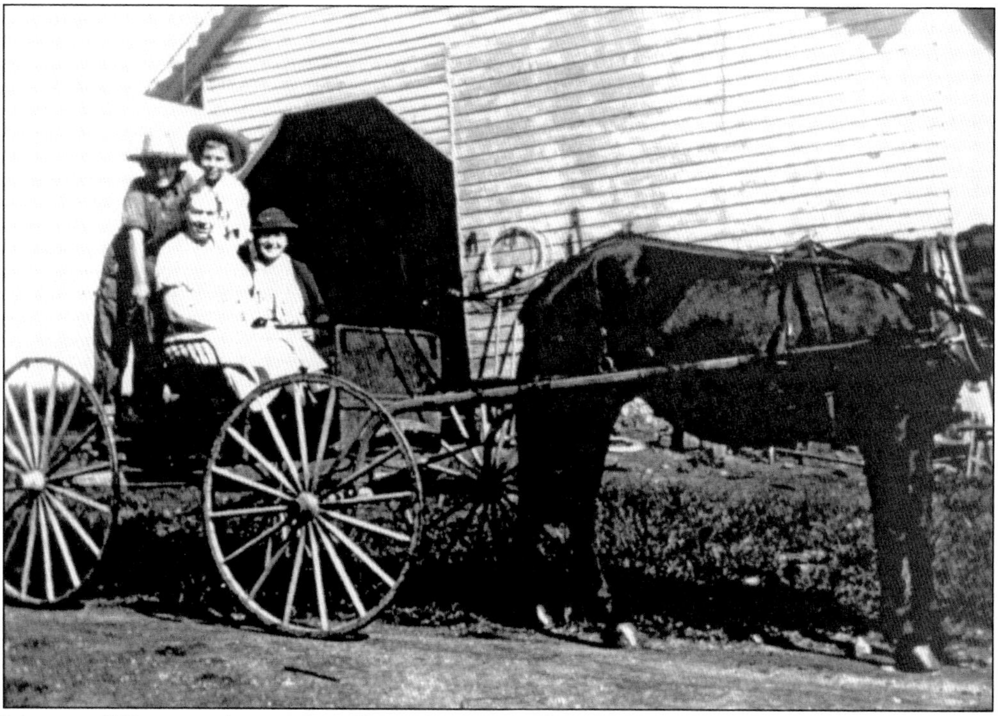

Maurice O'Bannon; his mother, Rena Armstong O'Bannon; Allan Stokes; and his mother, Katherine Scott Stokes prepare to depart for an outing in a carriage. (Courtesy of the Rappahannock Historical Society.)

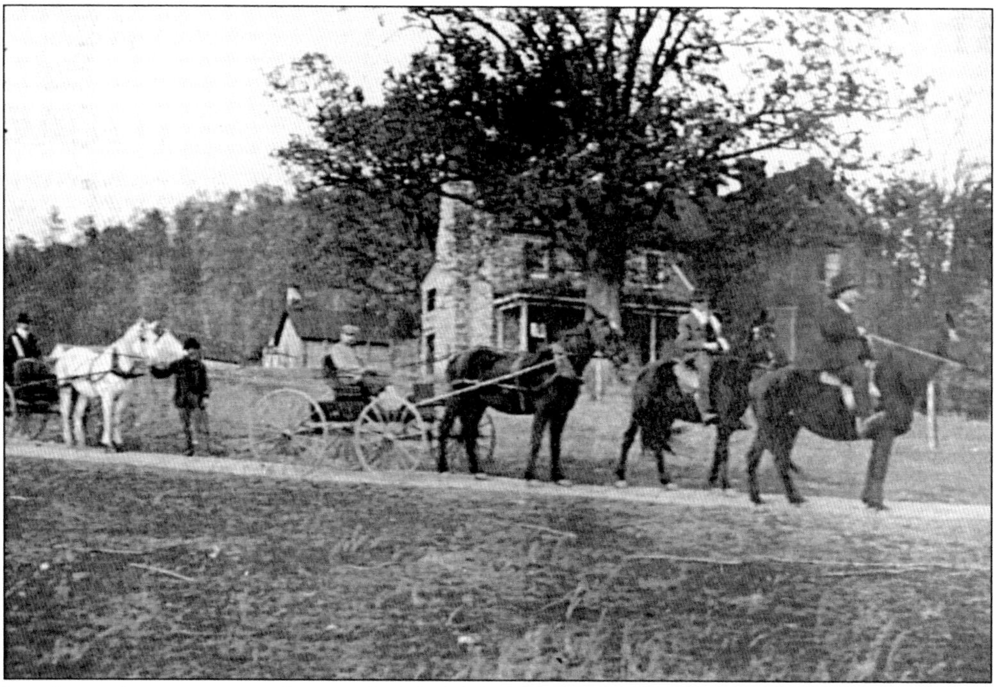

People are shown passing a farm on Red Oak Mountain in carriages and on horseback. (Courtesy of the Rappahannock Historical Society.)

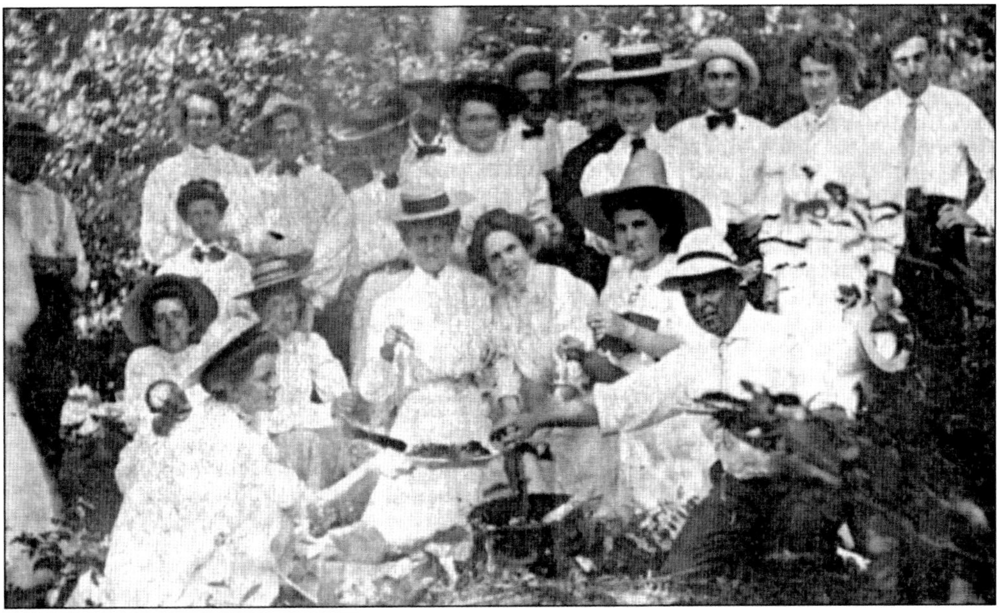

A group of friends gathered to fish and later fry their catch in Woodville in 1907. Among those in attendance were the Armstrong, Jones, Mason, Long, Kinsey, Browning, Smith, Yancey, O'Bannon, Fletcher, and Miller families. (Courtesy of the Rappahannock Historical Society.)

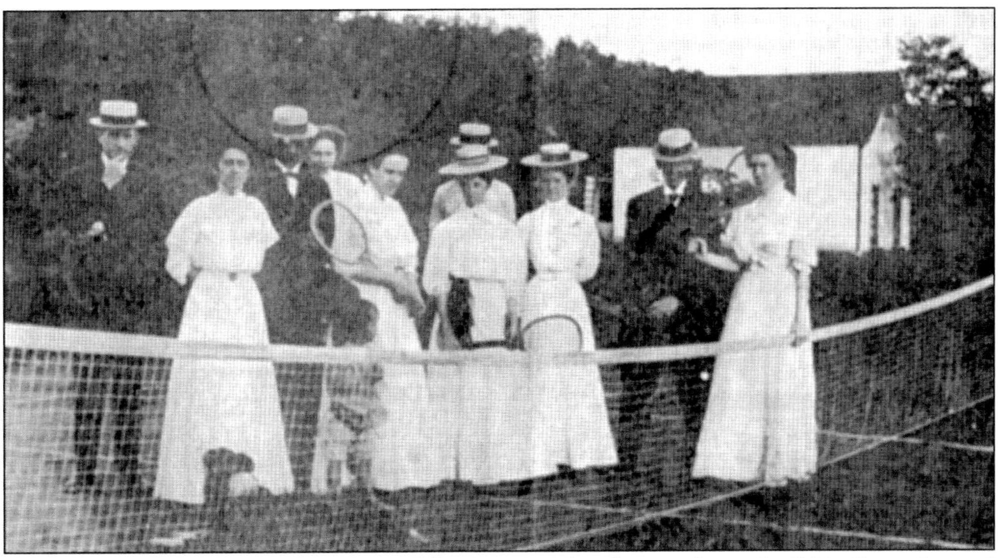

The Woodville Academy and Tennis Club was a popular place in the early 1900s. It was located on Rudasill Mill Road just north of Route 522. The building is no longer standing. (Courtesy of the Rappahannock Historical Society.)

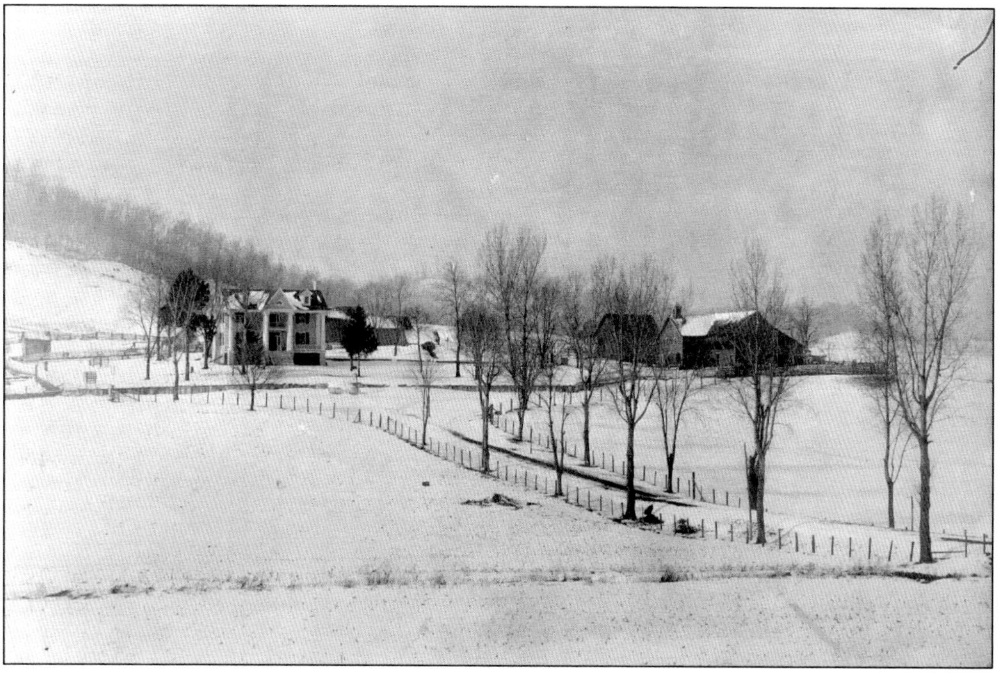

Clover Hill is located on Route 522 at Eldon Farms. Col. John Slaughter, a Revolutionary War soldier, built it in 1785. Beginning as a log cabin, the home was enlarged in the mid-1800s. During a later renovation of the home, a saber that was used in both the Revolutionary War and the Civil War was found in the wall and donated to the Rappahannock Historical Society. (Courtesy of the Rappahannock Historical Society.)

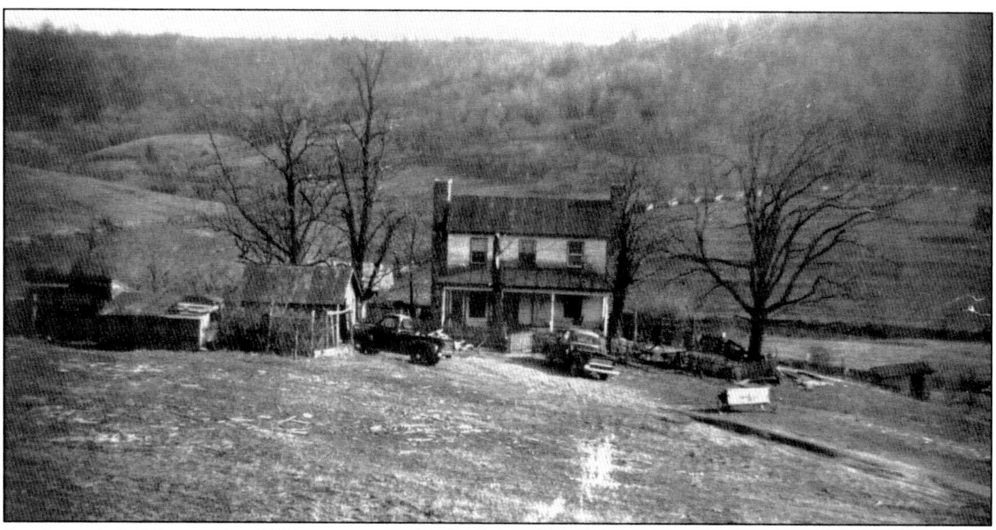

Reuben A. Kibler, a Civil War veteran, built the Kibler house in the 1870s. The house sits up a hill off Rudasill Mill Road. (Courtesy of Misty Hitt.)

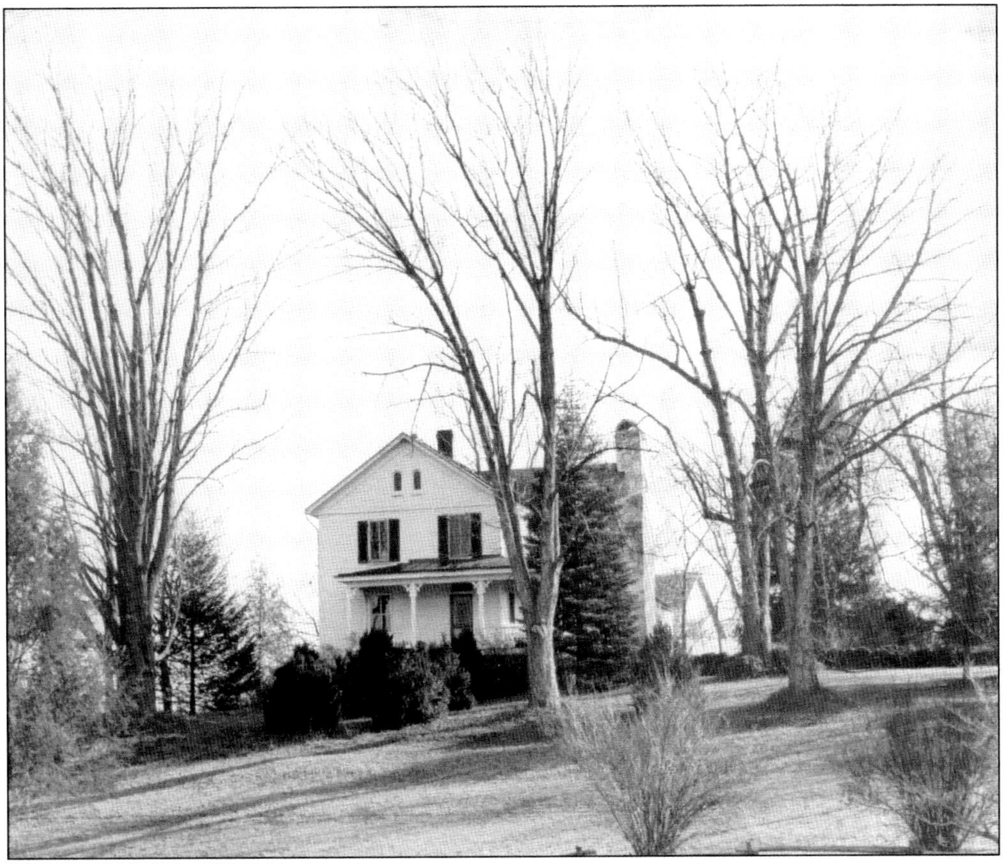

South Red Oak was known as Western View in the 1880s, when Mr. and Mrs. J. Macon Long owned it. (Courtesy of Carolyn and Jim Manwaring.)

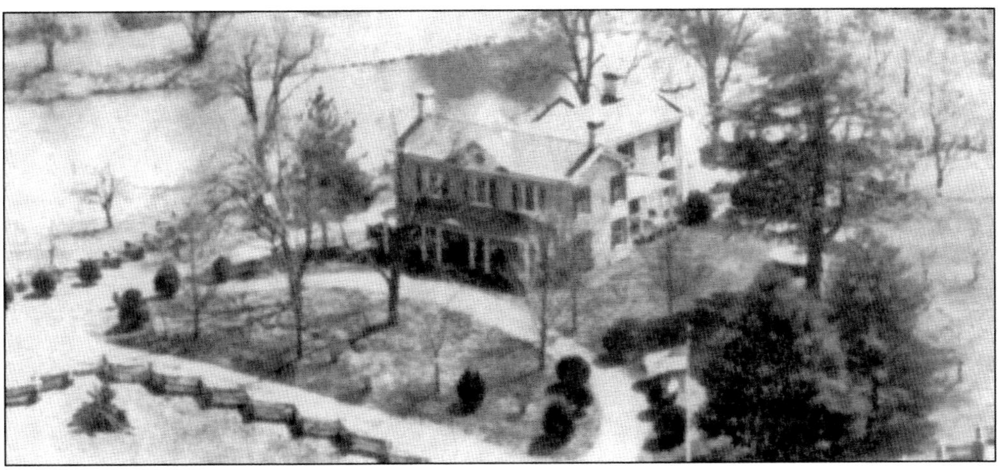

Dr. Aylette Hawes built Hawthorn, located on Hawlin Road, between 1790 and 1812 for his bride, Frances Thornton. She combined her maiden and her married names together and came up with Hawthorn. The stately, two-story brick manor house sits on 221 acres with numerous outbuildings, including a schoolhouse. Mrs. Hawes died suddenly and never lived at Hawthorn. (Courtesy of the Rappahannock Historical Society.)

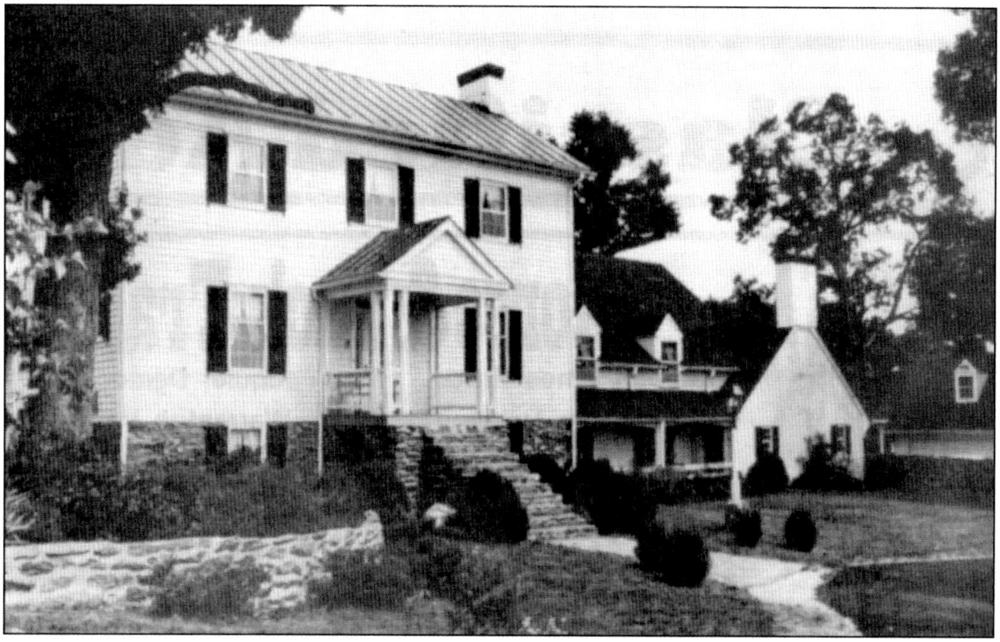

Joseph Reid built Millwood in 1836. The Colonial-style home is located on Route 522. The house remained in the Reid family for several generations until 1976. Noted blues musician John Jackson was born on the property. (Courtesy of the Rappahannock Historical Society.)

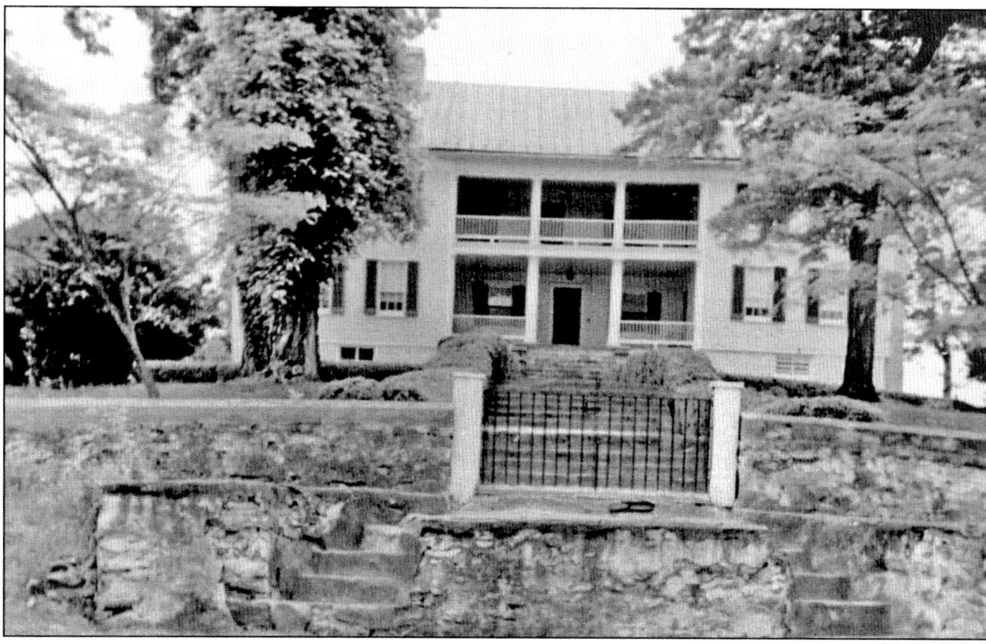

The Shade, on Rudasill Mill Road, was the ancestral home of the Green family and was built in 1780 by Charles Green. The 3,500-acre estate was obtained in a land grant from King George III. The Georgian two-and-a-half-story house stands in a secluded spot on the farm, surrounded by elaborate gardens containing boxwoods started from slips brought from England. The Shade was commandeered during the Civil War, and a large contingency of Union troops camped there. (Courtesy of the Rappahannock Historical Society.)

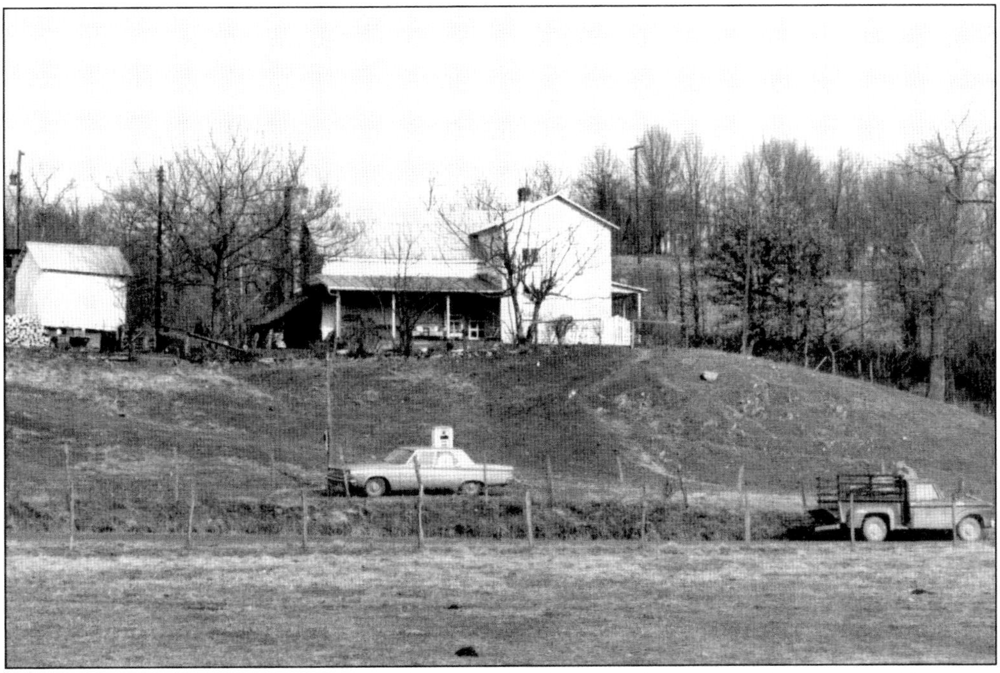

Rock Mills Farm is located on Aaron Mountain Road on a wide curve overlooking the Thornton River. The house began as a log cabin and was expanded over the years. (Courtesy of Carolyn and Jim Manwaring.)

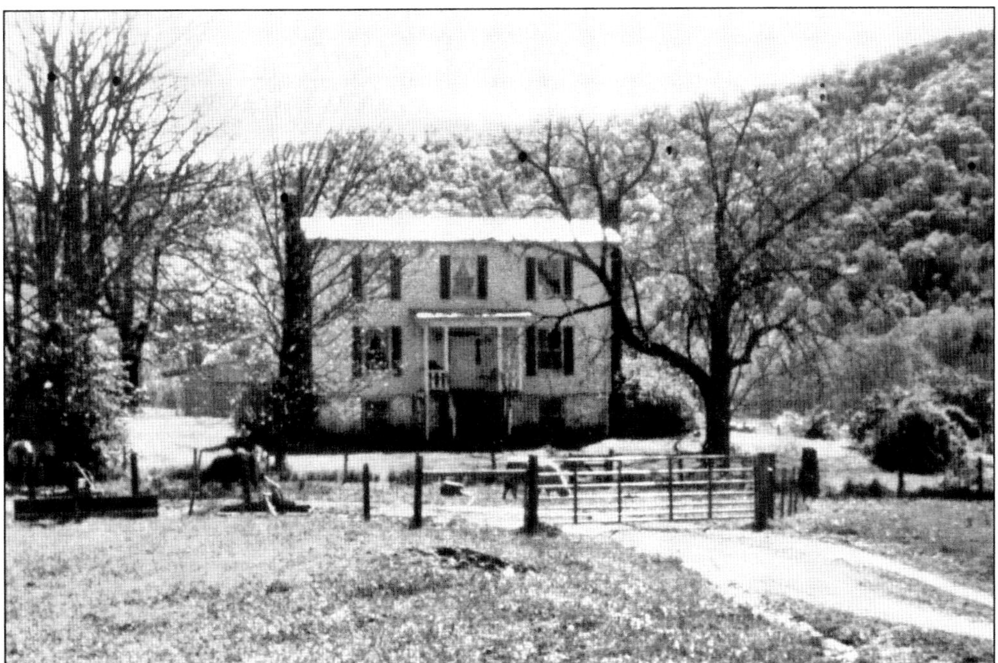

The Red Oak Farm house was built in 1880 on Rudasill Mill Road. The house sits far off the road surrounded by fields and is silhouetted by Red Oak Mountain. (Courtesy of Carolyn and Jim Manwaring.)

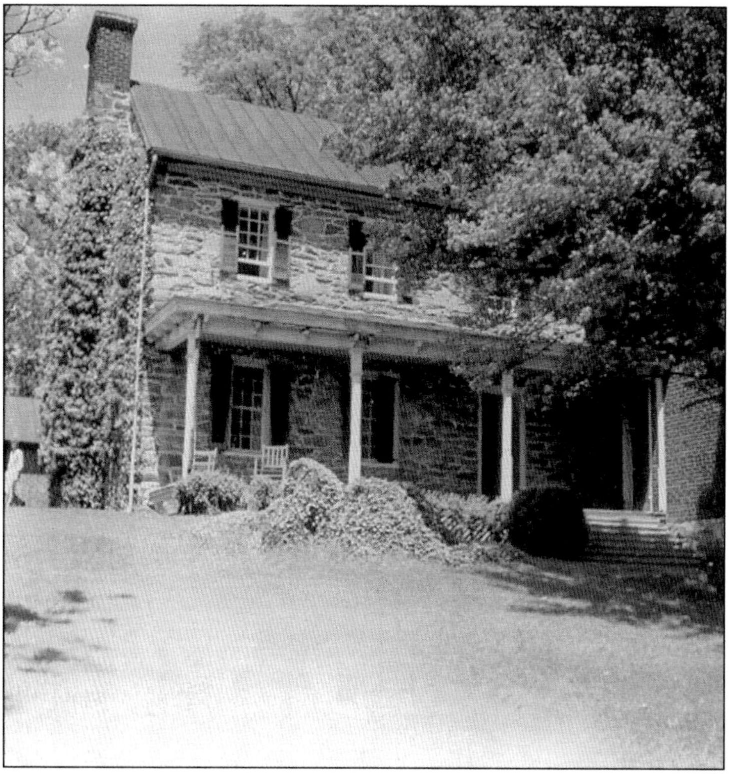

Oak Forest was the home of Col. William W. and Flossie Williamson. The Williamsons moved to the county in the 1950s. Following Colonel Williamson's death, Mrs. Williamson developed a reputation as a talented gardener. Along with Lois Snead and Dotsie Davis, these ladies organized the Trinity Episcopal Church's Annual Dried Flower Sale and House Tour. (Courtesy of the Rappahannock Historical Society.)

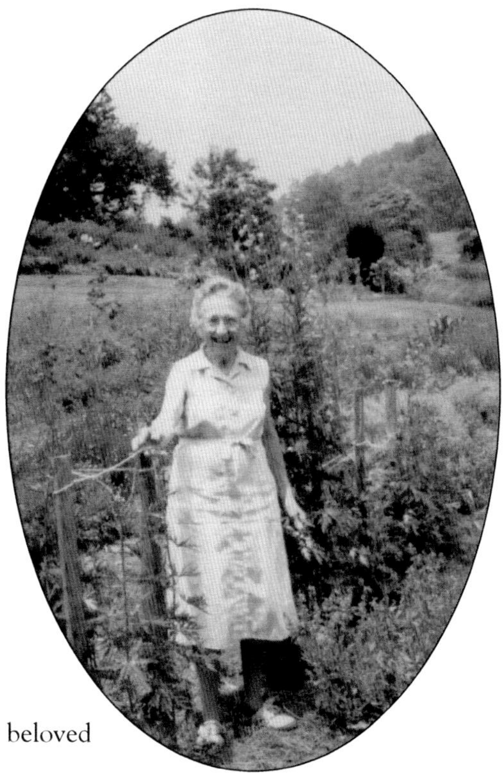

Flossie Williamson is shown standing in her beloved garden. (Courtesy of Cheri Woodard.)

Seven

Blue Ridge Crossroads and Villages

Numerous secondary roads, such as Route 626, lead to colorful vistas and interesting crossroads and villages such as Slate Mills, Laurel Mills, Castleton, Viewtown, Scrabble, Boston, Huntly, and Hawlin. Some of these waypoints contain a single landmark such as a church or historic residence. Others are defined by a cluster of houses, often located near a current or former general store or mill. (Courtesy of John Tole.)

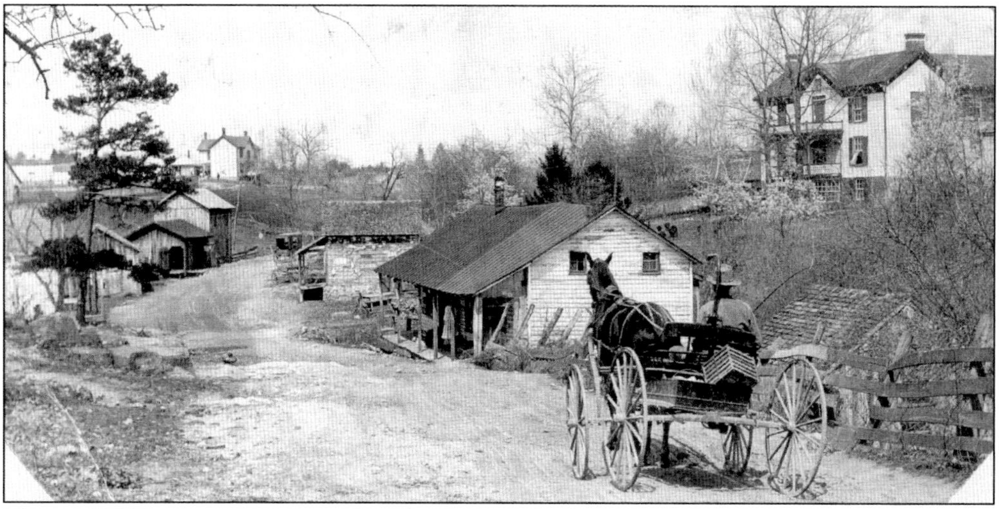

This is Old Boston as it appeared in the 1800s. The buggy is shown approaching Woodville. (Courtesy of the Estes family.)

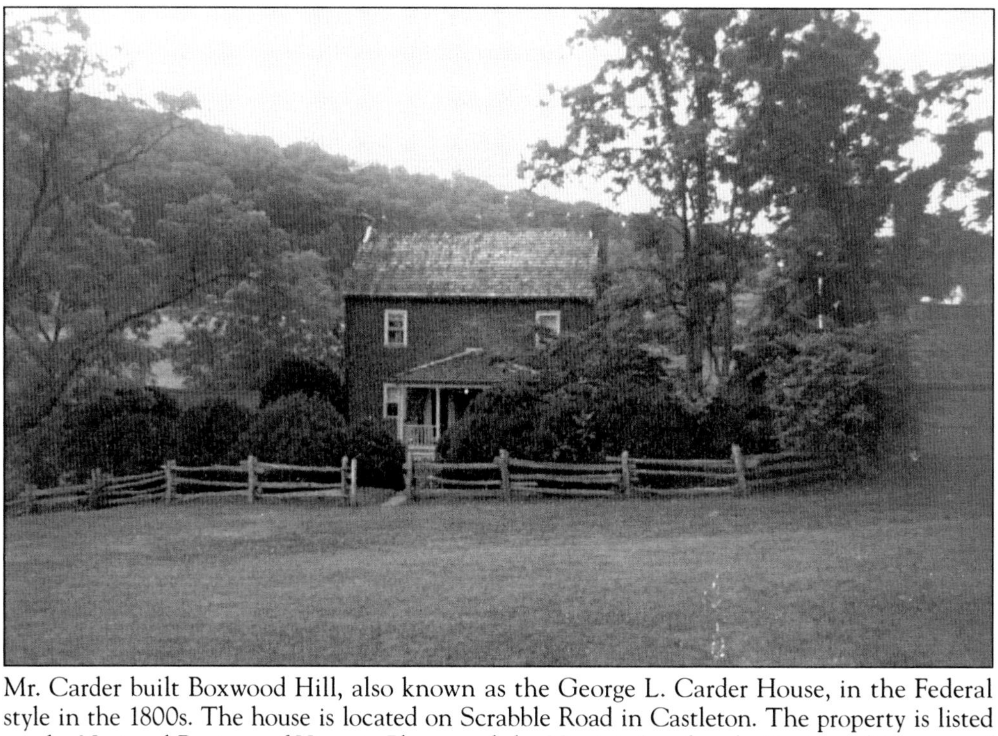

Mr. Carder built Boxwood Hill, also known as the George L. Carder House, in the Federal style in the 1800s. The house is located on Scrabble Road in Castleton. The property is listed on the National Register of Historic Places and the Virginia Landmarks Registry. (Courtesy of Donna Fisher.)

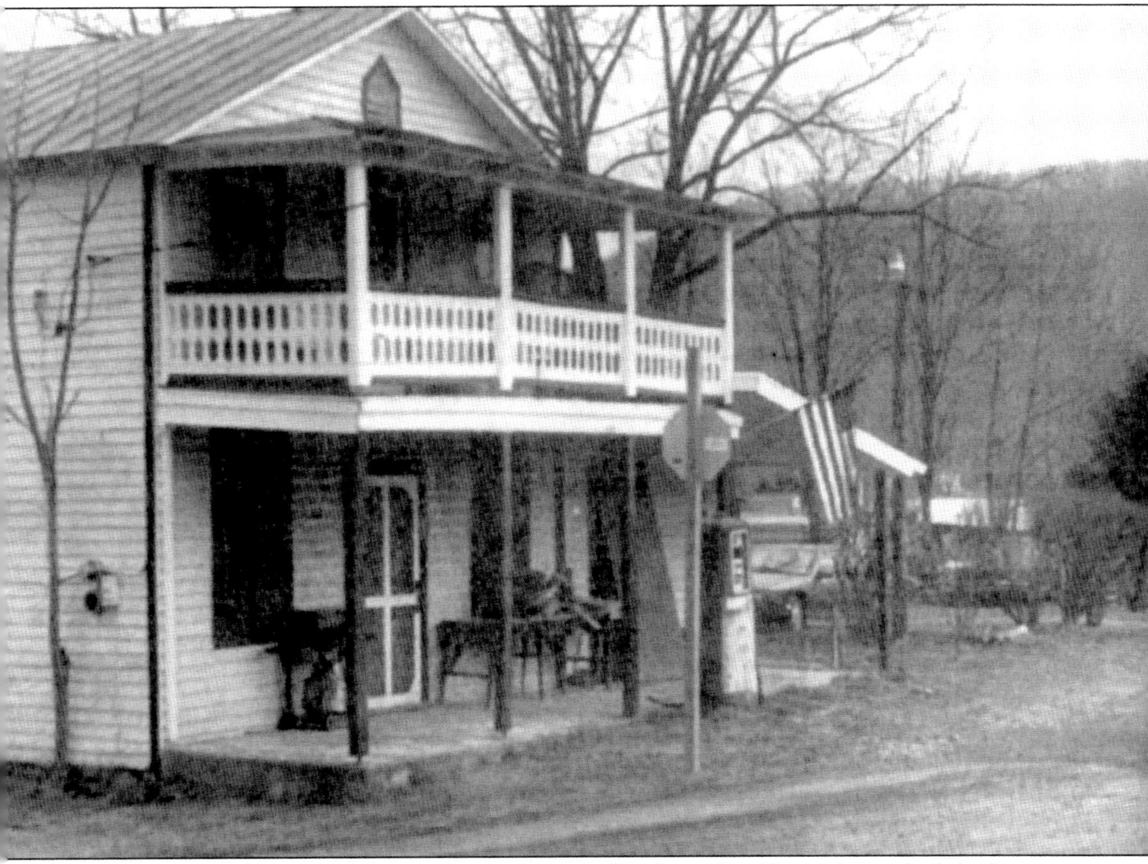

Cannon's Store is located on the northeast corner of Castleton Ford Road. It was built by James F. Cannon in 1914. (Courtesy of the Rappahannock Historical Society.)

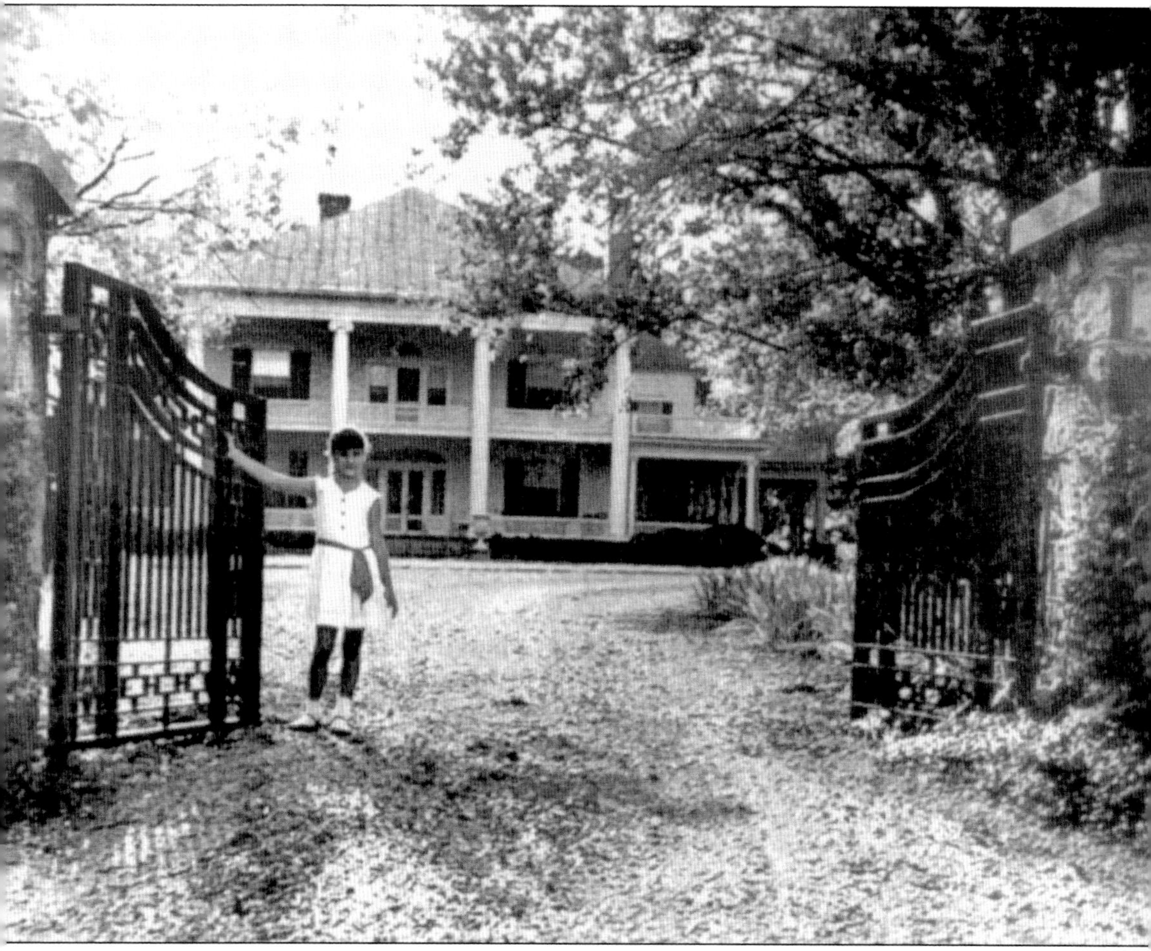

Meadowbrook Hall was once a 740-acre estate. It was built in the early 1900s. The Edwardian-style house was remodeled after 1915 to include a ballroom and solarium, both of which were used for Rappahannock Hunt Balls. A number of county children learned to swim in the pool here. The home burned in 1970 and was replaced with the current house located on Route 522. (Courtesy of the Rappahannock Historical Society.)

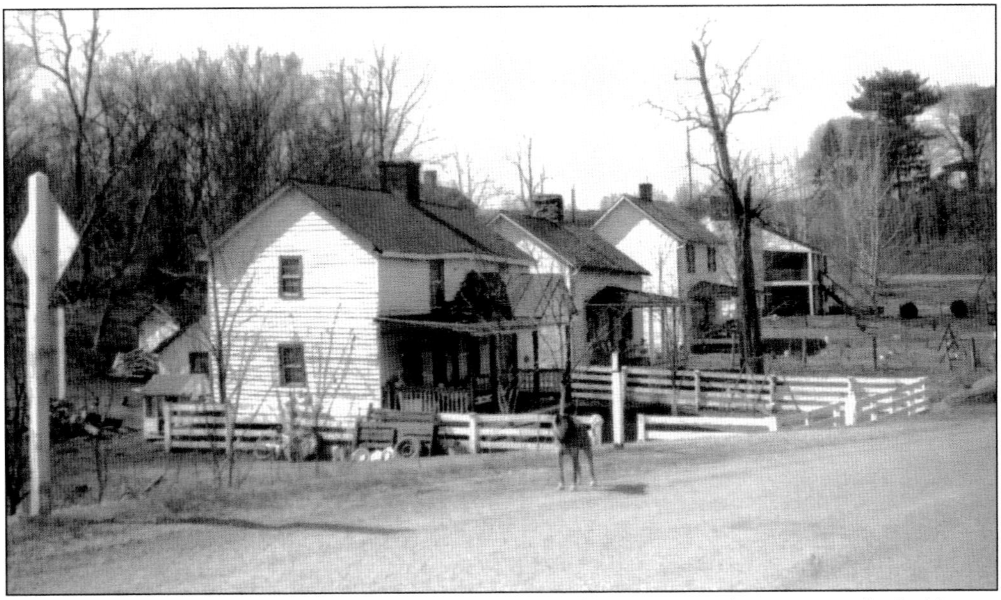

A group of workmen's houses were built at Laurel Mills in 1840. These one-and-a-half-story houses were wood-framed with a stone foundation and a side-gabled, standing-seam metal roof. The Laurel Mills Historic District is listed on the National Register of Historic Places and the Virginia Landmarks Registry. (Courtesy of the Rappahannock Historical Society.)

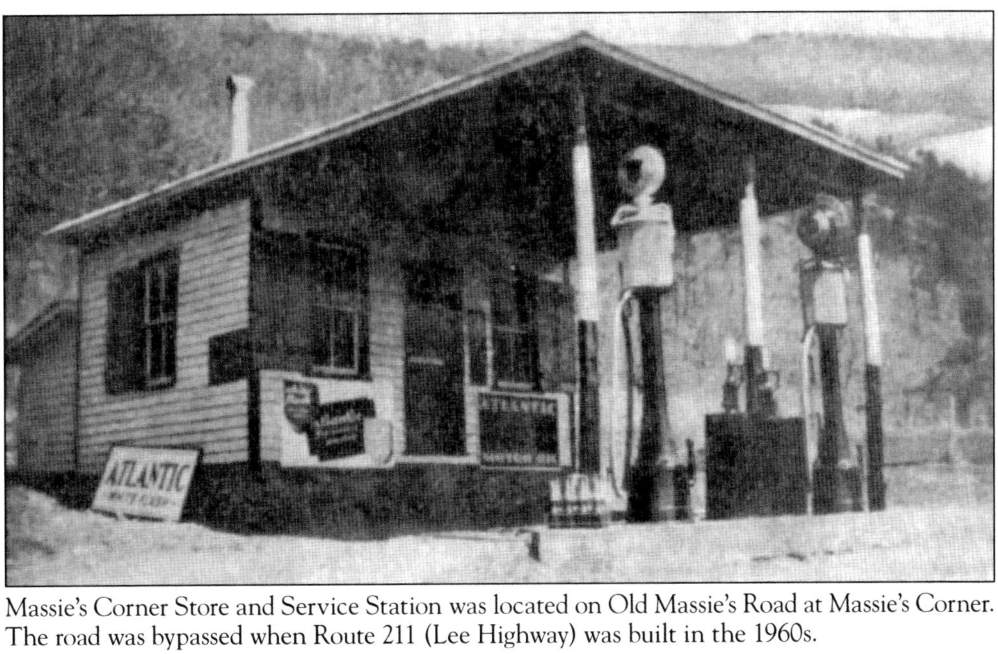

Massie's Corner Store and Service Station was located on Old Massie's Road at Massie's Corner. The road was bypassed when Route 211 (Lee Highway) was built in the 1960s.

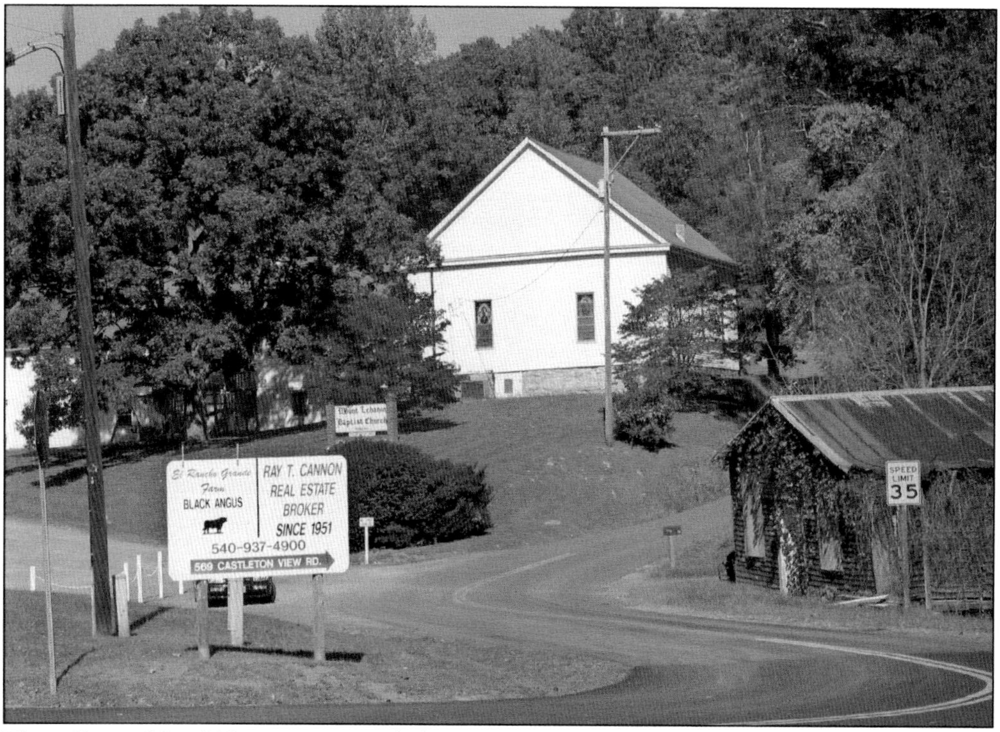

The village of Scrabble was commonly known as "Hard Scrabble" because the usual weekend recreation of the young men of the community was scrapping, or fighting. (Courtesy of John Tole.)

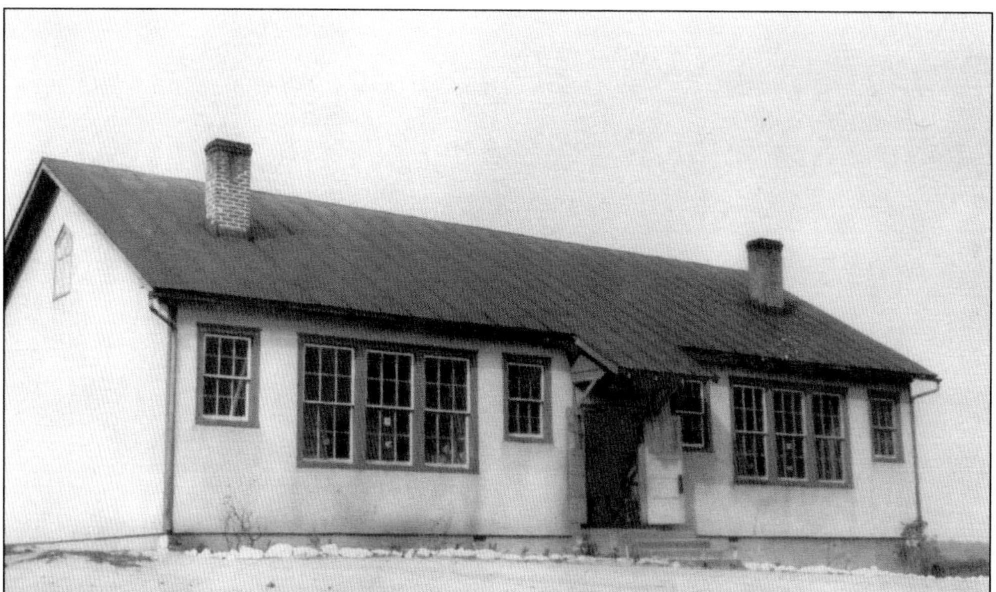

Scrabble School was built in 1922 with money provided by the Rosenwald Fund. The caliber of teaching was always high, and many students were inspired to achieve goals of distinction. (Courtesy of the Rappahannock Historical Society.)

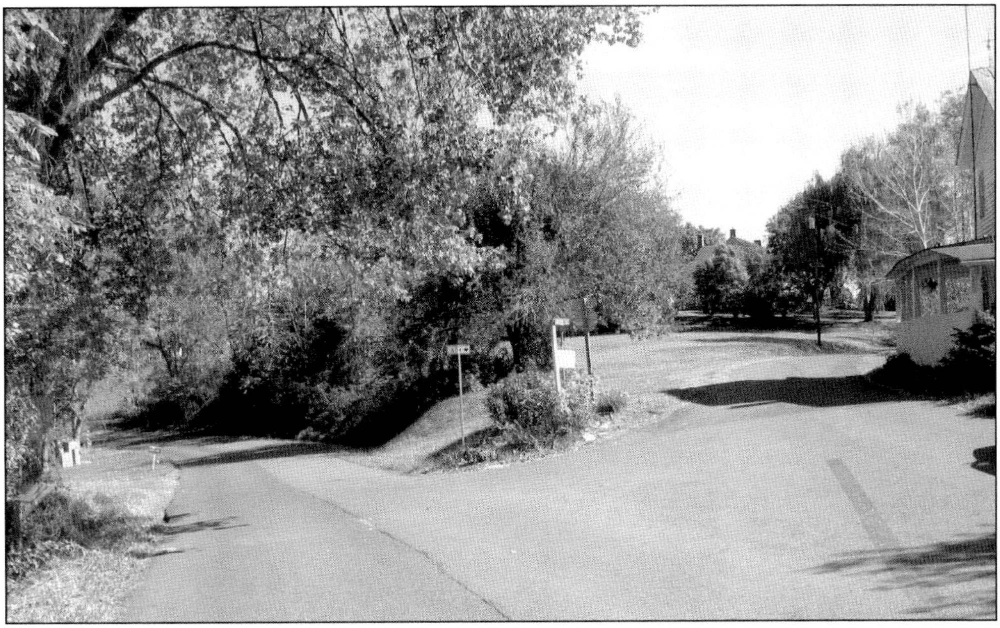

The village of Slate Mills lies at the intersection of Slate Mills Road and Green Road. (Courtesy of John Tole.)

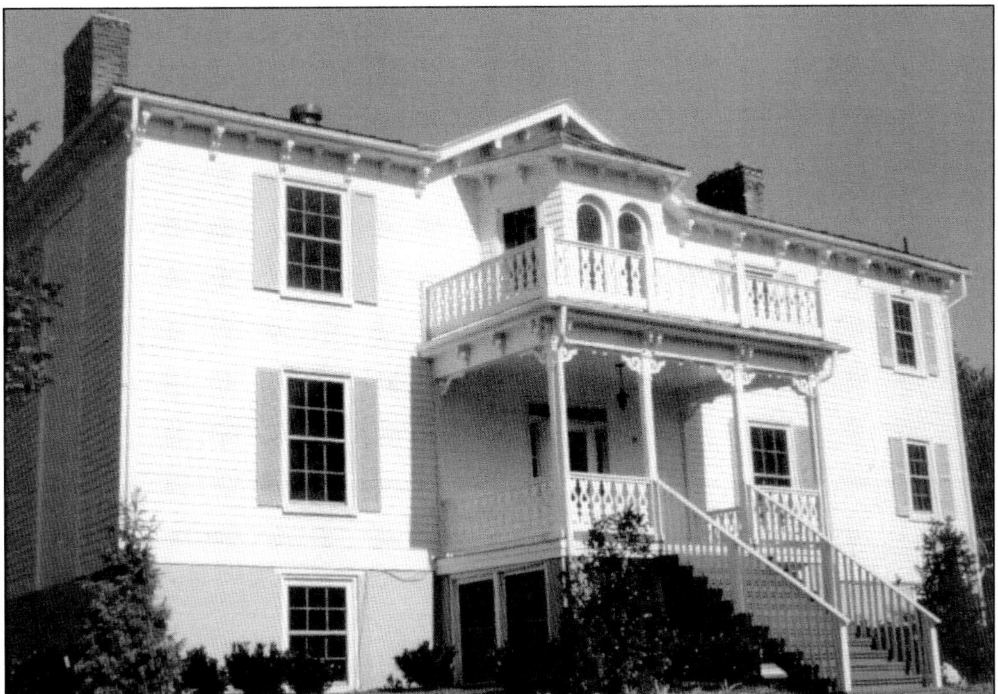

John W. Miller built the Miller House in the early 1840s. It is located at the corner of Routes 604 and 607. The home is an I-form farmhouse, later adorned with Italianate features in the 1880s. The Miller House is listed on the National Register of Historic Places and the Virginia Landmarks Registry. (Courtesy of the Rappahannock Historical Society.)

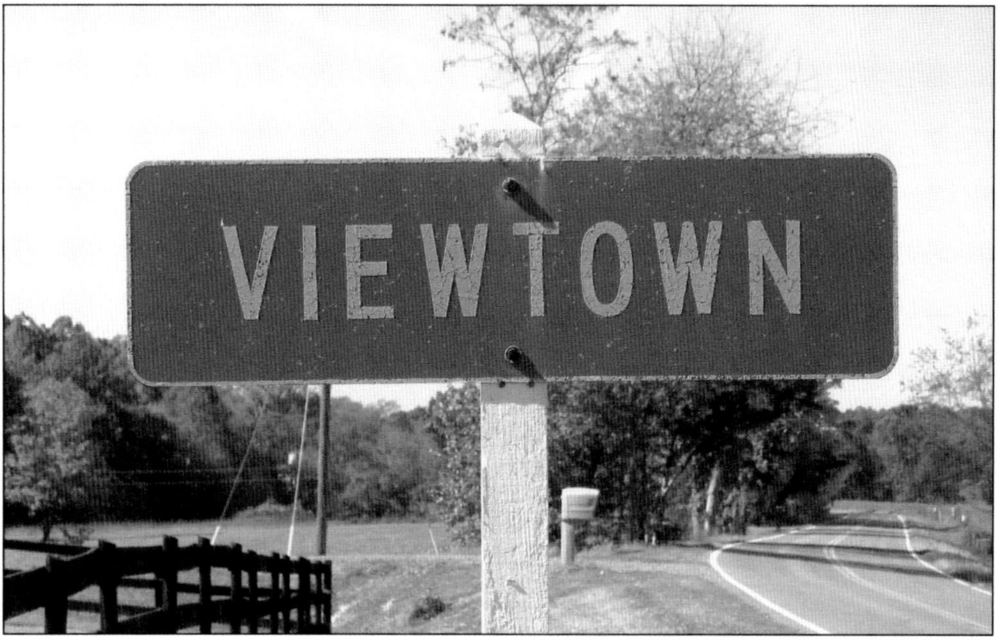

Viewtown is located about five miles southwest of Amissville near the Culpeper County line. (Courtesy of John Tole.)

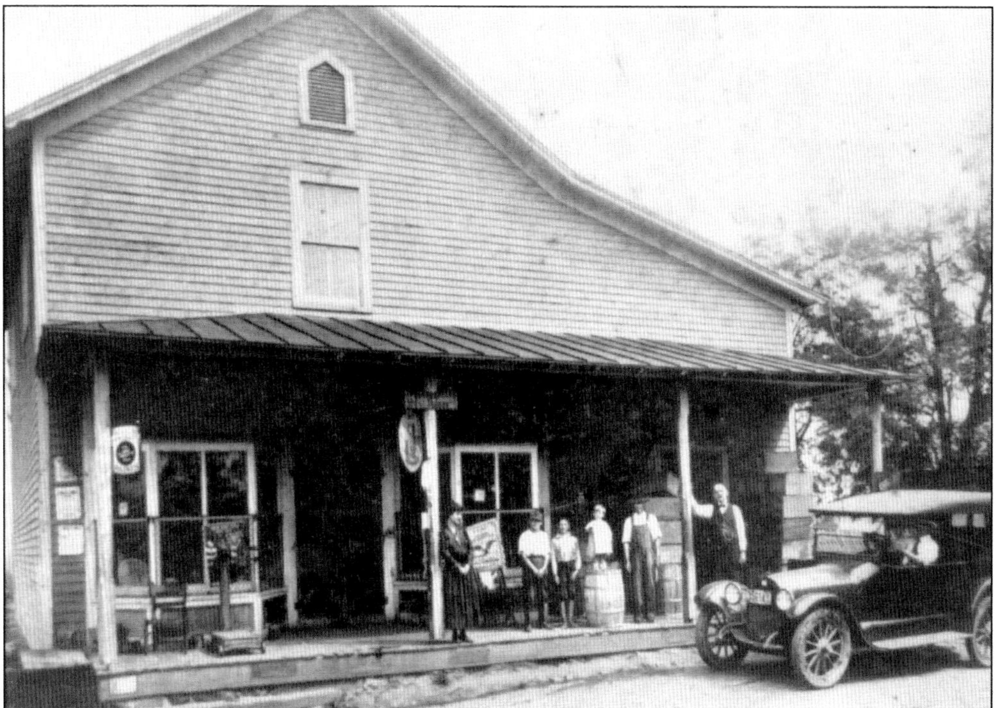

Viewtown Store was previously known as Spillman's Store in 1890 and then Barron's Store in 1918. The store served as a trading post in the old days, both buying and selling goods. A post office was housed in one section of the store. (Courtesy of Mary Priest.)

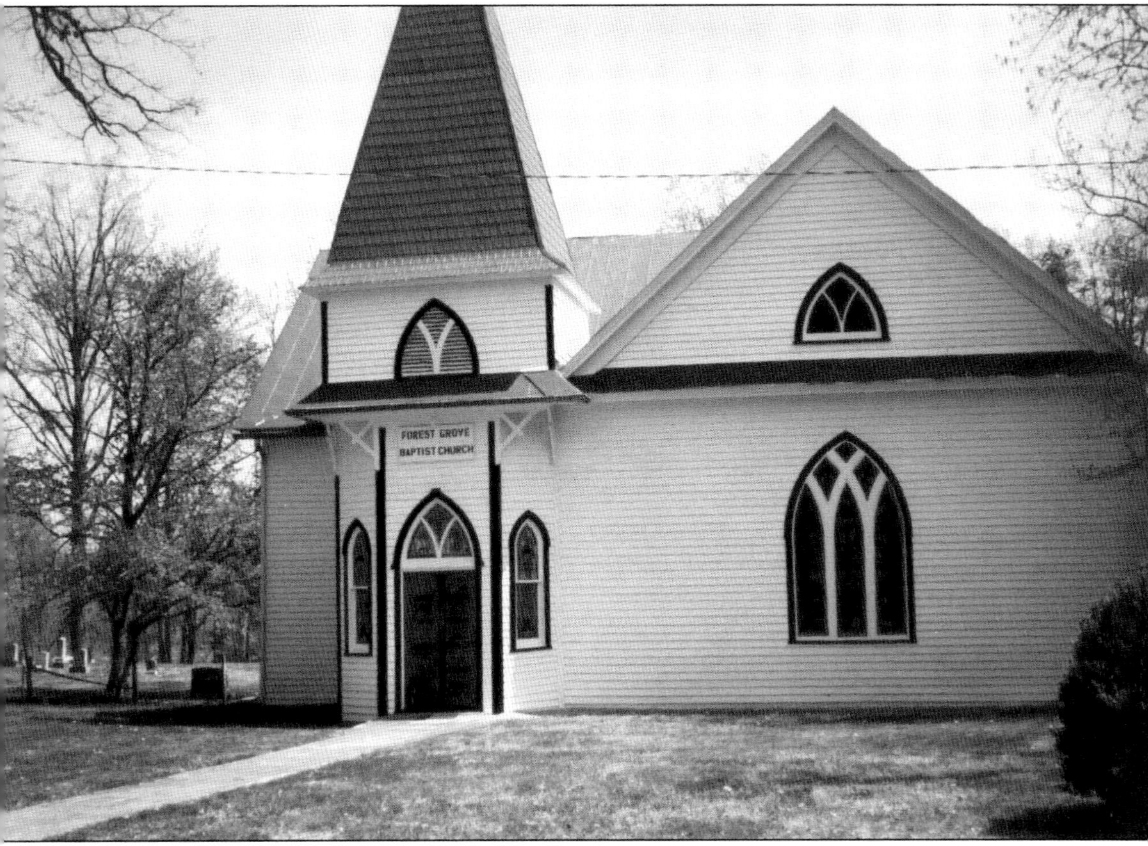

Forest Grove Church is located on Viewtown Road. It was organized in Viewtown in 1886 as the Chestnut Grove Baptist Church. The church was renamed Forest Grove Church and rededicated in 1887. (Courtesy of Mary Priest.)

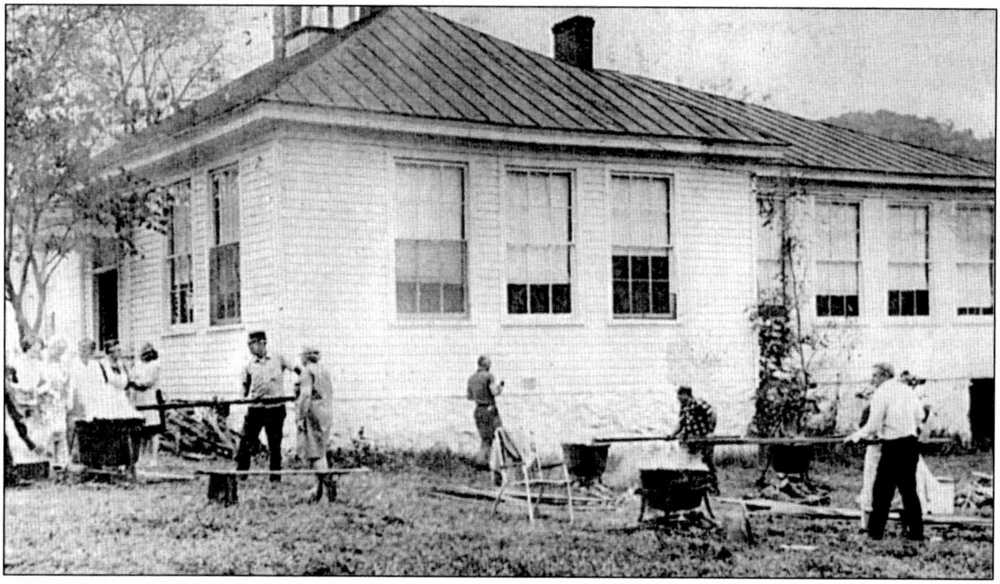

The original Forest Grove School was built in 1876 and contained one room. It was located on Viewtown Road beside the Forest Grove Church parking lot. A new Forest Grove School was built in another location in 1912. (Courtesy of Dan Hitt.)

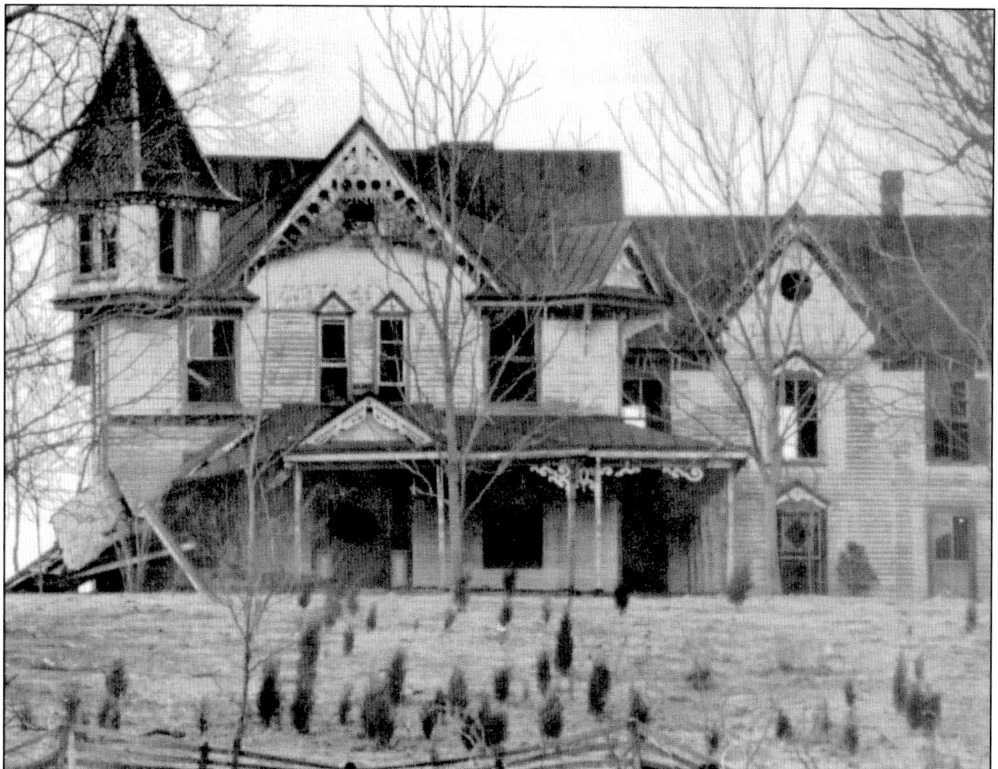

The Spillman/Settle/Corder/Zimmerli House, also known as Forest Hill, was located on Viewtown Road. It was a very large home containing 25 rooms, including a ballroom on the second floor. (Courtesy of the Rappahannock Historical Society.)

Eight

ROADS LESS TRAVELED

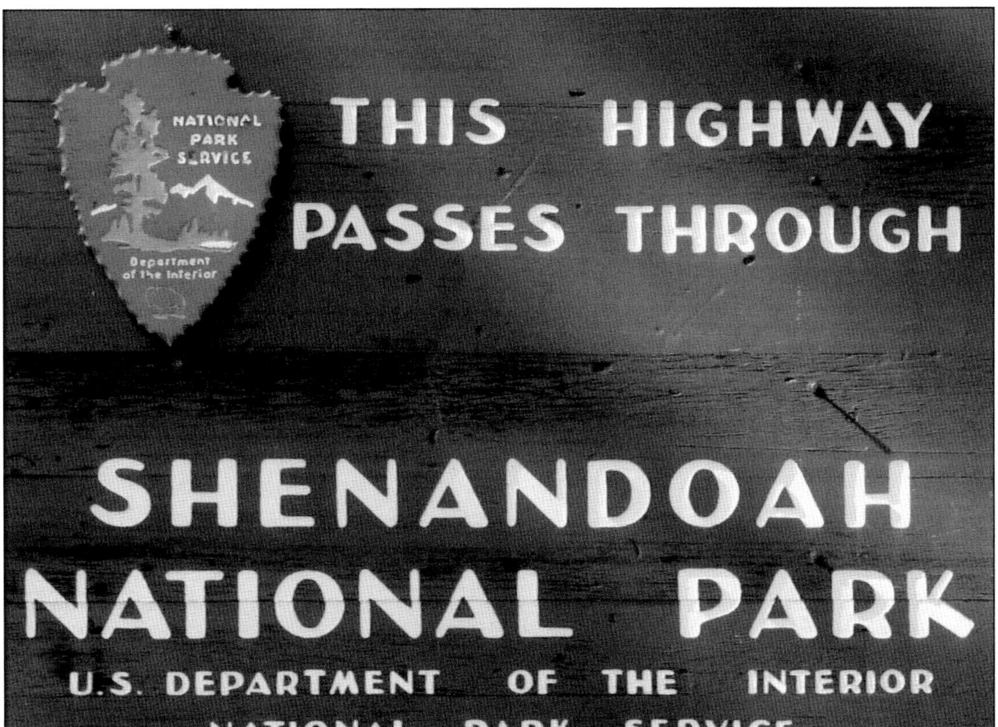

The Shenandoah National Park was dedicated in 1936. This sign is on Route 211 west of Sperryville. (Courtesy of John Tole.)

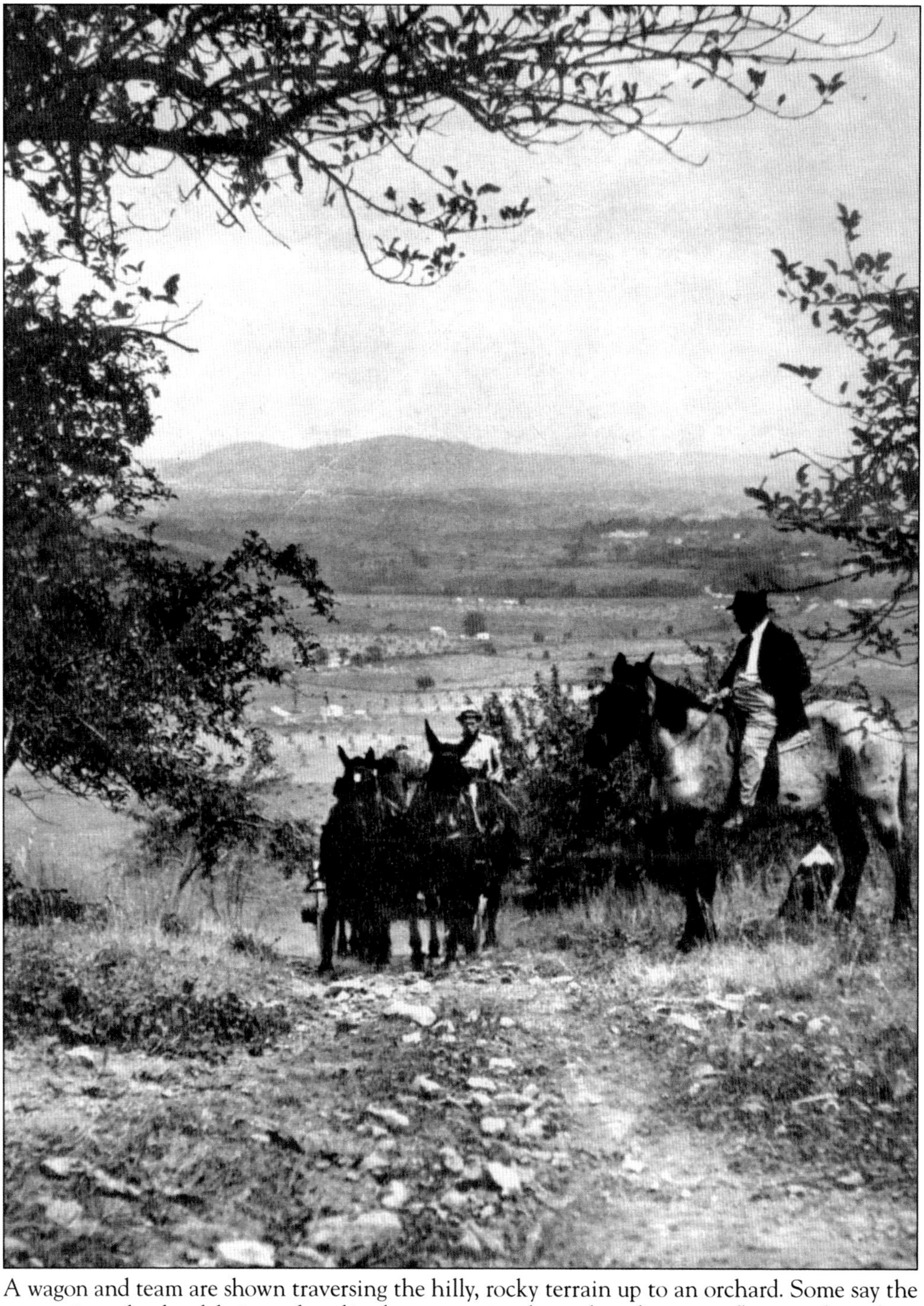

A wagon and team are shown traversing the hilly, rocky terrain up to an orchard. Some say the mountainous land and drainage found in the county give the apples a distinctive flavor, making them among the most desirable in the state. (Courtesy of the Rappahannock Historical Society.)

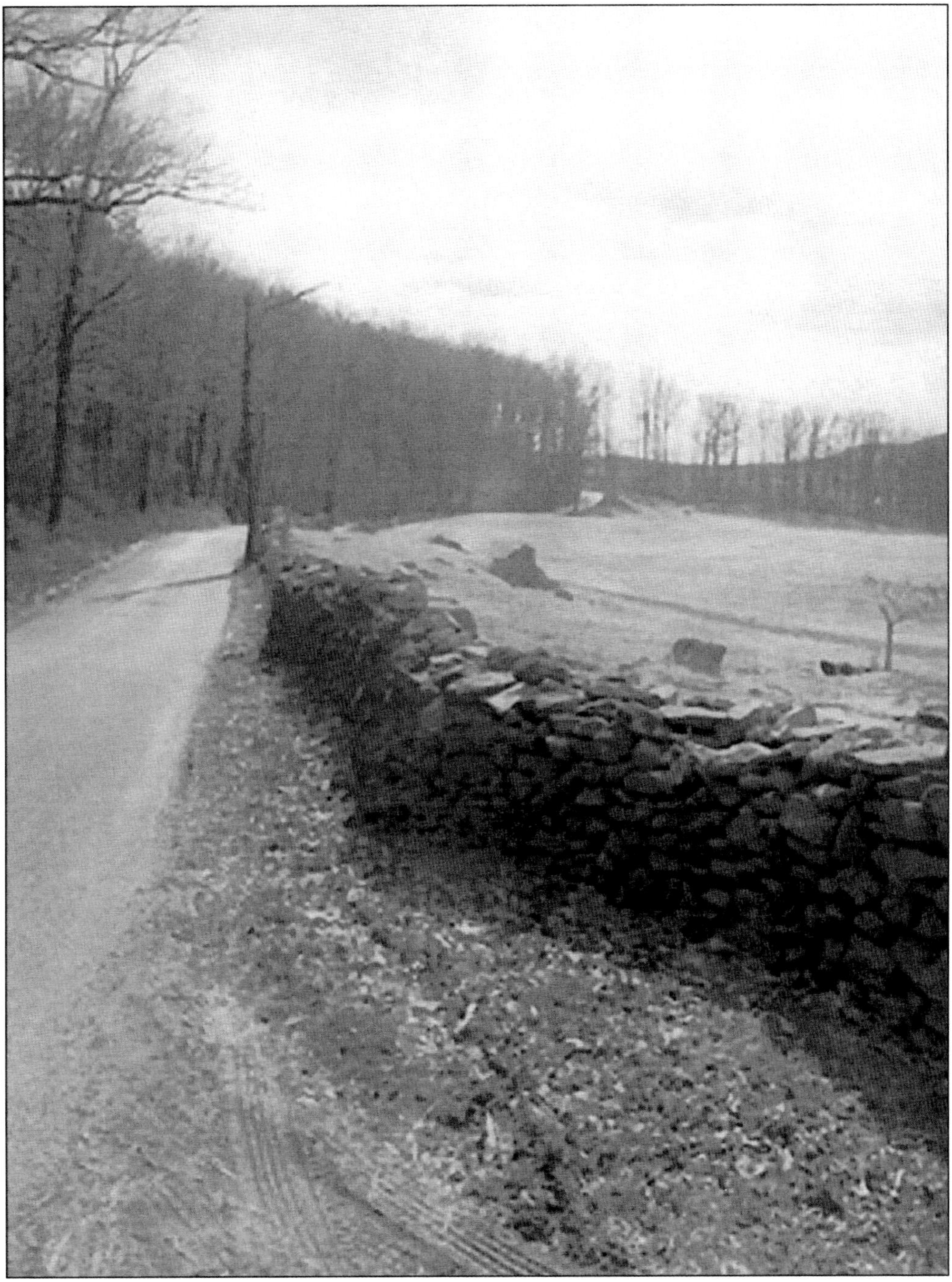

Ben Venue Road was once known as the Richmond Road. It was one of the first turnpikes that went from Richmond to Flint Hill. This section of the Richmond Road at Ben Venue was a major thoroughfare for both the Union and Confederate armies. (Courtesy of John Tole.)

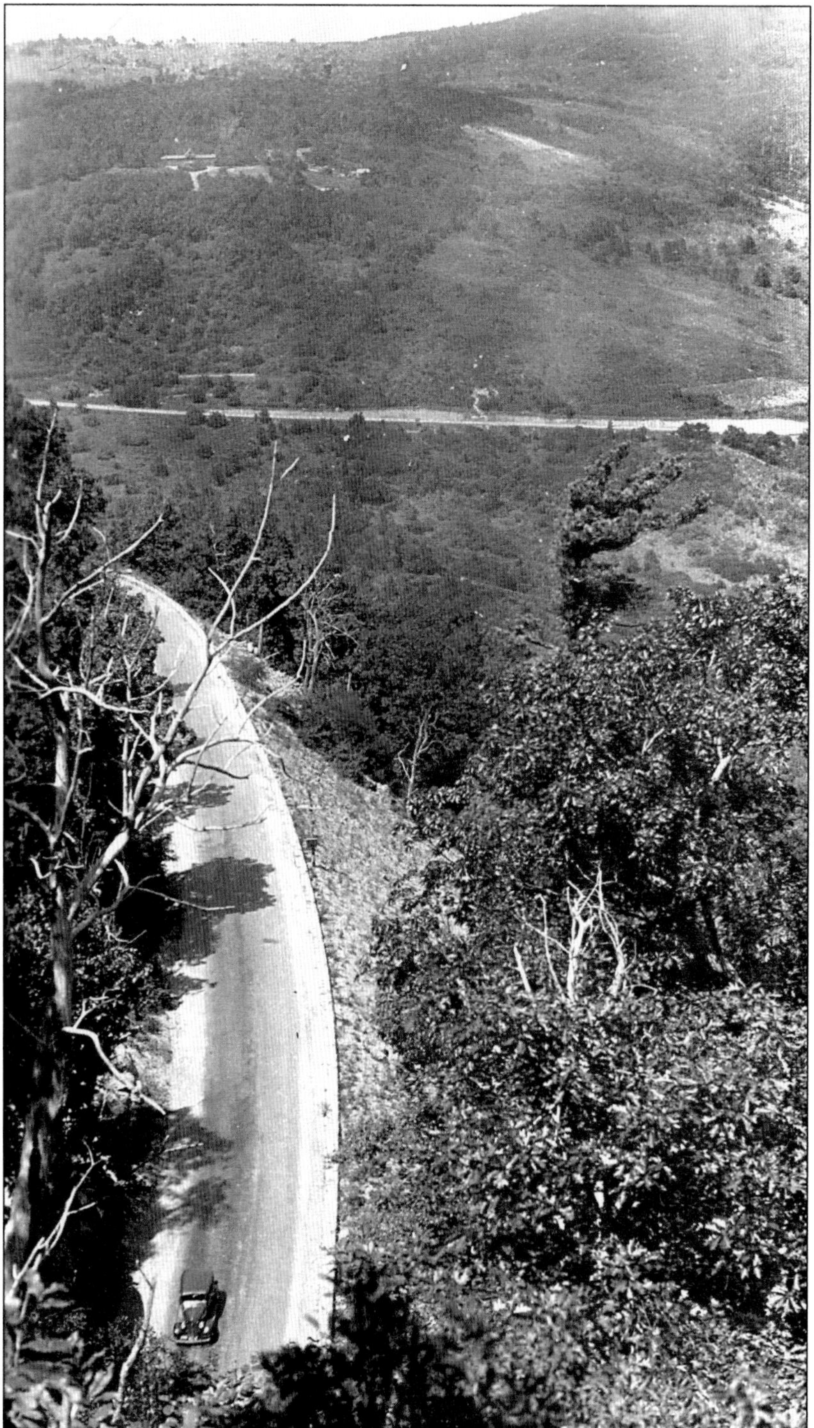

Route 211 winds its way up the mountains towards Skyline Drive west of Sperryville. There are places along the way for motorists to pull over and admire majestic views of the Blue Ridge Mountains. (Courtesy of the Shenandoah National Park Archives, Reed Engle.)